Lust, Commerce, and Corruption

TRANSLATIONS FROM THE ASIAN CLASSICS

TRANSLATIONS FROM THE ASIAN CLASSICS

EDITORIAL BOARD

Wm. Theodore de Bary, Chair

Paul Anderer

Donald Keene

George A. Saliba

Haruo Shirane

Burton Watson

Wei Shang

Lust, Commerce, and Corruption

An Account of What I Have Seen and Heard,
by an Edo Samurai

Abridged Edition

Translated by Mark Teeuwen, Kate Wildman Nakai,
Fumiko Miyazaki, Anne Walthall, and John Breen
Edited and with an introduction by
Mark Teeuwen and Kate Wildman Nakai

Columbia University Press
New York

Columbia University Press
Publishers Since 1893
New York   Chichester, West Sussex
cup.columbia.edu
Copyright © 2017 Columbia University Press
All rights reserved

Cataloging-in-Publication Data available from the Library of Congress
ISBN 978-0-231-18276-8 (cloth)
ISBN 978-0-231-18277-5 (paper)
ISBN 978-0-231-54435-1 (electronic)

Columbia University Press books are printed on permanent and durable acid-free paper.
Printed in the United States of America

Jacket design: Noah Arlow

CONTENTS

PREFACE vii

MEASURES x

CURRENCIES x

MAPS xii–xv

PART 1: BUYŌ INSHI AND HIS TIMES 1

PART 2: MATTERS OF THE WORLD:
AN ACCOUNT OF WHAT I HAVE SEEN AND HEARD
Buyō Inshi 35

Prologue 35

Chapter 1 39

Introduction 39

Warriors 41

Chapter 2   76
Farmers   76

Chapter 3   103
Temple and Shrine Priests   103

Chapter 4   128
The Blind   128

Lawsuits   136

Chapter 5   148
Townspeople   148

Lower Townspeople   175

Chapter 6   193
Pleasure Districts and Prostitutes   193

Kabuki   212

Chapter 7   235
Pariahs and Outcasts   235

On Japan Being Called a Divine Land   239

The Land, People, and Ruler   249

EDITIONS AND REFERENCES   255

CONTRIBUTORS   259

INDEX   261

PREFACE

The core of this volume is an abridged translation of a late Edo account of the ills of the day titled *Seji kenbunroku* (*Matters of the World: An Account of What I Have Seen and Heard*; 1816). Quite by coincidence a pocket edition of this work caught my attention in a Tokyo bookshop some years ago. I knew the text, by an unknown author presumably of samurai background, as a favored source of juicy quotes, with passages from it brightening up many books and articles on Edo-period history, and I was immediately attracted by the notion of a social critique written by a samurai who thought it best to stay anonymous (he uses the pseudonym Buyō Inshi). As I got to know the book better, I discovered that it was not only an informative historical source; it was in fact a very good read. Four collaborators and I embarked on a project to make Buyō's picture of late Edo society available in English.

Buyō is at times tiresome in his hammering at what he sees as the decline in people's customs and moral disposition. But unlike many of his contemporaries, he does not stop there. Buyō is at his best when he reveals the concrete details of the corruption that, in his view, permeated life in Edo. In these passages, he gives the reader a vivid look at the inner workings of his society. He writes, for example, about contractors who put in formal offers for construction work at daimyo domain compounds in what appears to be fair competition for a contract. Behind the scenes, however, jobs have been shared out beforehand, and all parties make a good profit—while the samurai officers who handle the paperwork enjoy evenings out in the pleasure quarters and a cut of the proceeds. Builders' groups in the townspeople's blocks double as firefighters, and they make sure that those house owners who fail to pay protection fees are on their own when the next blaze occurs—accidentally or otherwise. In the countryside, wealthy village leaders shift tax obligations to the low-quality fields left in the hands of the poor so that the good fields in their own possession become less burdened with taxes and can be sold for a higher price. And so on and so forth. Buyō describes in revealing detail how some people were doing very well, while others paid the price.

Buyō's analyses are premised on the traditional understanding that the economy is a zero-sum game, a view that was becoming old-fashioned even in his own time. His opinions on class and gender are, from a modern perspective, prejudiced to the point of bigotry. Yet at the same time, he consistently argues that moral indignation should be directed at the system that corrupts, rather than at the individuals who have no choice but to let themselves be corrupted. Buyō makes a convincing analysis of the systemic impossibility of living up to warrior-like ideals of principled uprightness and decisiveness in dealing with injustice. In this, he offers insights that are not easily found in other Edo-period materials.

The translation and the introductory essay that precedes it are the products of teamwork by the five collaborators. Each of us undertook an initial translation of different sections, which we then discussed and revised as a team. Kate Wildman Nakai and I are responsible for the overall editing of the translation and have added subheadings and paragraph divisions (the original has neither) to enhance readability. The introductory essay, "Buyō Inshi and His Times," is a cooperative piece by the two editors but also incorporates corrections and additions by the other team members. It has benefited as well from comments made by the anonymous readers of the manuscript. The maps were produced by Kirsten Berrum of Oslo University.

In 2014, Columbia University Press published a full translation of Buyō's text, under the same title as this volume. The current abridged version, which has been prepared by the two editors, comprises about half the original. Some sections have been cut in their entirety—for example, brief accounts of "The Medical Profession" in chapter 3, "The Way of Yin and Yang" in chapter 4, and "Mountains and Forests" in chapter 7. Elsewhere we have removed passages that appeared repetitive, general and abstract, or overly technical. In the interest of readability, cuts are not indicated in the text but can be readily identified by comparing this abridged edition with the full translation. Throughout we have endeavored to preserve Buyō's argument in both scope and emphasis.

We thank three anonymous reviewers whose detailed comments aided us in making the cuts. Thanks are also due to Morgaine Theresa Wood, who put together the files to be used for the final fine-tuning.

This abridged edition includes fifteen illustrations taken from woodblock-printed popular literary works and guidebooks dating from the same general period as Buyō's text. They have been chosen for offering corroboration of points Buyō makes, although they often do so from a far less critical perspective. We are indebted to the National Diet Library Digital Collection and Waseda University Library for the images.

Mark Teeuwen

MEASURES

Buyō uses the following measures (the U.S. and metric equivalents are approximate):

1 *sun*: 1 in; 3 cm
1 *shaku*: 1 ft; 30 cm (10 *sun*)
1 *ken*: 6 ft; 1.82 m (6 *shaku*)
1 *ri*: 2.4 mi; 3.93 km
1 *tsubo*: 36 ft²; 3.3 m² (1 sq. *ken*)
1 *tan*: 0.25 acres; 1,000 m² (300 *tsubo*)
1 *chō*: 2.45 acres; 1 ha (10 *tan*)
1 *shō*: 1.6 quarts; 1.8 L
1 *koku*: 5 bushels; 180 L (100 *shō*)

One *hyō* (bale) varied in quantity regionally between one-fifth and one-half of a *koku*; Buyō counts 1 *hyō* as roughly equivalent to one-third of a *koku*.

CURRENCIES

In the Edo period, gold, silver, and copper cash served as the basic mediums of exchange. Gold and silver were used for larger transactions, copper cash for smaller ones. The shogunate tried to maintain a stable rate of exchange between the different mediums, but in practice, exchange rates varied over time and in different locales. Rice prices were in principle geared to the basic currency units, with 1 *koku* (theoretically, the amount consumed annually by an adult male) equal to 1 *ryō* in gold or 60 *monme* in silver, but they too fluctuated. Between 1800 and 1816, the value of 1 *koku* varied between 50 and 70 *monme*.

The major monetary units in late Edo were as follows:

gold: 1 *ryō* (or *koban*) = 4 *bu* = 16 *shu* = 400 *hiki*
silver: ca. 60 *monme* = 1 *ryō* gold
copper: ca. 6,500 *mon* = 1 *ryō* gold
1 *kanmon* = 1,000 *mon* (coppers)

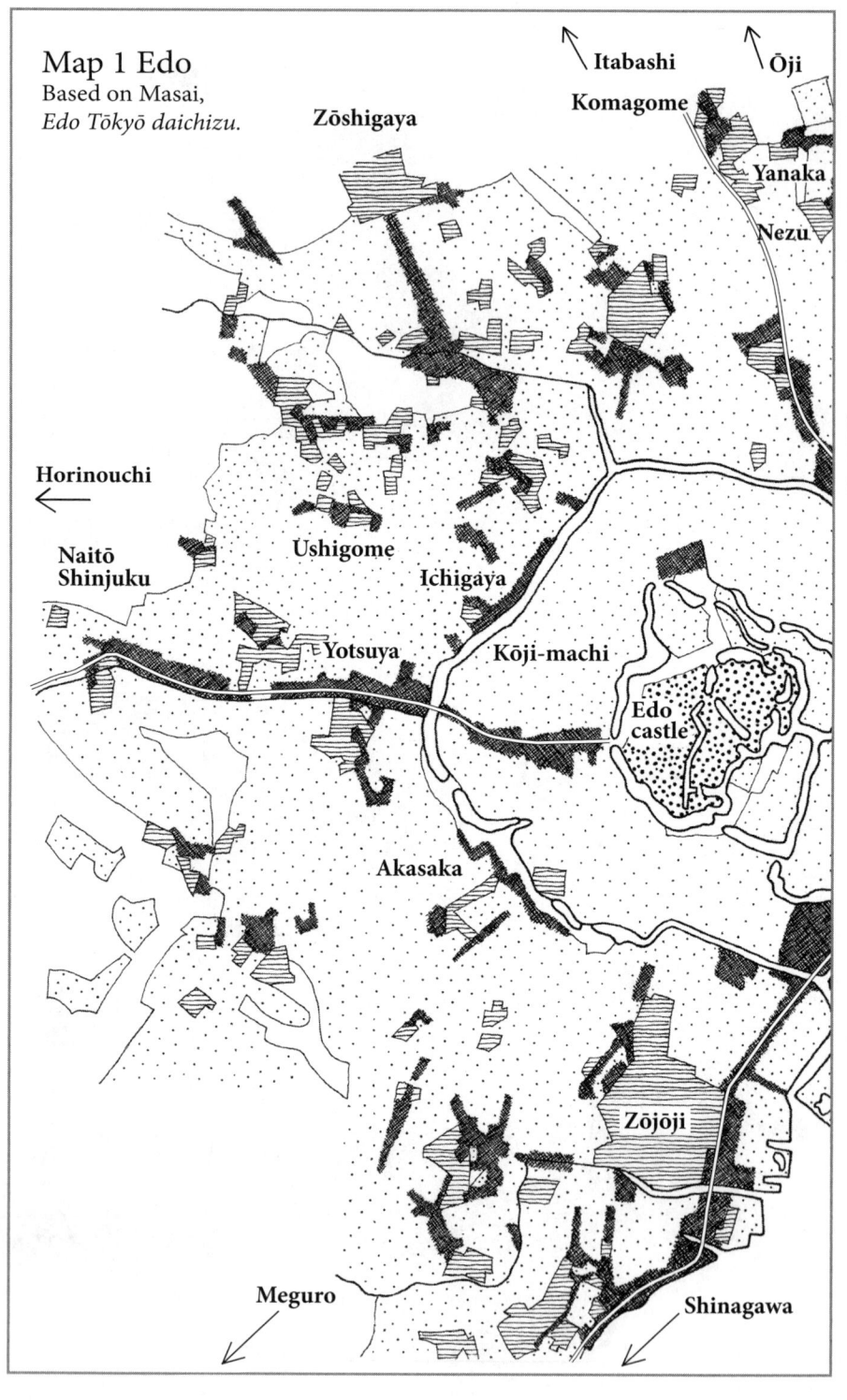

Map 1 Edo
Based on Masai, *Edo Tōkyō daichizu*.

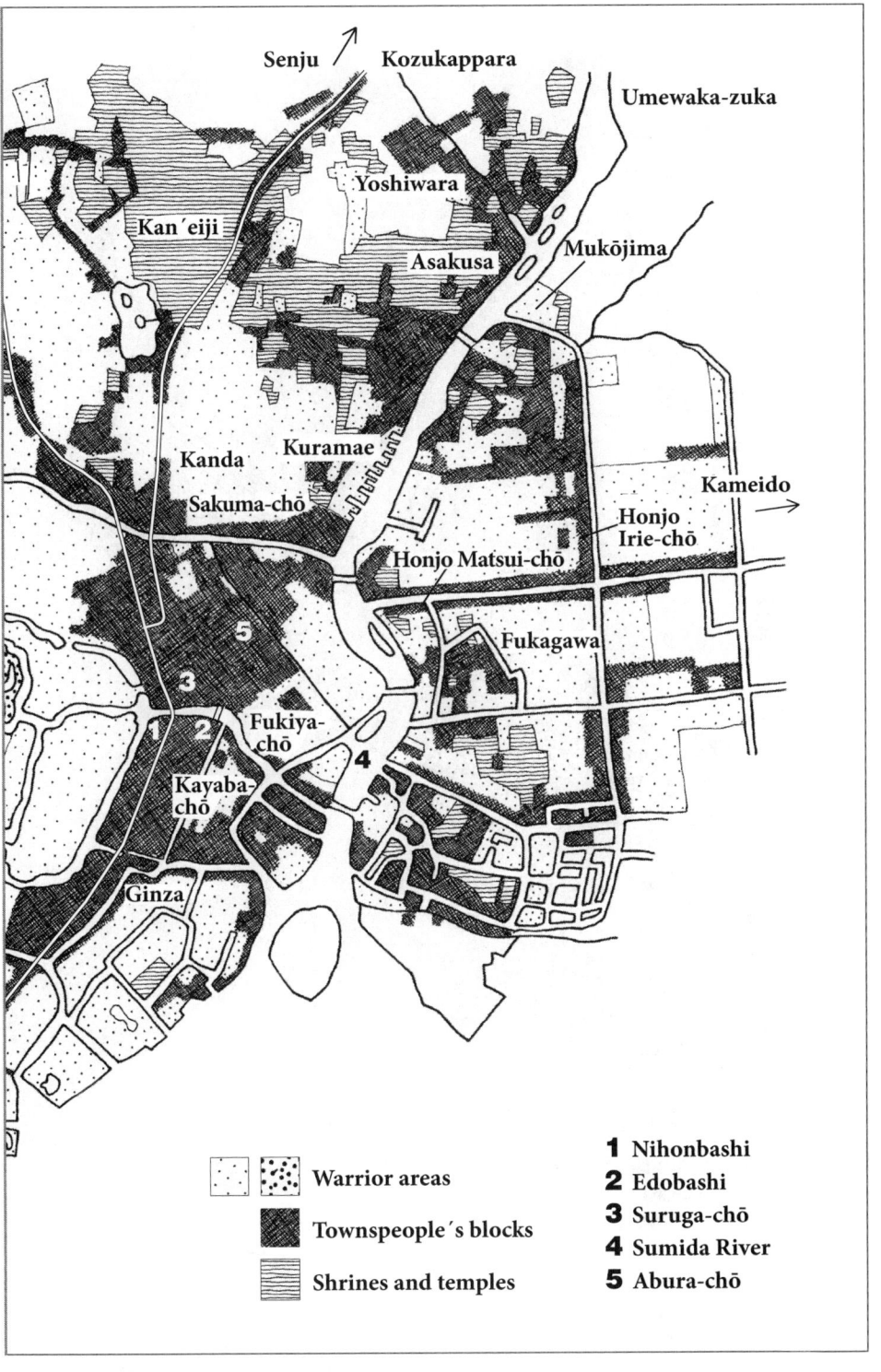

Map 2
The provinces of Japan

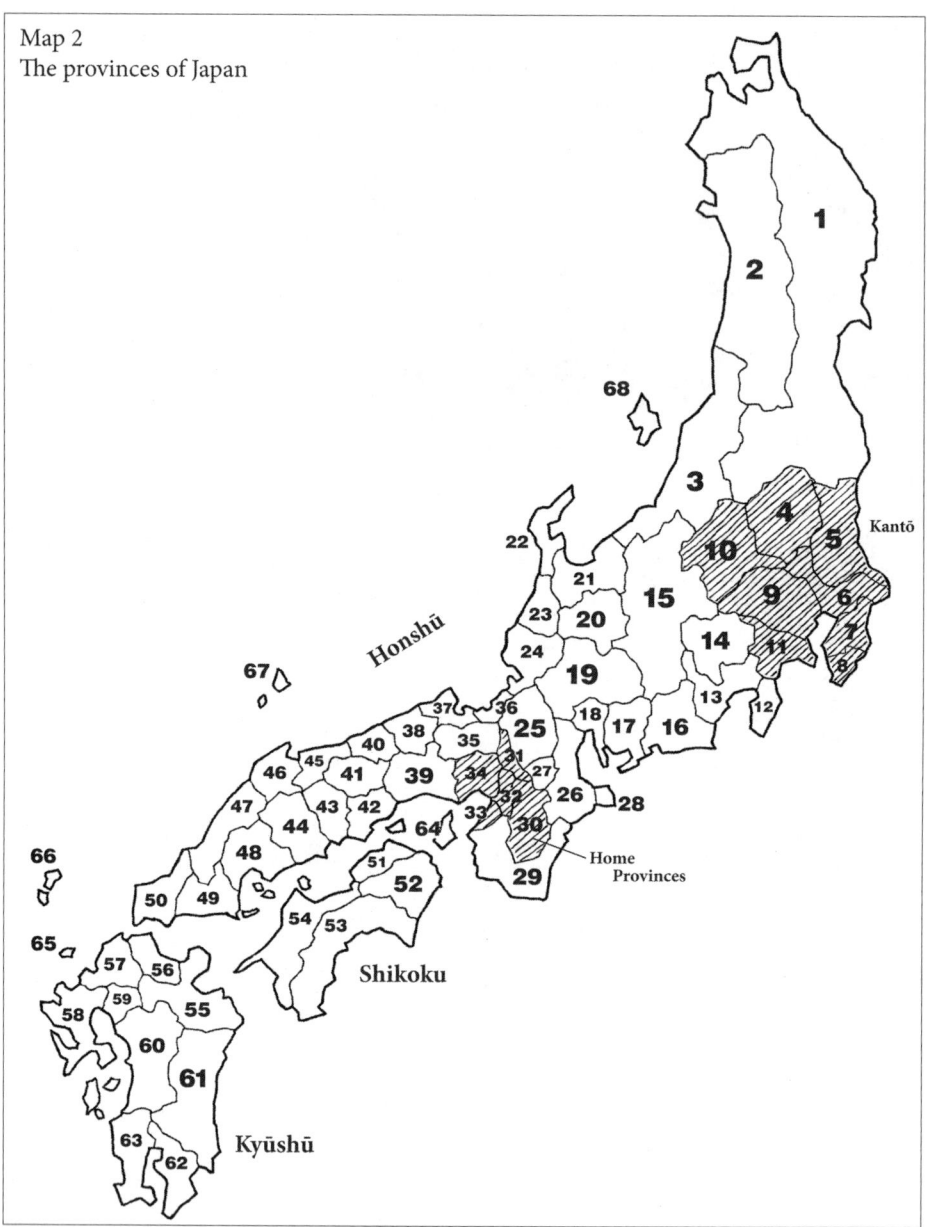

PROVINCE NAMES: 1. Mutsu; 2. Dewa; 3. Echigo; 4. Shimotsuke; 5. Hitachi; 6. Kazusa; 7. Shimōsa; 8. Awa; 9. Musashi; 10. Kōzuke; 11. Sagami; 12. Izu; 13. Suruga; 14. Kai; 15. Shinano; 16. Tōtōmi; 17. Mikawa; 18. Owari; 19. Mino; 20. Hida; 21. Etchū; 22. Noto; 23. Kaga; 24. Echizen; 25. Ōmi; 26. Ise; 27. Iga; 28. Shima; 29. Kii; 30. Yamato; 31. Yamashiro; 32. Kawachi; 33. Izumi; 34. Settsu; 35. Tanba; 36. Wakasa; 37. Tango; 38. Tajima; 39. Harima; 40. Inaba; 41. Mimasaka; 42. Bizen; 43. Bitchū; 44. Bingo; 45. Hōki; 46. Izumo; 47. Iwami; 48. Aki; 49. Suō; 50. Nagato; 51. Sanuki; 52. Awa; 53. Tosa; 54. Iyo; 55. Bungo; 56. Buzen; 57. Chikuzen; 58. Hizen; 59. Chikugo; 60. Higo; 61. Hyūga; 62. Ōsumi; 63. Satsuma; 64. Awaji; 65. Iki; 66. Tsushima; 67. Oki; 68. Sado

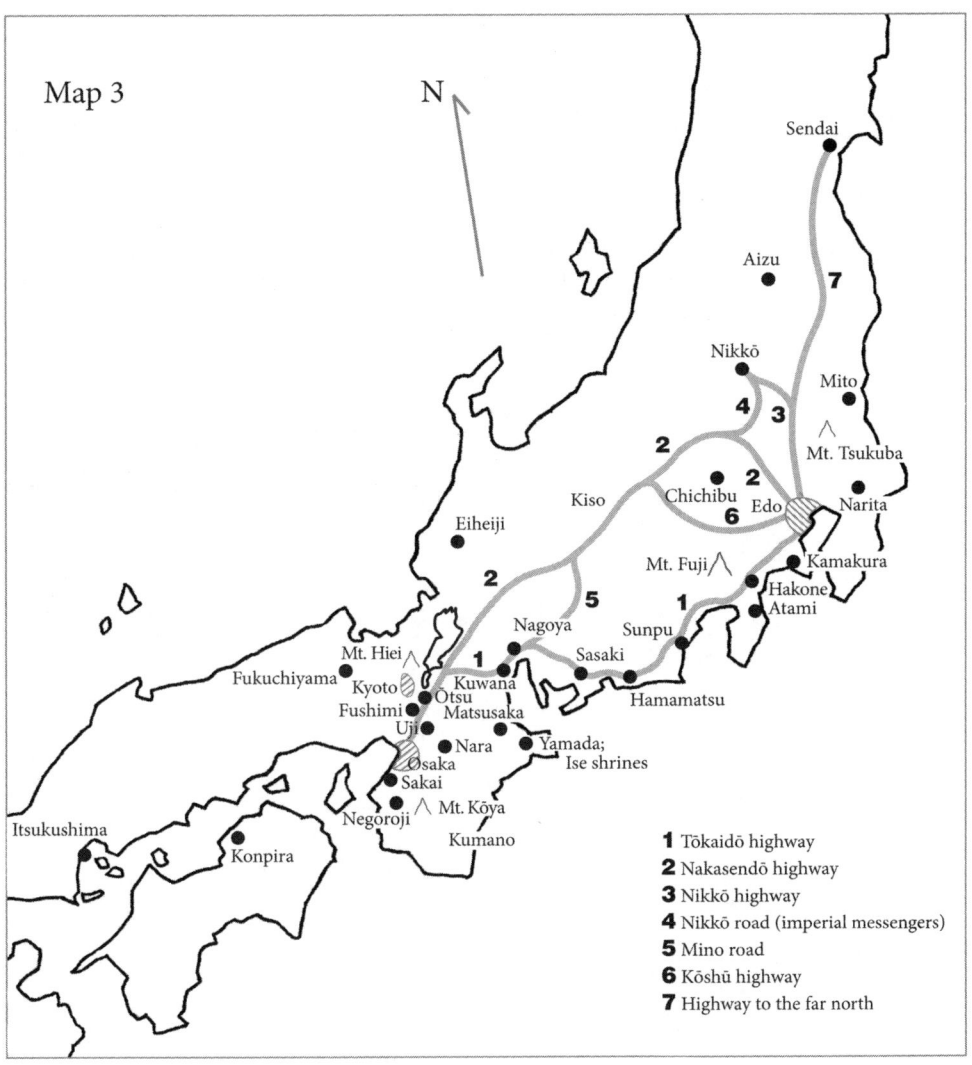

PLACE NAMES AND ROADS OUTSIDE EDO MENTIONED IN THE TEXT

Lust, Commerce, and Corruption

Part 1

BUYŌ INSHI AND HIS TIMES

What kind of society was Japan in the early nineteenth century? Many have contrasted Japan's Edo period (1600–1868) with the Qing of neighboring China as an early modern era of progress, stressing that developments during that time prepared the country for its rapid rise in the world after the Meiji coup of 1868. Others have taken a negative view, portraying the period as an age of isolation and stagnation. The latter describe Edo Japan as a country caught in a time bubble, from which it could be saved only by a tidal wave of catch-up Westernization. One school of thought sees the Edo period as an era of peace that produced one of the world's great civilizations, while another stresses the price that was paid for that peace. The former holds up Edo Japan as a highly urbanized society, boasting unrivaled literacy rates and ruled by a relatively humane bureaucracy. The latter protests that Edo society was as feudal as it was modern, based as it was on the principle that power should be hereditary and on a rigid system of class and gender discrimination.

There is some truth in all these perspectives. In the later Edo period, Japan was a country of as many as thirty-two million people (exceeding any state in Europe except Russia), of whom more than one million lived in the shogunal city of Edo. Only a limited portion of the country was ruled directly by the central shogunal government; much of the population came under the jurisdiction of semi-independent domains. Restrictions on geographical and social mobility and an approach to governance that favored self-administration meant that rural communities retained a high degree of autonomy. Yet at the same time, countless official channels and unofficial loopholes ensured that no village or domain remained unconnected to nationwide networks of trade, religion, and politics.

All societies, of course, are multidimensional—Edo Japan was perhaps even more so than most. It is little wonder, then, that contemporary understandings of Edo society were no less diverse than modern historical accounts. Writings analyzing, describing, and criticizing the society of the time were by no means rare. This volume contains the translation of one such work. Titled *Matters of the World: An Account of What I Have Seen and Heard* (*Seji kenbunroku*, or, in an alternative reading, *Seji kenmonroku*), it is among the Edo period's most sustained attempts to examine society critically in its entirety, from shogunal worthies at the top to outcasts of various kinds at the bottom. Both the prologue and the final chapter of this substantial work, which in the most accessible modern edition fills more than 440 pages, are dated Bunka 13 (1816). Little is known about the text's author, intended audience, or original purpose. The author's identity remains hidden behind the pseudonym Buyō Inshi, "a retired gentleman of Edo."[1] The text initially circulated only in manuscript form, with parts of it published for the first time half a century after it was written.[2]

---

1. "Buyō" likely refers to the "yang" (*yō*, that is, southern) part of the province of Musashi (*bu*), where Edo was located. The same pseudonym "Buyō Inshi" had earlier been used by the obviously unrelated compiler of *Jikata ochiboshū*, a large instruction guide for rural administrators dated 1763. In its blandness, this pseudonym offers no clues as to our author's identity.

2. Most modern editions go back to a manuscript kept at Kyoto University that Honjō Eijirō transcribed and published in 1926 (*Kinsei shakai keizai sōsho*, Kaizōsha) and again in 1930 (Kaizō Bunko). Honjō's edition was later republished by Seiabō (1966) with further corrections and an introduction by Takigawa Masajirō that remains the most thorough discussion of this work. Both the Kaizō Bunko and the Seiabō editions were consulted by Naramoto Tatsuya, who prepared the widely available Iwanami Bunko version that appeared in 1994. The text has been published as well in *Nihon shomin seikatsu shiryō shūsei*, vol. 8 (1969). The present translation is based primarily on the Iwanami Bunko edition of 1994. Compari-

Buyō (as we will refer to him) reveals remarkably little about himself in the course of his lengthy account. There is no doubt that he was based in Edo and that he belonged to the warrior class. He identifies closely with the shogunate and has little to say about the domains; this suggests that he may have been a retired shogunal retainer of some kind. On the other hand, Buyō reveals an intimate knowledge of many corners of society well beyond what one would expect of an elite samurai. In one passage, he recalls that for a while he "was able to make a little money" by means that he now regards as foul, but recently "stopped doing such improper things" and has "once again fallen into poverty" (see page 398).[3] From such remarks and from Buyō's interest in and knowledge of money lending, the handling of lawsuits, and Edo city life, researchers have surmised that he may well have had a connection with one of the protolawyers who unofficially assisted plaintiffs bringing suits (related mostly to debts and loans) in shogunal courts.[4] Readers of *Musui's Story*, the autobiography of another retired samurai written in the 1840s, may detect a certain resemblance to the multiple "fixers" on the margins of late Edo warrior society who populate its pages.[5] Whatever Buyō's background and earlier experiences, they evidently left him in a position of relative independence that allowed him to take an informed, if censorious, look at the world with some critical distance.

Buyō had an advantage over modern-day historians in that he could describe Edo Japan firsthand. The reader will soon notice, however, that this does not necessarily make his account more objective, balanced, or even true. Buyō holds strong opinions about the way the world should be and measures society against those standards. His agenda is not to produce a Balzac-like naturalist portrait of his time. The anecdotes and descriptions of social practices that he includes often show a moralistic, not

---

son with other editions revealed only nonsubstantive differences. One exception is that the Iwanami edition retains the censorship of the term *kōgō* (sexual intercourse) introduced in the Kaizō Bunko edition of 1930. A list of all published editions of *Seji kenbunroku*, both complete and partial, is included in the references at the end of this volume.

3. Not all the passages from *Matters of the World* quoted in this essay have been retained in the abridged edition. Page citations are thus to the unabridged version.

4. Takigawa, "Kaisetsu," pp. 8–12; Harada, Takeuchi, and Hirayama, *Nihon shomin*, pp. 641–42.

5. Katsu, *Musui's Story*.

to say reactionary, perspective on the social dynamics of Edo. One scholar of the period has aptly characterized *Matters of the World* as "an articulate loser's view of the times,"[6] and the book is unquestionably as much a work of ideology as of history. Much postwar historical research on the Edo period has endeavored to relativize such a view and offer less ideologically biased readings of the record. Thanks to this research, it has now become clear that a good deal of what Buyō describes should be taken with a grain (or lump) of salt. Nevertheless, Buyō's sharp delineation of the social and economic contradictions of late Edo life remains compelling, as do the vivid details he provides of financial and legal doings, and academic as well as more popular studies continue to cite him widely.[7]

When read as a window on Edo thought, *Matters of the World* introduces us to a section of the period's intellectual scene that has been largely neglected in the literature on Japan's history of ideas. Buyō does not number among the thinkers whom specialists of the period's intellectual history have typically singled out for analysis, such as his more "progressive" contemporaries Kaiho Seiryō (1755–1817) and Honda Toshiaki (1744–1821). Buyō's language is far from sophisticated, and his use of Confucian, Buddhist, and Kokugaku ("nativist") concepts is eclectic, to say the least. Buyō expresses disdain for intellectuals who do their studies "sitting at a desk" (p. 417), and although he mentions various authors in passing, he stresses that his knowledge of the world derives from his own observations. "Over the years," he writes, "I have used my free time to mingle widely with people in the world," making a conscious effort to befriend people from all walks of life (p. 35). In many ways, his views echo a broadly shared "common sense" that exerted considerable influence on warrior politics in nineteenth-century Japan. As such, these views offer something that more polished intellectual treatises may not: a picture of that common sense in action.

6. Totman, *Early Modern Japan*, p. 466.
7. Buyō has been widely quoted in English-language scholarship as well as in Japanese, beginning with Neil Skene Smith's 1937 compilation of sources on Edo society and economy and Thomas C. Smith's classic 1959 study of Edo village structure. See Skene Smith, "Materials," pp. xvi, 30; Smith, *Agrarian Origins*, pp. 176–77. Corroboration for many of Buyō's observations about Edo social and economic arrangements can be found in the translations of Edo court cases and shogunal records contained in Wigmore, *Law and Justice*.

Buyō's thesis is a simple one. In 1600, after over a century of endemic warfare, Tokugawa Ieyasu (1542–1616), whom he refers to as the Divine Lord (Shinkun), established a near-perfect society through his mastery of the military Way. Seventeenth-century Japan was, in Buyō's eyes, an era when frugal farmers supported a benevolent regime of enlightened warriors. These two classes, which together form the "foundation of the state," were bound together by a mutual sense of duty, respect, and even understanding. Over time, however, the superb order created by Ieyasu and maintained by his immediate successors gave rise to wealth. As the world filled with "splendor," merchants and "idlers" (*yūmin*) grew in number and consumed more and more of the state's resources. As a result, money took over the world, corrupting even the warriors and the farmers. The Way of duty and righteousness succumbed to the Way of greed. For every merchant or idler who grew rich, hundreds if not thousands of farmers and even warriors were thrown into poverty. As money entered into people's social relationships, natural intimacy and solidarity gave way to heartless calculation and alienation. A return to the golden age of the Divine Lord might no longer be possible, but at least it should serve as a guide to those currently in authority. To prevent the impending collapse of the realm, the number of townspeople and idlers—including nonproductive people such as popular writers, artists, and entertainers—should be reduced and the warrior class should reestablish its grip on the world. The key to such essential reform, Buyō argues, is to reassert the primacy of the military Way.

To understand Buyō's anger, his analyses, and his proposed solutions, we need some sense of the historical context in which *Matters of the World* was written. To that end, here we first take a closer look at the larger structures of society in the mid-Edo period. Then we address some of the events in the age that must have formed Buyō's worldview: the decades around 1800. Finally, we trace Buyō's major concepts and categories and sketch the intellectual landscape that informed his outlook.

SOCIETY IN THE MID-EDO PERIOD

How was society organized in Buyō's day? Traditional theory divided the population into four classes: warriors, farmers, artisans, and merchants (*shinōkōshō*). Reality was more complicated. In the broadest terms, one can arrange these different segments of society into two categories: the ruling and the ruled. The former included shogunal and domainal warriors (*bushi*), the court nobility in Kyoto, and the temple clergy. The latter can be divided into farmers (*hyakushō*), townspeople (*chōnin*), and outcasts (*eta* and *hinin*); "artisans" did not constitute a social category of their own in any meaningful sense. These groups were clearly distinguished from one another, entered into different census or household registers and subject to different laws and rules. Less easy to categorize were free vocations, such as physicians and performers of different kinds. There was also a considerable number of "unregistered persons" (*mushuku*), people who had fallen out of the register system and thus were no longer incorporated in the basic framework of social control. Buyō designed his work around a simplified version of this social hierarchy: warriors, farmers, townspeople, and idlers.

WARRIORS

Warriors of the Edo period differed fundamentally from their forebears in that, after the initial decade or so, they were not called upon to fight. Further, policies adopted by national and regional leaders in the late sixteenth and early seventeenth centuries had resulted in warriors' being removed from their landholdings in the countryside and gathered in the castle towns that consequently sprung up throughout Japan. The largest such castle town was Edo, built both literally and metaphorically around the shogunal castle, which occupied the large area that today serves as the imperial palace. In Buyō's time its resident was the eleventh shogun, Tokugawa Ienari (r. 1787–1837), whose reign was the longest of the fifteen Tokugawa shogun. The shogun held directly lands producing some four million *koku*;[8] controlled the main cities, harbors, and mines; had a monopoly on minting coins; and supervised the largest markets in Osaka and Edo. A further three million *koku* of land were distributed as fiefs (*chigyōsho*) among the upper ranks of some fifty-two hundred shogunal retainers called bannermen (*hatamoto*), although almost all the holders of these fiefs resided permanently in Edo.[9] Bannermen filled

---

8. Land was measured in terms of putative yield. One *koku* corresponded to approximately five bushels (180 liters) of rice, or the amount consumed by one adult male in one year.

9. It should be kept in mind that for a fief or stipend calculated in *koku*, the figure indicated the total putative yield of the landholding, not the feudal holder's

most civil and military positions in the shogunate, except for the very highest. Below them were some seventeen thousand housemen (*gokenin*). As a rule, these men did not hold fiefs but received fixed stipends of rice; the same was true for more than half the bannermen. What distinguished housemen from bannermen in formal terms was that housemen did not have the privilege of attending an audience with the shogun; Buyō often refers to them as "below audience rank."

Both bannermen and housemen were organized in units under a chief (*kashira*) of higher rank or placed under the supervision (*shihai*) of some office. Appointments to official duties were channeled through these chiefs and supervisors, as were disciplinary matters. Such duties, which could involve both extra income and extra costs, were far fewer than there were hopefuls: even among bannermen, less than half held administrative positions. Living on fixed stipends, payable in rice, in a large city was far from easy, and many warriors faced structural economic problems. Possible solutions included cutting costs and relinquishing the symbols of one's status; engaging in piecework and a variety of side jobs; borrowing money; renting out one's official accommodation and moving to cheaper lodgings; or even "selling" one's warrior status, via the adoption of a commoner heir in exchange for money.

Warriors with fiefs of more than 10,000 *koku* were known as daimyo. In the late Edo period there were some 260 daimyo, who, altogether, held around 22.5 million *koku*, or about 75 percent of all productive land. Daimyo kept their own armies, issued their own laws, collected their own taxes, and enjoyed a large degree of autonomy in governing their domains. At the same time, they were kept under close surveillance by the shogunate, which had the authority to confiscate, reduce, or increase domains; move daimyo from one location to another; and impose extraordinary obligations. Daimyo were categorized on the basis of their relationship to the shogunate. Pre-1600 hereditary vassals of the Tokugawa (*fudai*) occupied strategically situated smaller domains, many in the vicinity of the Tokugawa heartland. Daimyo drawn from this category filled the highest posts in the shogunal administration. Major collateral branches of the Tokugawa house (*gosanke*) occupied large domains in Mito, Kii, and Owari, while other Tokugawa-related houses (*kamon*), large and small, were dispersed throughout the country. Finally, the so-called

---

actual income. The latter, which depended on the tax rate, was generally about one-third of the total yield.

outside (*tozama*) daimyo, who had pledged fealty to the Tokugawa only after 1600, held some of the largest domains, located in more peripheral regions.[10]

In principle, only hereditary vassal daimyo held positions in the shogunal government; daimyo in the other categories were expected to concern themselves solely with the administration of their own domains. The main source of daimyo income was rice taxes and other levies on farmers in their domains. Many domains, particularly those situated in the western provinces, sent their rice to Osaka, where it was traded at the country's largest rice exchange. Compared with the shogunate, which had the option of trying to manipulate the price of silver and gold through recoinage and debasement, daimyo were more exposed to fluctuations in the price of rice. From the mid-eighteenth century onward, many larger domains developed local monopolies, stimulating within their lands the growth of industries whose products were sold in the cities by domain merchants. When facing deficits, domains "borrowed" money from their retainers by cutting stipends or from villages through special levies, printed rice bills that served as local currency, and took loans from city merchants.

All daimyo were obliged to spend part of their time in Edo, generally every other year, and to leave their heir, consort, and a support staff there permanently. Traveling back and forth between their domains and Edo and maintaining multiple Edo residences was a tremendous drain on daimyo finances. The roughly six hundred compounds kept by daimyo in Edo dominated the city landscape and added a substantial number of domainal warriors to the shogunal retainers of various ranks who resided permanently in the city.[11] There were also numerous *rōnin* (masterless warriors), who, having lost or failed to secure a regular vassal position, had to survive on their wits without a stipend from a lord. Scholars estimate that approximately half of Edo's one million inhabitants were warriors of one kind or another.

---

10. The complete picture was rather more complicated; for a map showing the situation in 1865, see Wigmore, *Law and Justice*, vol. 1, following the preface and editorial notes.

11. From the shogunate's perspective, samurai who served the daimyo and bannermen as retainers were rear vassals (*baishin*). For an account of daimyo compounds in Edo and the circumstances of those living in them, see Vaporis, *Tour of Duty*.

In the country as a whole, warriors numbered between one and a half million and two million in all, which amounted to 6 to 7 percent of the total population. In legal principle, warriors represented a hereditary class that was strictly separated from all others. The cities were divided into separate quarters for warriors and commoners. Warriors were not supposed to engage in either agriculture or trade and were expected to marry within their own class. Theoretically, they had the right to cut down obstreperous commoners at will (kirisute); Buyō refers to this privilege more than once and laments the fact that it is no longer practiced. As Buyō sees it, warriors should have free rein in exercising their heavenly calling to administer the affairs of the realm.

In practice, however, the dividing line between warriors and commoners was increasingly opaque. Warrior status had become almost a commodity, purchased by or bestowed upon many commoners who, in Buyō's terms, lacked "pedigree." Buyō bemoans the formally illegal use by commoners of luxury goods and status symbols that were supposedly reserved for high-ranking warriors alone. Not only did commoners impinge on warrior privileges, but they also benefited from the freedom that came with nonwarrior status. Buyō was particularly disconcerted by the impunity with which commoners filed lawsuits against warriors over financial matters—and, even worse, the tendency of shogunal officials to uphold commoners' claims and force warriors to compromise and humiliate themselves. Whereas commoners were free to pursue their greed with impunity, Buyō argues, warriors carried the burden of pride and risked damaging their reputation, which constituted their essential capital. The fact that commoners could treat warriors with such contempt was a sure sign of the decline of the world, and Buyō feared that in the long run this might "come to their even bringing the warriors down" (p. 217).

COURT NOBILITY

We can be brief regarding the imperial court, because Buyō has little to say about it. He never refers to Emperor Kōkaku (r. 1781–1817), the long-ruling imperial monarch of his time. The main functions of the court in Edo Japan were confirming the shogun's legitimacy and authority, awarding—conditional on prior approval by the shogunate—court rank to leading warriors and titles and privileges to religious institutions, and performing ceremonies for the protection and prosperity of the state. The court maintained close ties with important temples by providing imperial and noble offspring to be their heads. Such temples were known as imperial and noble cloisters (*monzeki*). The court included some one hundred fifty houses of nobility. Many of these houses specialized in specific court traditions, ranging from poetry composition and a highly ceremonial form of football to yin-yang divination, and they derived an income from performing, teaching, and providing certification for those arts. In addition, most held fiefs granted by the shogunate and corresponding in size to those of a mid- or lower-range bannerman.

Few of these functions met with Buyō's approval. He was not impressed by courtly arts, lamenting that even warriors and townspeople had begun to waste their time and money on them. Even more dubious were the financial dealings in which court lineages engaged. The house crests of court nobles inspired awe, and the nobility, Buyō argues, abused this asset. They lent money against exorbitant interest or leased the right to use their crest to other lenders. The Tsuchimikado house rubber-stamped licenses of yin-yang diviners in return for annual fees, without educating them or supervising their activities; the Shirakawa and Yoshida houses gained an income from shrine priests in much the same way. Buyō is even more appalled by the fraudulent way in which court nobles dispensed licenses to monks; according to him, the Kajūji house, for example, systematically secured imperial edicts for a modest bribe, allowing monks to become abbots without fulfilling the official requirements. The court, then, features exclusively in a negative light, as a useless institution that gives idlers a semblance of respectability in exchange for bribes.

CLERGY

Monks and priests are a matter of special concern to Buyō. Temples were involved, if only formally, in the shogunal and domainal administration of the populace. From the 1660s onward, all sectors of the population were required to affiliate with a particular temple, and these temples were called upon to guarantee that their parishioners (*danka*) were not Christians but Buddhists. Annually, local officials compiled census lists and had them stamped by temple priests. By various routes, census information from all domains and territories ended up in the office of the shogunal magistrates of temples and shrines. Even landless farmers and urban poor, who often led floating lives, were included in these temple registers. Sooner or later, those who fell out of this net of social supervision were likely to run into trouble.

The temples involved in this system were organized into mutually exclusive sects with strict hierarchies, from head temples in western and eastern Japan at the top to regional intermediary temples and local branch temples at the bottom. Head temples educated, certified, and appointed priests to branch temples, collected various fees from them, and stood responsible for their conduct. Buyō is less concerned with shrines than with temples, although he senses that the former were even more numerous. Most shrines were small and controlled by temples, and they had no role in the administration of the populace.

Temples typically were endowed with land. The largest temples held so-called vermilion-seal lands (*shuinchi*), land granted by the shogunate in the same manner as a warrior or noble fief and left to the temple to exploit. However, few temples had sufficient land for their needs, and most raised additional funds by various other means. Most important were funeral and memorial services for parishioners, which were more or less obligatory; others included prayer ceremonies, public displays of sacred images (*kaichō*), solicited donations, lotteries, and money lending. Although most temples were underfunded or even destitute, Buyō expresses disdain at the money flow generated by these activities. He decries the enthusiasm with which parishioner households of all classes embraced Buddhist ritual and laments the fact that many gave precedence to temples' fund-raising activities over their duties to lord and family.

Even though temples were integrated into the Tokugawa administration, many intellectuals were critical of Buddhism and of the role played by temples and priests. Buyō goes so far as to argue that faith in Buddhism is an obstacle to performing one's duties as a warrior because it replaces loyalty and courage with an overriding concern for the afterlife. Buddhist temples might be useful if they concentrated on teaching the lowly some basic self-control, but, he contends, this was not what temples did. Quite the contrary, they acted as parasites, sucking up enormous wealth while inspiring in the faithful selfish greed and a fancy for extravagance. Even more damage was done whenever Buddhism infected warrior leaders, as it had already in the days of the first shogun, Minamoto no Yoritomo (1147–1199). When it was allowed to meddle with matters of the state, Buddhism would destroy the military Way and plunge the realm into chaos; this explained the dire state of Japan in the centuries before Tokugawa Ieyasu restored order.

Buyō displays a particularly aggressive distaste for priests. Not only were they idlers; they were idlers with an official status, ranks, fiefs, and a guaranteed income. In Buyō's view, giving public recognition of this sort to idlers added insult to injury.[12]

FARMERS

In contrast, Buyō underlines the central importance to the state of the farmer class. Farmers are the foundation of the realm, together with the warriors who tax them so as to provide benevolent government. This perspective is clear from the alternative term he applies to the farmer class: *kokumin*, meaning "people who sustain the state." Needless to say, Buyō's conception of the state as a hierarchical system of classes has little in common with the modern nation-state (*kokumin kokka*) of "equal" citizens that defined Meiji Japan. Yet his use of the term *kokumin* to denote productive people who form the state's foundation and thus deserve its protection seems to point forward to that later transformation of the word.

In late Edo, Japan's countryside consisted of some sixty-three thousand villages, in which resided about twenty-five million of the overall population of approximately thirty-two million people. The majority of villages were agricultural, although a substantial minority engaged in fishing, lumbering, or other trades. Whereas all villages came under the jurisdiction of the shogun, a daimyo, a bannerman, or, in a few cases, a temple or court noble, they were managed without too much interference from such higher authorities by a farmer elite, consisting of the village officials (*mura yakunin*)—the headman (*shōya* or *nanushi*) and a small group of leaders—and a larger body of landowning farmers (*hon-byakushō*). Below these were small-scale farmers (*komae-byakushō*) and a class of landless laborers, who in the seventeenth century had typically survived as hereditary subordinates of major farmers but in the later Edo period were more likely to enter into tenancy contracts or to engage in temporary wage labor.

---

12. For an analysis of Buyō's views on religion, see Teeuwen, "Early Modern Secularism?"

Villages had their own regulations, managed their own common lands, and were taxed collectively, with the allocation of the tax burden among cultivating households left to the village officials. Most substantial was the annual land tax (*nengu*), consisting nominally of 40 to 50 percent of rice and other crops (the latter mostly payable in coin); in practice, as a result of discrepancies between putative and factual productivity, actual taxes were in the range of 20 to 30 percent. Public duties and corvée works were assigned to villages, which either divided the work among locals or paid wages to others to do it; not a few of these duties were, in effect, additional annual levies thinly disguised as corvée. Villages also made contributions to infrastructural work on rivers and roads, as well as paying extra levies to cover projects or deficits as and when they occurred. In sum, these various taxes, corvée duties, and levies constituted a considerable burden on most villages.

These taxes and levies formed the main source of income of both the shogunate and the domains. It was, therefore, of overriding importance to keep farmers in their villages and to make sure that they obeyed orders from their absentee warrior lords. This function fell to the village officials, who transmitted orders from above, reported on irregularities and incidents, and, on occasion, conveyed villagers' needs to the warrior authorities. Collective responsibility was an important mechanism for keeping order in the countryside, and farmers were organized in five-household groups (*goningumi*) that were supposed to see that their fellows did not step out of line. In the early Edo period, in particular, warrior governments also set restrictions on the sale of land, the kinds of crops that could be grown, trading activities, and crossing domain boundaries.

Legal constraints of this sort could be real enough whenever fief holders saw themselves forced to intervene in village affairs. In normal times, however, many of these measures were riddled with loopholes. Selling land, or at least the right to cultivate it, was a common practice. By the late eighteenth century, much agricultural land was the private property of a farmer elite that took rents from those who actually tilled the fields and invested its capital in commercial crops such as cotton, tobacco, and vegetables or in the production of consumption goods for sale in the cities. This undermined the ideal of a coherent village community in which landholding farmers shared responsibility for production, taxes, corvée work, and order on a basis of relative equality. Other restrictions were equally ineffective. Villagers traveled widely, even across domain borders; many sent their sons and daughters into service in city households. Many poorer farmers abandoned their fields and drifted into towns and cities, looking for employment as day laborers, peddlers, or servants. Especially in the Kantō area, fief holders struggled to maintain village populations and to keep fields in cultivation.

By Buyō's time, village life was a far cry from the ideal envisioned by the warrior government. For Buyō, the farmer should be a humble person who eats coarse food, dresses in rough clothing, exposes himself to the winter cold and the summer heat, tills the soil in the company of oxen and horses, obeys the fief holder's rules, performs his corvée labor, and "nurtures everyone" with his produce. Buyō laments the fact that the urban vices of calculation, extravagance, and greed had infected the countryside. As a result, a small number of rich farmers monopolized the wealth and plunged all those around them into destitution. To make things worse, the evil habits that follow money's trail had made farmers wayward and stubborn in their dealings with fief holders, fostered crime and murder, and obfuscated class distinctions. On the other hand, Buyō is critical of what he saw as the oppression of farmers by greedy fief holders. He argues that fief holders should strive to reduce the numbers of destitute people, or at least should grant them the freedom to leave and find a livelihood somewhere else.

TOWNSPEOPLE

Edo-period Japan had three large cities: Edo, Osaka, and Kyoto. In Buyō's time, Edo was still growing at the expense of the other cities. Osaka had topped out at around 500,000 inhabitants but was now declining; Kyoto had been shrinking for a longer time and had fallen below 300,000. In addition, there were some two hundred castle towns, as well as a fair number of temple, harbor, post-station, rural market, and mining towns. In total, the urban population may have reached some three million to four million people—*excluding* the warrior class, which also, as noted, lived almost entirely in the towns and cities. This means that some 15 percent of Japanese were urban, a percentage higher than in most of contemporary Europe, with the exception of the Netherlands and England. Only London, Paris, and Naples were larger than Osaka in 1800; Edo was probably more populous even than London.

The warriors, townspeople, and temples and shrines in towns and cities fell under different administrative jurisdictions and tended to be situated in physically separate districts. In Edo, almost 70 percent of the city area was taken up by daimyo compounds and warrior housing, and of what remained, half was temple land (see map 1). This left approximately half a million townspeople cramped into a very small space. Initially, some 300 blocks (*chō*) were laid out for townspeople's use; by Buyō's time these had increased to 1,678.[13] Shogunal officials of warrior status presided over the top echelons of each jurisdictional pyramid and adjudicated matters involving people from different jurisdictions via the Supreme Judicial Council (Hyōjōsho). In the case of Edo, the shogunal officials primarily responsible for overseeing commoner matters were the two town magistrates (*machi bugyō*). Among other things, these magistrates received lawsuits lodged by townspeople, although if the person being sued was of a different status (such as a warrior) or from a different jurisdiction, the case would be referred for ultimate decision to the Supreme Judicial Council, on which the town magistrates sat together with other warrior officials, such as the finance magistrates (*kanjō bugyō*), responsible for overseeing shogunal lands classified as rural.

Underneath this supervisory and policing apparatus, townspeople, like the farmers, largely ran their own affairs. Edo had three commoner town elders (*machi-doshiyori*) who took turns managing city matters. Below them were about 260 headmen (*nanushi*), each of whom was responsible for from two to four or, in some cases, as many as ten-plus city blocks. The headmen performed specialized tasks under the town elders as well. These positions were hereditary and came with salaries; also, fees were payable to town elders and headmen for various administrative procedures, such as the sale of house plots.[14] In Osaka, the system was different in its details but not in its overall conception.

Blocks typically consisted of a street with facing shops, enclosed at both ends with gates that were closed at night. Although the term is often used more loosely, "townspeople" (*chōnin*) proper, comparable to the major

---

13. Osaka, in contrast, had only a few warrior blocks around the castle to the east and a temple district to the south, leaving some 90 percent of the city for the townspeople.

14. For the Edo town administrative system, see Katō, "Governing Edo."

landowning farmers (*hon-byakushō*) in the villages, were the house owners. Renters, many living in rows of tenements behind the houses that faced the street, constituted the main body of the city population—in Edo in Buyō's time, approximately 70 percent.[15] House owners were organized in five-household groups that played a central role in the block's self-administration. They paid fees and levies covering the costs of city and block administration, were responsible for keeping an eye on their tenants, and assisted the headman on a rotating basis in overseeing block affairs. In contrast to farmers, however, townspeople paid no regular taxes on the fruits of their labor and were not subject to the many restrictions applied to villagers.

Trade guilds (*nakama, kumiai*) were another important element of urban administration. From the mid-Edo period on most branches of trade were monopolized by such organizations, in many cases with shogunal sanction. Guilds paid annual license fees to the warrior authorities or provided services in return for protection of their monopolies. The members of such guilds held shares (*kabu*), which could be transferred or sold to others only with the guild's permission. Members shared access to the guild's trade network, rendering business more secure.

Merchants belonging to the largest guilds were closely integrated in the daily running of warrior affairs. Much of the rice collected as taxes by western domains and some from shogunal lands was channeled through Osaka, where it was bought and sold by rice brokers and converted into money. Through shipping and wholesaling guilds, a substantial amount of this rice was then sent to Edo, as were other items marketed through the Osaka exchange. The operations of Osaka merchants thus had a major impact, both direct and indirect, on the warriors' financial circumstances.[16] In Edo, a comparable role was played by the rice agents (*fudasashi* or *kurayado*) who handled the disbursement of stipends to shogunal bannermen and housemen. Three times a year, warriors of this level went through such townsman agents to have their stipends, allocated in rice, converted into coin. Rice brokers and agents frequently acted as financiers to daimyo and lesser warriors, advancing loans against the security of incoming tax rice, sometimes for years to come. As a conse-

---

15. This number is taken from *Ōedo happyaku yachō*. Kitō Hiroshi cites a number of "over 60 percent" (*Bunmei*, p. 98).

16. On Osaka's role in the national economy, see McClain, "Space, Power."

quence, it was by no means rare for merchants of townsman status to manage the financial affairs of daimyo compounds, and if a storehouse agent refused to renew a loan to a daimyo at the end of the year, when bills needed to be settled, this could mean economic disaster for that domain and its retainers. Similarly, how much income an individual warrior received from his stipend depended on rice prices and the amount of deductible interest on his debts. Buyō is outraged that such important matters as the pricing of rice and supply of provisions were left to market mechanisms and argues that it would be impossible to rule the realm effectively unless such matters were brought under shogunal control.

Of course, not all townspeople wielded such power. The cities also attracted paupers and fortune seekers from the countryside and housed a large number of unregistered persons, people no longer included in one of the census registers either because they had absconded or because their families had formally expelled them as a punitive or self-protective measure. Buyō shows some sympathy for those who had been forced to flee to the city by hardships beyond their control. He sees preventing such eventualities as a test of the government's benevolence (a test that, in his eyes, the shogunate did not pass). Fortune seekers, of course, were a different story altogether. And ultimately the poor, too, were certain to be corrupted by city customs. Even those who tried to survive by honest labor soon ran into trouble with guild monopolies, fell prey to moneylenders, and were forced into committing crimes.

In the end, Buyō has no use for city dwellers. Townspeople produced nothing and wallowed in unlimited consumption, easily becoming parasitical idlers. They were "worms" that devour the state's wealth and "fester in the flesh of the warriors and farmers" (pp. 308, 376). As followers of the "inverted Way" (*gyakudō*)—greed and calculation—they undermined the martial virtues that formed the foundation of the realm.

OUTCASTS

Unregistered people who made their way to the city soon found that Edo life was strictly regimented even at the bottom of the heap. Various groups on the periphery of mainstream society laid claim, with shogunal sanction, to exclusive begging turfs, for example. Such groups included, among others, different categories of outcasts, known as *eta* (pariahs), *hinin* ("nonhumans"; translated in the following as "outcasts"), *koyamono* (hut dwellers), and similar terms.

Eta and *hinin* were denied townsman status and were physically segregated from the rest of the population, but they were by no means cut off from society; in fact, they constituted an important link in the system of social control. There were major regional differences, but in most places outcasts were organized in hierarchical structures under a designated chief (*kashira*). In Edo, chiefs carrying the hereditary name Danzaemon supervised the *eta* of the city and the surrounding provinces. The *hinin* were divided among smaller bosses, the most important of whom were called Zenshichi and Matsuemon. By the 1800s, both had fallen under Danzaemon's authority. The prototypical trade of the *eta* was the production of leather goods from horse and cow hide, but they also acted as prison guards, executioners, and police assistants; worked at graveyards and as cleaners; and engaged in more ordinary activities such as making and selling lamp wicks and straw sandals and cultivating marginal land. *Hinin* made periodic door-to-door rounds collecting alms, performed dances and sketches on street corners, did jobs dealing with sanitation, acted as guards, and formed a general workforce that could be ordered out by their bosses at the authorities' request. Whereas *eta* was a hereditary status, *hinin* were not necessarily born such. By origin, many were unregistered vagrants who had drifted into the city and resorted to begging on the streets. *Hinin* bosses sent out regular patrols to round up such "unofficial" beggars and often then enrolled them among their underlings.[17]

Although the large majority of *eta* and *hinin* lived in a state of abject poverty and exploitation, those at the top did not necessarily do so badly. Danzaemon received a large compound and a stipend of three thousand *koku* from the shogunate, a great deal more than the average bannerman. (His case was unique; no other *eta* or *hinin* leader enjoyed such treatment.) *Eta* monopolies on leather goods were also profitable. As semi-official guards and watchmen, the outcast bosses were in a good position to collect bribes and kickbacks. Yet outcasts confronted many obstacles to raising their living standard even when they had the means to do so. In a famous case from 1805, a middle-ranking *hinin* was sent into exile when it became apparent that while officially living in a ghetto hut he ran a

---

17. Howell, *Geographies*, pp. 30–31.

wealthy household in another part of town, complete with a garden, tea ceremony room, and a large staff of servants. The scandal was such that it resulted in the arrest of many dozens, including two block headmen.[18] To Buyō, rich outcasts provided another example of the age's blatant incongruity between hereditary status and real-life wealth and power.

IDLERS

Priests and various town residents were the major representatives of what Buyō sees as the inverted Way of idlers. Another problematic type was what he refers to as "troublemakers" (*akutō*), people akin to the yakuza of later times who formed gangs, promoted gambling, and engaged in extortion and other unsavory activities. Still others may have posed less of an immediate challenge to the preservation of law and order but likewise exemplified the ills Buyō attributes to idlers. Three groups that stand out in *Matters of the World* are blind moneylenders, prostitutes, and Kabuki actors.

Many blind people were organized in yet another guildlike group, called Tōdōza (the Guild of Our Way). The major occupation of guild members was playing the *biwa* (Japanese lute) and singing the medieval warrior epos *The Tale of the Heike*; others served as acupuncturists and masseurs. As with the *hinin*, the shogunate recognized the Tōdōza as having the prerogative to collect alms on a regular basis. The guild claimed ancient links with the imperial court, and members paid annual dues to a house of nobility in Kyoto (the Koga); in Edo, this proved helpful in resisting attempts by Danzaemon to incorporate the blind into his empire. Buyō cites as historical facts the origination legends that the guild developed in its struggles to maintain its independence in the mid-Edo period.[19] He shows little interest in the majority of blind persons in Edo, who were either outside the guild altogether or filled its lowest echelons. His concern is with the highest ranks, who were close to warrior leaders and who secured official backing for their financial dealings.

---

18. Groemer, "Edo Outcaste Order," pp. 291–92.
19. On the development of these legends, which had medieval roots, see Fritsch, *Japans blinde Sänger*. On the Tōdōza's struggles with Danzaemon, see Groemer, "Guild of the Blind," pp. 352–55.

Already in the seventeenth century, Tōdōza members began to lend funds to warriors and merchants. The income from such loans provided the blind with the means to obtain higher rank (*kan*) in the guild, and, as a charitable measure, the shogunate granted special protection in its courts to loans made from guild members' "rank funds" (*kankin*)—a term that also carried the connotation of "official funds." The shogunate exempted Tōdōza rank funds from the "edicts ordering the parties to resolve matters on their own" (*aitai sumashi rei*) that it issued periodically to clear out the backlog of old debt cases clogging shogunal courts. Basically, such orders stated that the parties should handle current disputes over debts by themselves rather than rely on official adjudication and enforcement. The protection of Tōdōza rank funds from the danger of becoming subject to such an order drew nonblind lenders to try to funnel their money through them as well, even if this meant they had to pay a cut to the Tōdōza. The shogunate moved to stop such practices on several occasions (e.g., in 1765 and 1815), explicitly censuring the noisy techniques of harassment that the blind sometimes adopted to shame debtors into paying. Even so, banking became the main occupation of Tōdōza members. In 1779, an investigation triggered by the flight from Edo of a shogunal retainer of considerable rank revealed that the guild's outstanding loans amounted to no less than 360,000 *ryō*, a sum corresponding to the annual income (in *koku*) of a major daimyo.[20] To Buyō, the blind represent a blatant case of idlers of the most evil sort, who, like priests, enjoyed official protection. He even considers blindness to be a heavenly punishment for greed. The blind epitomized the inverted Way, and they certainly did not deserve a better fate than *hinin* beggars and street performers.

An even more blatant example of that evil Way was the prostitution business. Brothels of various kinds were ubiquitous in Japanese towns and cities; Edo, which had a considerable surplus of males, was no exception. The city sported the country's largest authorized red-light district (Yoshiwara), as well as scores of unauthorized but often tacitly tolerated brothel areas known as *oka-basho* (a term meaning something like "side place"; Buyō refers to these as "restricted areas," *okamai basho*, places

---

20. This case backfired on the lenders, with some dying in custody and others exiled, fined, or thrown out of the guild; see Groemer, "Guild of the Blind," p. 358.

where, officially, prostitution was off-limits). Unauthorized prostitution also took place at tea shops, restaurants, pleasure-boat inns, bathhouses, and in the street. In Buyō's time, some five thousand girls and women were confined within Yoshiwara's moat alone; unauthorized brothels housed as many again. Occasional crackdowns hardly put a dent in this business. The authorities closed more than fifty *oka-basho* in 1795, but at least thirty appear to have survived, and in the first decades of the nineteenth century new ones popped up, especially on the far side of the Sumida River. Stern action against illicit brothels was limited to short periods and tended to dissipate at Edo's boundaries. Yoshiwara burned down completely in 1800, 1812, 1816, and 1824; but the number of prostitutes continued to grow.[21]

For Buyō, sexual misconduct was a central component of the inverted Way of money. Those he accuses of greed are also often charged with debauchery, and it is clear that for him material and sexual desire are two sides of the same coin. Yet toward those who were sold into prostitution Buyō shows unexpected sympathy. He sees them as innocent victims or even as paragons of filial piety, submitting to a life "in hell" so as to enable their impoverished parents to survive. The real villains of this trade were the brothel keepers, who lived lives of extravagance and depravity by exploiting hapless girls. On the other hand, Buyō leaves little doubt that once they had become professionals, prostitutes could never redeem themselves. He describes their transformation, mediated by a debilitating sickness, in almost metaphysical terms. Through their exposure to men's desire, prostitutes depleted the "roots" of their feelings and ceased to be human beings endowed with heavenly virtue. They became barren "beings that are no longer human" (*ninpinin*), unable to do even the simplest kind of productive work. Forcing a woman to violate her "natural chastity" in this fashion was as bad as a warrior abandoning loyalty: prostitution destroyed the very foundations on which society was built (pp. 324, 319).

---

21. According to Amy Stanley (*Selling Women*), prostitutes in both Yoshiwara and the entertainment districts enjoyed some protection by the ruling authorities because they worked under contract, their earnings going to a parent or guardian. Streetwalkers did not deserve protection because they worked for themselves.

Buyō also worries about sexual norms beyond prostitution. He notes that more and more men had taken up the custom of installing "kept women" (*kakoimono*) in houses around the city. Sometimes they even bought these women from their proper husbands, destroying families for the sake of private lust. Instead of keeping it a secret, Buyō observes, they bragged about it as a status symbol. All sense of discretion appeared to have been lost, and as people's taste for luxury spilled over in a general decay of sexual morals, "the Way of men and women has become a matter of buying and selling, and sometimes even stealing" (p. 360). As an obvious cause of this decay Buyō points to the world of entertainment: Kabuki theater, popular light novels (*gesaku*), samisen songs, puppet shows, and erotic prints (*shunga*) all conspired to promote lasciviousness and corrupt people's sense of propriety. The only pastime that is to Buyō's liking is sumo wrestling; yet even this admirable sport was in decline because people no longer liked something as clear-cut as a fight for victory or defeat, preferring instead "something sexy" (p. 338).

All in all, Buyō perceives the world as a place where idlers thrive while honest warriors and farmers fall into poverty. The straight Way of martial uprightness was being undermined by its inverse, the Way of money and sex. Even warriors were presented with the choice between honest ruin and corrupt prosperity. Only the appearance of "a virtuous and able figure" who could correct the age's "deleterious customs," "restore the ancient style [of the Divine Lord], and establish a regime of good rule, peace, and order" could turn the tide (p. 433). How exactly such a savior might achieve this, however, Buyō fails to clarify.

BUYŌ'S HISTORICAL PERSPECTIVE

Buyō is quite specific about his dating of the world's decline. As he puts it in his prologue,

> The period from the Keichō and Genna eras [1596–1624] until the Genroku and Kyōhō years [1688–1736] was an enlightened age of supreme peace, sincere courtesy, and warm magnanimity. After that time, however, things appear to have gone awry, and although we may well revere that age of goodness today, we are unable to recover it. (p. 36)

What above all led Buyō to point to the early eighteenth century as a watershed was his belief that from this time, warrior government had become inextricably caught up in an increasingly commercialized economy. Fundamental to his perspective was his acceptance—widely shared by Edo-period thinkers and policy makers—of three related premises of classical Chinese political thought. One was the assumption that as the state was built on agriculture, its prosperity depended on its ability to realize the ideal pithily expressed in the *Book of Rites* as "no abandoned fields, no idlers."[22] The second was the identification of excessive consumption as the root cause of impoverishment: "Let the producers be many and the consumers few. Let there be activity in the production, and economy in the expenditure. Then the wealth will always be sufficient."[23] The third was the conviction that, as Mencius put it,

> If the people have a steady livelihood, they will have a steady heart; if they have not a steady livelihood, they have not a steady heart. And if they have not a steady heart, there is nothing they will not do in the way of self-abandonment, moral deflection, depravity, and wild license.[24]

Buyō refers repeatedly to this notion, which in his eyes fit exactly the circumstances he saw around him: farmers and warriors should in principle belong to the category of people with a "steady livelihood," while townspeople and idlers, by definition, fell outside it.

Buyō does not conceptualize economy, politics, morality, and nature as separate domains, each with its own dynamics; for him, they are all subsumed in a single "Way of Heaven" that is inextricably tied to moral practice in human society. He does not look for ways to promote progress or growth; rather, he yearns for the state of equilibrium that, he imagines, existed in the past. Blaming excessive commerce for the increasing disparity between rich and poor, he disapproves of the ever more pervasive circulation (*yūzū*) of money, which, he believes, had spread the evil habit of calculation (*rikan*), a mode of behavior that was antithetical to loyalty, sincerity, and all other virtues. Because commerce brought with it more circulation and calculation, it could only worsen

---

22. *Book of Rites* (*Liji*), chapter 5, "Royal Regulations." James Legge, who uses a slightly different wording to translate this phrase, also uses a different numbering system for the chapters. See Legge, *Lî Kî*, 1:230.

23. *The Great Learning* 10:19; Legge, *Chinese Classics*, 1:379.

24. *Mencius* 3.A.3; Legge, *Chinese Classics*, 2:239–40; the translation has been modified slightly.

the imbalance between rich and poor, corrupt social morals, and undermine the warrior control on which the social order depended.

Looking at the first two hundred years of Tokugawa rule from this perspective, Buyō sees the "splendor" that resulted from the orderly and peaceful environment established by the Tokugawa founders as having given rise to a proliferation of "evil customs" that had thrown the world out of kilter. Until the Genroku-Kyōhō years, even the lowliest had had a sense of moral obligation, but from this time on, greed, extravagance, and deceit had taken hold and corrupted society. Beginning in the reign of the fifth Tokugawa shogun, Tsunayoshi (r. 1680–1709), the wealth accumulating in the hands of townspeople had caused all others to become ever more impoverished, while under the eighth shogun, Yoshimune (r. 1716–1745), the government itself had come to adopt a mercantile outlook. It was in the Kyōhō period that the shogunate began to offer loans from government coffers (a practice that Buyō likens to the government engaging in usury), recognized the monopolies of the rice agents, and—in a reversal of previous policy—began to encourage the formation of closed merchant guilds, guaranteeing their monopolies against the payment of annual fees. As Buyō sums up the situation, "On the occasion of the Kyōhō reforms, the shogunate openly decided things on the basis of the calculation of profit" (p. 393).

Buyō thus does not subscribe to the characterization of the Kyōhō period (1716–1735)—still found in some history textbooks and general historical studies—as marking the first great effort at restoration in an alternation of eras of "rout and rally." Such a view, now widely criticized as an overstatement, structures Edo history as a succession of waves of excessive consumption, commercialization, and corruption (routs), followed by reforms that restored feudal order through strict sumptuary laws, attempts to strengthen agriculture and reduce commerce, and anticorruption measures (rallies). Buyō presents Yoshimune as a promoter rather than an enemy of commerce. All in all, Buyō sees the Kyōhō years as a time when, although there was still a degree of decency in the world, the Way of profit was rapidly gaining ascendancy.

Buyō takes a similar view of what has traditionally been regarded as the second great rally, the Kansei reforms of 1787–1793, which were enacted during his lifetime. Led by the senior councilor Matsudaira Sadanobu (1759–1829), Yoshimune's grandson, the Kansei reforms were carried out in the wake of a series of disasters in the preceding decade.

Bad weather caused a sustained series of crop failures, exacerbated by a catastrophic volcanic eruption of Mount Asama in 1783. Hundreds of thousands died of malnutrition or starvation, rice prices exploded, and refugees from northern Japan flooded into Edo. In 1787, three days of rioting shook the city, with mobs plundering and destroying up to one thousand rice-dealer shops and pawnshops; Buyō must have lived through this time of turmoil as a young man. In response, Sadanobu sought to strengthen shogunal control over "gold and grains," to stabilize rice prices, and to bring down the prices of other commodities. To increase rice production, farmers who had fled their villages for Edo were encouraged to return. Sadanobu also took measures against the rice agents and other brokers who had invited the wrath of both commoners and retainers in Edo. The agents were ordered to cancel long-standing debts owed by bannermen and housemen and were forced to reduce the interest rates of more recent loans. Together with these economic measures, Sadanobu launched an attempt to improve public morals, because, like Buyō, he saw moral corruption as the root cause of the crisis. New sumptuary laws were aimed at reducing consumption and clarifying class differences. There was a clampdown on "decadence," including illegal brothels, mixed bathing, popular prints, and novels of an "immoral" nature.

Such policies might be expected to meet with Buyō's approval, and indeed he praises Sadanobu's establishment of granaries as a buffer against famine as an example of "benevolent governance"—although he also adds that "the fact that things cannot be managed without such a policy is a sign that the world is coming closer to the end" (p. 306). On the other hand, Sadanobu also pursued further the accommodation with the commercial economy that Buyō decries as a negative legacy of the Kyōhō period. The Kansei reforms utilized the financial power of a select group of Edo financiers, and public funds were loaned to rural investors, who were ordered to use the proceeds for measures to support destitute farmers and return abandoned fields to cultivation. The shogunate expanded the policy of trying to regulate supply and pricing through the formation of closed guilds. Both in cities and villages, the shogunate depended on the investment skills of designated merchants to finance measures intended to underwrite a warrior-led rice economy. As a consequence, in Buyō's eyes, the reforms failed to bring about any real improvement. His general assessment can be gleaned from a passage in which he ridicules the shogunate's attempt to ban extravagance in Edo's theaters:

> Ever since the Kansei reforms, there have been so-called clothing inspections, with officials occasionally coming to make an examination. On that single day the actors deliberately wear old and plain clothing to pass the inspection. Because the actors have to wear ugly rags when the officials come to inspect their clothing and the officials get in the way of the performance, the latter just peer in for a little while and leave almost immediately. When they come to see the spectacle for their private enjoyment, they bring along their wives and concubines or entertainers and see it through to the end. What was supposed to be an inspection by the public authorities ends up being nothing of the kind, and the actors are left free to indulge in their usual splendor. (p. 332)

If anything, the measures adopted in the Kansei years contributed, Buyō holds, to a tendency for warrior authorities to become more "weak-kneed." The reforms "did no more than stress ordinary proper manners" and in that way ended up aggravating the imbalance between rich and poor (p. 417). It is by no means certain what Buyō means by the term "manners" (*sejō no gyōgi*) here, but other passages make it clear that he had serious doubts regarding what he saw as the age's stress on protocol and propriety, based on a predilection for Confucianism. Rather than as proof of order, he takes the imposition of Confucian rites on warriors to be harmful to Ieyasu's true legacy. Although the government had managed to gain control over the rioters in 1787, he was not at all convinced that this would still be possible in his own time.

THE BUNKA YEARS

Buyō finished *Matters of the World* in Bunka 13 (1816). By this time, the shogunate was facing quite a different range of problems from the Kansei years. A long spell of largely favorable weather produced bountiful harvests, which drove rice prices down. The prices of other goods did not decrease proportionately, leaving both individual warriors on stipends and the shogunate as a whole with growing deficits. To resolve this problem, the shogunate continued the policy of trying to concentrate trade in the hands of merchants' guilds. In the same decades, however, emerging rural producers who linked up with nonguild traders succeeded in opening new channels into Edo's markets, frustrating shogunal attempts to gain control over pricing. The shogunate then resorted to increased lending of public funds against interest, new sumptuary legislation, and, in 1818, the minting of new coins and the debasing of others.

The Kantō area was particularly vulnerable to the economic changes of these decades.[25] The countryside around Edo had remained relatively backward for multiple reasons. It was fragmented among countless small fiefs (including the holdings of thousands of bannermen), it suffered badly in the 1780s, and it profited relatively little from proximity to Edo because the bulk of goods consumed in the city was shipped in from Osaka. The latter situation began to change in the early nineteenth century, when the region developed its own Edo-linked networks of production and trade. Well-to-do villagers took part in and benefited from these developments, but commercial growth had an adverse effect on the traditional village structure and agriculture. The farming population shrank, and taxable harvests dwindled away. As noted, Buyō makes frequent mention of floating groups of troublemakers and unregistered persons; these groups included many people who had abandoned their villages and agriculture, and they emerged in part because of the vacuum of authority characteristic of the region. Administrative fragmentation made it difficult to deal with any of these problems. By 1827, the situation had grown so serious that the shogunate created a range of new administrative policies, regulations, and offices (the so-called Bunsei reforms) to restore order in the Kantō countryside.

When Buyō was writing *Matters of the World*, many of the problems specific to the Kantō were already apparent. Buyō's horizon was limited largely to the city of Edo and its surrounding provinces, and his analyses project the problems of the Kantō on Japan as a whole. His sense of crisis over the powerlessness of warrior authorities in the face of falling rice taxes, rising prices, extravagant and guileful farmers, and increasing numbers of "floaters" is best read as a reflection of realities on the ground in the Kantō area in the first two decades of the nineteenth century.

25. Howell, "Hard Times."

INTELLECTUAL INFLUENCES

Matters of the World falls into a category of works known loosely as "discussions of government and society" (*seidōron*). Buyō states that he is not learned and, as mentioned, takes conventional scholars to task for being overly attached to abstract theory of one sort or another. Nevertheless, he also indicates a familiarity with the central works of such scholars, from Kumazawa Banzan's (1619–1691) *Daigaku wakumon* (*Questions and Answers Regarding The Great Learning*) to Ogyū Sorai's (1666–1728) *Seidan* (*A Discourse on Government*) and *Taiheisaku* (*A Policy for Great Peace*) and Motoori Norinaga's (1730–1801) *Hihon tamakushige* (*The Jeweled Comb Box: A Private Memorial*). Echoes of these writers' observations on contemporary ills can easily be detected in *Matters of the World*.[26] For instance, Buyō criticizes Ogyū Sorai for focusing excessively on forms of social propriety (*kaku*), but he also reprises Sorai's concern about the vacuum of authority in the Edo hinterland and praises his diagnosis of the problematic consequences of the accumulation of wealth in the hands of townspeople: "Considered from the present state of affairs, [Sorai] indeed hit the mark. On many other points also things are just as he said" (p. 393).

Despite such parallels, *Matters of the World* differs in a number of regards from other well-known Edo-period discussions of government and society. Above all, whereas other authors set out often elaborate proposals for rectifying the problems they identify, Buyō makes virtually no specific policy recommendations.[27] His idiosyncratic modification of a term central to Sorai's discourse, *seido*, meaning "regulative institution" or "system," encapsulates the difference. Holding that the lack of appropriate *seido* was the root cause of the problems of the time, Sorai called for the adoption of a wide range of new institutional arrangements. Buyō, by contrast, frequently uses the term *seido* as a verb, meaning something akin to "control" or "clamp down." Seeing the recommenda-

---

26. The abridged version largely omits the sections where Buyō discusses the views of other thinkers, including most of the passages cited here. For a fuller picture of his intellectual outlook, see the unabridged version, particularly chapter 7.

27. At various points in his narrative Buyō notes cryptically that he has a plan that he will set out "elsewhere." If he did so, though, it is not known to us today.

tions of Sorai and other scholars as overly abstract and visionary, Buyō argues that to correct the current sorry state of affairs and restore a truly benevolent regime, what was essential was to to implement "the military Way" (budō):[28]

> The Way of benevolence is to bring benefit to others without harming oneself. To benefit those below without diminishing those above can be called benevolent government. This is the benevolence of the great Way. This great Way cannot readily be established without the military Way. (p. 417)

What does Buyō mean by the "military Way"? He contrasts it to Confucianism, noting that warriors were unable to act effectively and easily fell victim to the machinations of townspeople, idlers, and farmers "because the shogunate has sidelined the military Way and placed the circumspect ways of Confucianism at the center" (p. 73). He does not, however, define the military Way in concrete terms. One clue to his understanding of it comes from the character of a work that he sets apart from "scholarly" discussions of government and society and praises as coming "very close to hitting the mark on this great Way": *Honsaroku* (*The Records of Lord Honda*), attributed traditionally to one of Ieyasu's advisers, Honda Masanobu (1538–1616). As Buyō puts it, "Masanobu may have been unlearned, but since he was accomplished in the military Way, the Confucian scholars mentioned above could in no way match him" (p. 417). Unlike the other works Buyō mentions, *Honsaroku* does not prescribe specific measures. Rather, it offers the ruler more general, no-nonsense advice—advice that corresponds quite closely to Buyō's own view. Rulers should keep a distance from Buddhist priests, townspeople, and idlers. They should choose advisers carefully, keeping on guard against people likely to prove sycophantic, self-serving, or unreliable and seeking those who would unswervingly take the steps necessary to ensure the ruler's welfare and that of his regime. They should deal with farmers and agricultural resources in such a way as "to see that farmers are left with neither an excess of wealth nor an insufficiency."[29]

---

28. *Budō* is the usual term; *bushidō* (Way of the warrior) occurs once (see p. 72).

29. *Honsaroku*, p. 289.

Buyō often prefers a telling anecdote to a theoretical argument. It is just such an anecdote, about Ieyasu and his trusted adviser Itakura Katsushige (1545–1624), that provides perhaps the best clue as to how Buyō imagined the military Way should be practiced:

> When the Divine Lord traveled to Kyoto in the Keichō years [1596–1615], he was received by the Kyoto governor, Lord Itakura Katsushige, who had an audience with him at the Awata entrance to the city. The Divine Lord asked him, "Now you have been governor for three years. How many criminals have you had executed?" Lord Itakura replied, "Three criminals have been condemned to death and executed." "Three people in three years is a lot," the Divine Lord said, and next he enquired whether everything was all right at the court. Lord Itakura's reply, that there had been just three executions, was a lie. In reality, the number of executions was several score, and "three" was nowhere near the truth. Lord Itakura's lying in this manner was an expression of his loyalty to the Divine Lord. A number of low-ranking Kyoto townspeople [known for being assertive toward their governors] were present when the Divine Lord asked this question. When they heard his exchange with Lord Itakura, they thought, "His Majesty is a merciful person indeed to imply that even a mere three executions in three years is too much. And how gracious of him to ask about this even before he enquires about the court itself. In contrast, Lord Itakura is truly callous to say that he has had only three persons executed, while in fact he has killed scores. He is a man one should be wary of!" Due to their fear of Lord Itakura, the city was peaceful and orderly. The loyalty of people of that age was of a different caliber. (pp. 419–420)

Through this tale from shogunal lore, Buyō offers a model for the balancing of military and civil means, for the intelligent loyalty that the shogunate should inspire in its retainers, and for the attitude that government leaders should take toward the populace.

Such references suggest that, for Buyō, the military Way meant a capacity to gauge the situation from a broad perspective and act in a tough-minded and decisive manner. It also meant a readiness to employ force when necessary. The current age, in his eyes, was one of virtual "war," in which people preyed on others with no restraint; soon, he feared, matters would deteriorate into an "actual clash of weapons and a renewed age of upheaval." Since the ultimate cause of the crisis at hand was unlimited consumption by townspeople and idlers, the only real solution was to reduce their numbers. To do so, a bold "attack" (*kōgeki*) was needed; and "unless one uses the force of the military Way, it will be difficult to carry out such an attack" (pp. 401, 407).

BUYŌ IN HISTORY

An outright military attack on townspeople and idlers was, of course, not a realistic option for shogunal policy makers. Many of Buyō's arguments resonate, however, with the thinking behind a string of measures that the shogunate would adopt three decades later. In the Tenpō reforms of 1841–1843, it tried to forcibly dissolve merchant guilds and monopolies, return people who had gathered in Edo to the countryside, and sharply reduce the place of theaters, brothels, and popular entertainments in Edo life. The results were highly mixed; the dissolution of guilds, in particular, disrupted economic life and long-standing administrative mechanisms. That the reformers were prepared to push such measures suggests that they looked at the situation from a perspective not so different from Buyō's. Similarly, the hostility Buyō shows toward the Buddhist priesthood as greedy and corrupt was widely shared and anticipates the anti-Buddhist measures adopted in the last decades of the Edo period and following the Meiji Restoration.

If in these ways Buyō's views may be taken to illustrate a quite general samurai "common sense," it is also revealing that he pays little attention to new ideas that by 1816 must have been readily accessible to an avid observer like him. Notably, he demonstrates no interest in the place of the imperial court in Japanese life, an issue that was attracting increasing attention from a range of thinkers. Buyō represents a worldview that placed the Tokugawa shogunate squarely in the center. He never refers to the shogun as the emperor's deputy, a notion that gained currency from the late eighteenth century onward; for him, the "present reign" began with Ieyasu's pacification of the realm. The Tokugawa regime was legitimated not by imperial commission but by the Way of Heaven, which had responded to Ieyasu's benevolence and mastery of the military Way by giving him the realm. Buyō's frequent allusions to the Way of Heaven (*tendō, tentō*) hark back to a discourse with roots in the seventeenth century—*Honsaroku* is an important exemplar of the genre—in which the Way of Heaven appears as the "lord of Heaven and Earth," a semipersonalized, ultimate source of authority that rewards the worthy and punishes those who ignore its commandments.[30] In Buyō's view, the military Way and the Way of Heaven are two sides of the same coin. The Way of Heaven would back those who, like Ieyasu, employed the military Way appropriately, and without such use of the military Way it would be impossible to secure the Way of Heaven's lasting support.

Together with his focus on the shogunate and disdain for the imperial court, Buyō keeps a distance from matters that animated a number of contemporary thinkers, including the growing Kokugaku movement, such as the nature of Japanese antiquity as an age of divine perfection and the character of the Japanese polity compared with that of other countries. He titles one chapter "On Japan Being Called a Divine Land" and, in an apparent nod to Kokugaku concerns, begins it with the statement "I have heard it said that Japan is a Divine Land and that in ancient times the feelings of its people were clear and bright, without duplicity and never obscured by a single cloud or wisp of mist. Those times are thus called the Age of the Gods" (p. 381). In what follows, however, he finds no use for that divine age, the imperial ancestor and sun goddess Amaterasu, or any other of the ancient deities.[31] Neither does he show an interest in the theories of warrior-scholars who trace Japan's martial essence back to the islands' formation from the brine that dripped from the creator deity Izanagi's spear in that same "Age of the Gods."[32]

Buyō also fails to touch on another issue that was already looming in the writings of some of his contemporaries: the potential danger of Western economic and territorial ambitions. Russian military action in the north in 1806 and 1807 and the appearance of a British warship in Nagasaki in 1808 caused a minor panic even in Edo, and the Western threat became a topic of some debate. For Buyō, however, Japan remained a

---

30. For more on this notion in Buyō, and also the significant differences with seventeenth-century *tendō* discourse, see Teeuwen, "Way of Heaven."

31. Pilgrimages to Ise, where Amaterasu is enshrined, figure primarily as regrettable occasions for wasting money (see pp. 258, 334) or committing crimes (p. 323), although Ise itself is associated with laudable frugality, in contrast to the extravagance of Buddhist temples (p. 160).

32. For this discourse on Japan as a "martial land" (*bukoku*), see Maeda, *Heigaku*.

closed system, unaffected by what might be going on in the rest of the world.

Buyō's lack of concern for matters such as those in the preceding suggests the need for a degree of caution in estimating their weight in the general discourse of the day. Preoccupied with identifying the seeds of the ideas on which the Meiji state was founded, historiography of Edo-period thought has tended to focus on thinkers who sanctified the imperial line or who saw beyond "feudal" understandings of class and the economy. In English, the 2005 revised edition of *Sources of Japanese Tradition* is a good illustration of this tendency: it introduces imperial loyalists, untraditional economic thinkers, critics of the class system, and "forerunners of the Restoration."[33] To the student who has read this selection of sources, Buyō might appear as an anachronism, an eccentric relic out of tune with his own time. We argue that he was not. The modern reader may query Buyō's proposed response to the contradictions of Edo economy and society but cannot but admire the acuteness with which he observed them. Beyond that, the interest that others took in his indictment of the ills of the day reminds us of the danger of reading history backward, in the light of later events. *Matters of the World* seems to have secured a substantial audience by the end of the Edo period. An undated printed version of the first two chapters appeared late in the period, and a manuscript copy of the first chapter with reading notes attributed to the daimyo Tokugawa Nariaki (1800–1860), who was a major presence on the national political scene in the 1840s and 1850s, exists in the former archives of the Mito domain.[34] Surely the thinkers who did make it into *Sources* should be situated in an intellectual context that continued to find much of Buyō's worldview congenial.

33. De Bary, Gluck, and Tiedemann, *Sources*.
34. Aoki, "Seji kenbunroku no sekai," p. 34.

Part 2

MATTERS OF THE WORLD: AN ACCOUNT OF WHAT I HAVE SEEN AND HEARD

Buyō Inshi

PROLOGUE

Ever since I reached the age of discretion, I have noticed that people's dealings with one another are not straightforward. Some win and others lose, some make a loss and others gain. People's desire to win and their competition for gain troubled me, and many a time I thought to find out the source of this mental disposition and to clarify where it might end.[1] Over the years, I have used my free time to mingle widely with people in the world. From farmers I learned about their hardships, and I reflected on profit by investigating market prices. I consciously sought to make friends with those idlers who exemplify the manners of our age, and I came to know the fickleness of their feelings. Seeing derelicts,[2] I found out what had brought them to their present condition and gave thought

---

1. "Mental disposition" (*ninjō*); Buyō uses this and related terms (*kishō, jinki*, etc.) to refer to people's moral, mental, and spiritual orientation or mood, rooted in their *qi* (Jp. *ki*), the East Asian notion of a fundamental psychophysical endowment.

2. *Haijin*, which is translated as "derelicts" throughout, refers to those who, as a result of degenerate behavior or otherwise, are no longer able to lead a normal life.

to their future fate. As I observed the customs of the present and compared them with the good times of the past, it became clear to me that people's dispositions have grown corrupt and their conduct negligent, that the principles of the Way have become hidden, and that the indiscriminate struggle for profit has created an extraordinary imbalance between rich and poor. As a rule, the strong and the shrewd win and the weak and the stupid are duped. Here, I will give an unvarnished account of such matters, though they are unbearable to watch and insufferable to hear.

Peace has reigned for more than two hundred years, and from one generation to the next the minds of the people have grown lax, their spirits have deteriorated, their commitment to trustworthiness and uprightness has worn thin, and they concern themselves solely with extravagance and lust. To be sure, that this is an age of peace also has its advantages, and some people behave in a calm and moderate way. However, it is hardly necessary to elaborate on such advantages, and here I will record only the evil aspects of our age. There is much more that is not at all well, but some of it involves the shogunate, and I will omit all points where it might appear as if I were castigating the shogunal government. Also, I will not touch upon those evils that it would in fact be detrimental to the state's interests to correct. Vulgar matters of little importance will also be passed over, since they are limitless. I will concentrate on the larger outlines and focus especially on those below middle rank and the baseborn.

The period from the Keichō and Genna eras [1596–1624] until the Genroku and Kyōhō years [1688–1736] was an enlightened age of supreme peace, sincere courtesy, and warm magnanimity.[3] After that time, however, things appear to have gone awry, and although we may well revere that age of goodness today, we are unable to recover it. Yet it is hardly satisfactory to spend one's days in resignation, abandoning all concern for the present situation, and therefore I have noted down the evils of the world wherever they have caught my eyes or reached my ears. Indeed, I have a distant hope that the world will be rectified once again. I am neither knowledgeable nor lettered. My account is bound to stray from the rules of logic, there will be mistakes in the characters I use, and my choice of words will be coarse and rustic. This work will remain the profound secret of my life; it hardly bears showing to others, nor passing down to my

---

3. Buyō refers to dates and spans of time by era name (*nengō*). We have supplied the Gregorian calendar equivalents.

descendants. Therefore, I will leave it to those wiser than me to decide what should be kept and what discarded, and I will simply let my brush run to my heart's desire, without embellishment or ornamentation.

Bunka 13 [1816]
A certain retired gentleman of Musashi

Chapter 1

INTRODUCTION

The history of ages past teaches us that order is difficult to maintain and disorder hard to put down. From medieval times, fighting continued throughout the provinces with not a moment's respite from the clash of weapons. The principles of the Way disappeared from the world, courtesy and deference were abandoned, and the Way of lord and vassal was lost. Those above turned their backs on the virtue incumbent in a lord; those below ignored the Way of the vassal. Vassals schemed to overthrow their lords, while lords, in turn, attempted to rid themselves of their vassals. Without the support of the structure of rank and office, the hierarchy of high and low was lost, the minds of the people became as unstable as clouds or water, and their situations became as precarious as walking on thin ice. Fields were left untilled, and the land was full of widows, orphans, and people without anyone on whom to rely.

But then, the Divine Lord, through his martial virtue, succeeded in bringing the entire land, from one seashore to the other, to bow to his majestic authority.[1] For quite a long time thereafter, the entire country remained at peace. The Way of Heaven and Earth was opened up and the Way of lord and vassal was correctly observed. Rewards and punishments were administered with strictness, loyalty and filial piety flourished, the country was affluent, and the military was at peace. Down to the lowest of the baseborn, all were able to keep order in their households, live in peace and security, and exert themselves in their proper occupations. The transforming effects of great peace spread throughout the state. Has any such thing been achieved since the origin of Heaven and

---

1. Buyō typically refers to Tokugawa Ieyasu as the Divine Lord.

Earth? Is it not without precedent in both Japan and China, past or present? It would be foolish indeed to believe it possible to describe the vastness of the Divine Lord's benevolence and virtue.

However, it appears that in the past two hundred years, people have grown weary and self-conceited from living in this splendid order, and perhaps because of too much ease and plenty, customs have changed greatly in recent times. Excessive luxury has caused both high and low to ignore the limits pertinent to their status. Opulence increases by the day and reaches ever greater heights by the month. People's dispositions have become unstable, and the bedrock of trust and duty is worn thin. As the gratitude that this great order should inspire is forgotten, even the lowliest become conceited. Thinking only of their own good, they seek solely to surround themselves with luxury and become ever more obsessed with private greed. They bully those who are of lower status while flattering those above them, and they seek to dupe others with lies and deceit. In all matters duty is disregarded.

Yet no one speaks out against this state of affairs, no one condemns it. The custom of the day is to condemn the poor and praise the rich. Therefore, both high and low have cast off duty, courtesy, and deference. Instead, they all exert their minds and exhaust their strength in running after profit. Today, those who have a warped talent for the Way of profit will win fame, and the affairs of the world are all tilted toward greed. Whereas relatives or friends should offer mutual assistance, greed drives them apart. Pretending not to notice even acute hardship, people run away from it. The faithless become rich, while the dutiful are robbed and reduced to poverty. Because of this, the true meaning of all ways of life is lost. Profit comes first and duty last. It is as though the differences between the four classes of people and between high and low no longer exist. What is considered honorable or lowly is determined solely by wealth or poverty. The order between high and low has been turned upside down in a manner that is utterly beyond words.

How regrettable! Orderly rule has given rise to too much splendor, and great peace has transformed the world. Things have become reversed, the root has gone awry, and the branches have become disordered. Below I will provide an outline of how the four classes of warriors, farmers, artisans, and merchants, as well as all others, have lost their sense of trust and righteousness, turned toward superficiality, and become obsessed with luxury and greed.

WARRIORS

The comportment of the warrior is meant to constitute a model for the world as a whole. It is the warrior's calling to interrogate the rights and wrongs, the good and the evil that men do, and to determine due rewards and punishments. Warriors are thus not to be remotely arrogant, nor are they to fawn; they are to be utterly immune to desire. They must be prepared to offer their lives for the state and to be paragons of loyalty and filial piety. Even the least and lowliest warrior is to comport himself with dignity, to put moral obligation first, to resist desire. His intent should never deviate from loyalty and filial piety. However, brought low by indulgence in long years of peace, the warrior character that the common people have as their model today is warped and off-kilter. To begin with, the warriors of today do not know their proper place, they are inadequately prepared militarily, and they give no thought to public service. Having no ingrained sense of propriety, in all matters they act without consideration;

Warriors and others at the Yotsuya gate on the road leading into the district surrounding Edo castle (see map 1). In the foreground a high-ranking warrior riding in a closed palanquin and surrounded by a procession of retainers leaves the castle district. Behind him two lower-ranking warriors on foot head into it. *Edo meisho zue* (1834). National Diet Library Digital Collection.

they are incapable of completing the task at hand. Instead, they are concerned solely with convenience, with making good the immediate situation.

The Faults of Daimyo and Other Highborn Warriors

These observations apply especially to those warriors born into daimyo houses and other houses with large fiefs. From the start of their upbringing, they are doted upon by others and praised for the most meager accomplishments, and their wrongdoings treated as virtues. Day in and day out from morning until night, they are the objects of unfailing respect. They know nothing of shame and so fail to understand the duties demanded of them. Warriors born to high rank have no sense of perspective, and as their housemen set before them only those matters that are designed to please, they become ever more headstrong. As their every whim is heeded, they become arrogant. They think that if what is before them is fine, everything is fine. If something displeases them, they, in their headstrong manner, are quick to anger, regardless of what is for the best. They force others to submit to them and think they are clever for having done so. They have no qualms about causing trouble or doing harm to others as a result, and they spare no thought either for the unfortunate consequences of their actions. They loathe anything that might constrain them; they hate to be told anything not to their liking. Indeed, they delight to see others at a loss, and thus they grow ever more self-indulgent.

As a man matures, he should become increasingly wise and sincere. This is not the case, however, with the daimyo and other major warriors of today. They are habitually impulsive and quick to anger; they are given to prejudice and, incapable of consideration, cause no end of trouble to their retainers. Retainers manage all the general affairs of the domain without informing the lord. The lord leaves all his personal affairs up to his young male personal attendants or his wives and concubines; he indulges them as if he were watching children at play. In past ages, it was common for warriors to mock those who pursue elegance as "courtiers." Now, though, it is the better warriors who behave like courtiers; the majority have become like women.

The fact is that, though entrusted with authority over a province or district, daimyo and other major warriors remain ignorant for their entire life of the actual conditions of the place with which they have been entrusted. They do not carry out the governance demanded of their role. Rather than looking on the people with compassion, they allow their gaze to be distracted by their maidservant favorites. Taking advantage of the lord's fecklessness, his housemen assume control over various matters, and because the lord is himself so lacking in purpose, the housemen do not deal with anything in an upright manner and do not carry out the administrative matters of the domain with any rigor. Since the lord abhors uprightness and rigor, his housemen dither and end up knocking some solution together on the spur of the moment. They bend things to find an easy solution and simply try to smooth things over. The lord is in truth the most vital presence: if his heart is in the wrong place, the many beneath him will be led astray. In such a situation, the relationship between lord and vassal, high and low, will be in disarray, and the end result will be that those below cheat those above, for when it comes to deceit, it is hard to better the lowly.

It is entirely natural for housemen to praise their lords; if the lord does something good, a houseman should praise it as welcome, attend to him with renewed vigor and loyalty, and spread word abroad that his lord is an especially wise man. And yet this does not happen. The aforementioned lazy and weakhearted stance means that there is nothing to praise. Since there is nothing but foolishness, inevitably the lord gains a bad reputation abroad as well. This is not a matter of shame enduring for the lord's lifetime alone: the reputation of a foolish lord endures for generations to come.

Even those major warriors who have their wits about them have instincts that are only fleetingly correct and a sense of duty that is ephemeral. They are incapable of sincerity of any duration. Even should they come up with a plausible statement on some matter or other, it is simply a case of stringing together fine words to impress others; never will they put those words into practice. Or they may make inappropriate statements, without thinking through the consequences; they are unable to achieve anything courageous or compassionate.

Major warriors of this sort are oblivious to the fact that in places beyond their sight people are enduring insufferable tribulations. Giving favors only to those whose apparent difficulties catch their eye, they imagine they have done all that might be asked of them. They are boastful, rejoicing when others show them gratitude in public for their beneficence. They treat well those for whom they feel fondness and delight in their own reputation among these, bestowing on them unwarranted favors. They pay not the slightest heed to the utter destitution among the people of the soil in the land entrusted to them. They may decry the injustice of a situation in which people, owing to the iniquities of the officials who rule over them, engage in wrongdoing, flee the land, or engage in unlawful acts out of desperate poverty and end up being punished. And yet they make no effort to adopt measures that will prevent people from falling into poverty and thereby forestall such lawbreaking. The grain and wealth they obtain from the people they spend entirely on satisfying their own personal desires.

Of course, the accumulated wealth of the warrior is the product of the sweat of the people, so it should not be lightly distributed elsewhere.[2] If there is a surplus, it should be used to bring succor to those who produced it. Yet daimyo and other major warriors do not dispense such surplus where it is needed. Instead, distracted by the desire to secure their own glory, they make donations to temples and shrines and extravagant offerings to buddhas and gods. Or they use their wealth on pastimes and entertainment for their own satisfaction. Or they use it to buy extravagant gifts for their beloved pages and servant girls. This extreme favoritism displays an utter lack of compassion for the impoverished people of the land.

The present age is a splendid one, and people have come to see military activity as something no longer necessary; that is why daimyo have forgotten the attitude a military commander should take toward his vassals and why they pay no heed to the people's welfare. With regard to the relations between lord and vassal, there is little communication between them until a looming crisis requires concerted action. They simply aim to keep up appearances and maintain conventional politeness; they avoid speaking plainly even about matters where principles are at stake. Vassals chatter away about things that take their fancy and simply fawn before their lords. Even when lord and vassal are unsure what to do, they will never sit together and discuss pros and cons. If the timing does not suit them, they will postpone the matter indefinitely. Thus, there can never be a meeting of minds between a lord and his vassals. Lord and vassal both become feckless. Sometimes each will yield to the other, leaving

---

2. For Buyō, the "people" (*tami*) always means the farmers.

vital matters unsaid; their minds thus grow distant from one another. Sometimes a crafty vassal will espy the growing distance between a lord and his other retainers and take advantage of it to confound the lord. Ignoring normal obligations and casting aside established regulations, he may go on to beguile the lord into establishing new [tax or trade] policies intended to enrich the domain. In this way, he may set before his lord the possibilities for profit and lure him into greed.

The upright and loyal vassal's mind is resolute; he can never perform the flashy tricks of the crafty vassal. Immediate profit has always some hidden loss lurking behind it; profit is, in brief, bound to impose suffering on the common people. Everybody knows it is not right, yet nobody is possessed of the wit to produce an alternative or to say stop it and do this instead. As a result, people are unable to thwart the proposed measure. Rather, they can do nothing but follow the crafty vassal's lead, saying that such a measure suits the present age; as a result, his undertakings come to hold increasing sway. Pursuing ever more frivolous plans of this sort, the crafty vassal becomes the hero of the day.

A vassal of this kind espies the lord's frailties and anticipates his delights; he takes actions designed to please the lord before he is told what to do. He sets before the lord only what is auspicious and happy and conceals anything unpleasant. He reassures the lord that cosmic calamities are nothing to be feared and flatters him into believing all is well. Such a vassal encourages the lord in superstitions so that he becomes timid and suspicious and acquires new prejudices and new likes. In this way, the crafty vassal makes himself indispensable and comes to take sole charge of matters both within the lord's household and in the domain at large. As a result, the other retainers grow yet more distant from the lord; loyal vassals increasingly hold their tongues and offer no advice. Lord and vassal grow apart in their understanding of the world. Each is content to spend the years looking out only for his own well-being.

Such, in this present age, is the way things have come to be. Daimyo have become caught up in the arrangements made by fawning, ingratiating vassals of this sort. They fail to understand the moral standards demanded of their position; they abandon irreplaceable virtue and allow themselves to be lured into compromising situations that they had hardly anticipated. They become addicted to their own pleasure and desire. They let the old ways lapse, disrupt the traditions of their house, and bequeath nothing but trouble to their descendants.

The Fecklessness of Smaller Fief Holders

Turning to the case of small-scale fief holders, they too have no awareness of their proper place in the world.[3] They have no capacity to make decisions on their own, and, faced with a crisis, they are incapable of response. They make a show of forbearance, but in reality they are craven, so everything they do is ineffective. To start with, they cannot enforce frugality even within their own household. Many cannot keep even their wives, children, and other dependents under control, let alone their servants. Others get caught up in some untoward obligation and end up incurring unforeseen expenses. Or, having a taste for splendor, they exercise no restraint over expenditures for weddings or funerals and act extravagantly. For example, if their income for the current year [derived from the taxes they collect from their fief or coming from their stipend] is inadequate to their needs, they appropriate what can be expected the next year. Never do they reflect for a moment that one year's glory might bring a decade of misery; nor does it occur to them to try to make up the loss. Rather, ever more unable to keep up financially, they end up relying on others and think nothing of incurring debts of gratitude. They delight in receiving gifts. Whenever they themselves are asked a favor, they are careful first to weigh what gratitude and recompense can be anticipated in return before responding accordingly.

When it comes to the performance of their official duties, they never consider whether their abilities might or might not be suited to the particular task at hand and are simply guided by greed in seeking a post. They request a position too lofty for one of their status, get themselves a supplement to their stipend, and indulge themselves in a luxurious life.[4]

---

3. In the following paragraphs, Buyō focuses primarily on the situation of shogunal bannermen, whom he often refers to as *shōshin* (small-scale), an allusion to the smaller size of their fiefs or stipends as compared with daimyo domains.

4. Buyō refers here to *tashidaka* supplements, a system introduced by the eighth shogun, Yoshimune, to encourage the employment of capable bannermen in shogunal administration. On the assumption that holding office was a feudal duty and that appointees would pay for the costs of that office out of their stipends, eligibility for office was geared to status and the size of the appointee's stipend. *Tashidaka* supplements involved temporarily raising the stipend of a lower-ranking prospective appointee to the level deemed necessary to hold the office in question.

Many small-scale warriors deploy their guile in this way in an attempt to make good their financial affairs that have fallen into disarray through their own mismanagement. Although, by rights, they should take the greatest care in performing the official tasks entrusted to them—after all they have received the honor of an appointment to an office in the shogunal government—they do nothing of the sort. Instead, they devise schemes to get promoted to some still loftier post before they have accomplished anything in their present position. This is a distraction, and they expend a mere 50 to 60 percent of their energies on service but a full 100 percent on getting promoted.

Because their only concern is for promotion, they are afraid of making mistakes. They can never take bold action; they are always timorous, so they lose the authority that attaches to the office allotted to them. They maneuver to ensure that their reputations are upheld, fawn to all and sundry, and turn a blind eye to any vices on the part of their subordinates. They think it appropriate to treat even servants with respect, and their behavior is ever more craven.

In line with the habits of the day, such people feel no shame about the disarray and mismanagement of their own personal finances. Indeed, they flaunt their financial problems, making a song and dance about them as though they were something to be proud of. They tell their superiors in the hope of a compassionate response from the shogun. They plead for a position that would bring a substantial supplement to their stipend. They seek positions of weighty responsibility when they lack the capacity to manage even the affairs of their own small house or to carry out the duties of their service. What an outrageous way to carry on! If their finances are in such a state that they cannot perform their duties, they should resign them of their own accord. But such is the way things are today. Their own disarray they use as grounds for pleading. They beg for compassion and mercy endlessly in pathetic tones that are fit only for the lowliest of servants.

It used to be the practice for warriors to endure their trials and tribulations in silence. As in the old saying, "The samurai proudly keeps a toothpick in his mouth even if he has no food to eat," there used to be a taboo on warriors' pleading for mercy and compassion, even if it meant dying of starvation. Samurai today have no such forbearance; they are forever complaining to others, fawning, seeking favors. They spend their days searching for immediate fixes. They think it desirable to equip themselves with money and fine garments, landing themselves in debt far beyond their capacity for repayment. In recent years especially, bannermen with fiefs use [the prospective taxes from them] as security to obtain those "loans" from the shogunate that are so popular today;[5] or they borrow so-called entitlement money from imperial cloisters and elsewhere.[6] They end up using half or even more of their allotted stipend to pay interest and other [handling fees]. They become totally unable to manage their finances and fail to repay the debts they have incurred. The shogunal administration tries to enforce repayment strictly, but the debtor, seeking to avoid his obligation, sends his retainers to the pertinent office to make hollow excuses and obtain a slight extension. In some cases, the office will summon the farmers who have stood as guarantors and threaten them with confinement or handcuffing.[7] Even then, repayment proves impossible.

Warriors of this sort spend much on miscellaneous matters and pile loss upon loss as they paper over their poverty. When they take out a loan, it may well give some temporary respite, but in the long run their finances become more and more constrained. Even when being dunned for repayment becomes a daily occurrence, they fail to find the funds to settle. And as for the lands that make up the bannerman's fief, farmers are brought low by repeated demands that they pay future years' dues in advance. As bannermen borrow from elsewhere, the debts to repay pile up to the point where their houses incur grave damage. For the glory of one generation, or the convenience of a single moment, three genera-

---

5. A number of shogunal offices, most particularly the Kantō supervisor (*Kantō gundai*), operated such loan funds. These supplied impecunious shogunal retainers with loans at lower rates of interest than they might be able to obtain elsewhere, but as Buyō points out in chapter 5, the shogunate was also strict about enforcing repayment. See also Ōguchi, "Reality," pp. 300–301.

6. "Entitlement money" (*myōmokukin*) here is a reference to loan funds managed by high-ranking temples and similar entities under the premise that the fund's ultimate purpose was to support the temple's preservation and the like. Because the money was "entitled," shogunal courts enforced repayment more rigorously than with ordinary townspeople's loans; they were thus the resort of those whose credit was no longer good enough to obtain ordinary loans.

7. If a bannerman used the future income from his fief as collateral for a loan, he might get the farmers living on the fief to cosign the debt instrument.

tions of descendants end up suffering. The impact on the economic situation of large numbers of farmers is profound.

The lands distributed to bannermen as fiefs have been bestowed as benefices from the shogun in return for the service [rendered by the holders' ancestors]. It is most regrettable that the shogunal government should lend the holders money, using [the taxes from that land] as security, and extract interest in addition to repayment of the principal. How lacking in compassion, too, the persecution of farmers who are unable to find the funds for repayment! Lord and vassal dispute over loans and profits and losses, and the upshot is that the lord seizes profit at his vassals' expense. Surely this undermines the shogunate's aura of authority! This is too much even for these latter days of warrior law.

On the other hand, those bannermen and shogunal housemen who receive stipends [instead of fiefs] build up enormous debts to the officially designated rice agents.[8] As a consequence one-third or one-half or even more of the warrior's stipend ends up being subtracted as interest. He has to keep on the agent's good side, fawn before the agent's clerks, tell lies, and offer excuses. He spends year in and year out in a state of permanent debt to those townspeople. Such warriors are recipients of a stipend in name, but in reality it is all taken away from them. They end up being unable to survive for a single day without the townspeople's goodwill. Here again, such rice agents may seem to meet the needs of the moment, but the happiness they bring is fleeting. From the day [a warrior receives the advance] onward, interest accumulates to the calamitous extent that he is robbed of most of his income.

In this age in which we live, lending and borrowing are the fashion. Warriors are deprived of most of their income by walking the Way of debt. In recent times, almost all houses, great and small alike, are in dire straits. They might reduce their servants or their horses. Where they employed ten servants, they might now employ five; they may relinquish the single horse they once kept. They might reduce their retainers' stipends, calling it "borrowing back," or fail to hand over monthly rations. Insisting that they can no longer manage, they seek help from the farmers of

---

8. These agents of townsman status, called *fudasashi* or *kurayado*, handled the conversion of the stipend from rice into cash and provided advances with future stipend allocations as security. For further discussion of the relationship between shogunal vassals and rice agents, see chapter 5, pp. 158–62.

their fiefs, who have no understanding of warrior standards, or from townsfolk with no pedigree. They display before them the house's internal and outer circumstances so as to obtain an "allocation" to cover their immediate living expenses.[9] They end up subject to the machinations of such people.

Such warriors beg farmers of means within their fief for monetary contributions [in addition to taxes], and they offer greater or lesser rewards depending on the size of the gift or contribution provided. They might give a kimono with the family crest or bestow a stipend or rations [prerogatives that should be reserved for warriors], or allow the farmer the use of a surname and two swords, or accord him privileges of status [not open to ordinary farmers]. These farmers of means are by nature tightfisted, cruel, and incapable of compassion, but through the authority of their money they have acquired their current high position. Domain and fief holders favor them with awards of status; their authority is thus enhanced, and they give free rein to their greed.

Warrior "Fixers" Who Prey on Feckless Fief Holders

When a warrior nowadays takes on a new retainer, he almost always does so on the condition that the person will arrange to raise a certain amount of [additional] income [from the fief's resources]. Referring to this person as his "subsidies assistant" or something similar,[10] the lord entrusts his official and private matters to this newcomer, beginning with administration of the domain or fief. All now depends on the newcomer's abilities. When it comes to giving instructions, this person casts aside correct procedure and precedent, and all turns on the calculation of profit. Even so, it becomes impossible for the warrior [and his other retainers of long standing] to contradict the newcomer; the warrior's own authority is nat-

---

9. The term "allocation" (*ategai*) usually indicates a grant from a superior to an inferior. Buyō uses the term here ironically to refer to a situation in which farmers or rice agents would reduce the amount currently being withheld from the fief holder's stipend to cover outstanding debts. For an example of such arrangements, see Ōguchi, "Reality," pp. 295–302.

10. Buyō's term, *shiokuri yōnin*, conveys a disdainful note. *Shiokuri* is normally a subsidy provided to someone in need. The assistant's task was to secure such subsidies for the lord.

urally undermined and, in the end, he himself becomes subject to the sanctions of the new man.

A retainer taken on in this manner is single-minded in his pursuit of profit, but he has never a consideration for his lord's ultimate interests. If the lord is of an upright character, the retainer is not free to indulge in his crafty wiles. However, when the lord is profligate and given to luxury, there is nothing to prevent the retainer from pursuing those wiles. He beckons his lord toward extravagance and profligacy, and what happens to the lord when his retainer recommends extravagance and profligacy? Even though he knows that the retainer will cause harm to his household, he is swept along by the retainer's urging. He believes no man between Heaven and Earth is as valuable as his retainer.

The new retainer is never sure when friction may occur, or whether he will encounter the malicious words of envious long-standing retainers, or meet some unexpected obstacle. As a consequence, he is constantly on the lookout for his own well-being. He devotes his energy to ensuring he will incur no financial losses should he suddenly find himself dismissed from service. For the rest, though, he has no concern as to whether he acts morally or immorally. He is merciless toward the domain's farmers; he dupes others into lending him money. His one concern is to exercise control over his lord's finances. He pays no heed to his lord's military duties or governmental obligations; in these matters, he cuts corners. He is loath to give any attention to legal cases brought by fief or domain inhabitants and is derelict in dealing with them properly. He takes bribes and grants favors in return to one party while he oppresses the other, even if it means the ruin of the latter's household.

When eventually things go wrong, and the retainer is released from service, he refuses to budge until every penny that he claims to have advanced is paid back to him. He takes care to pocket enough money to ensure that life will not be difficult if his service is terminated. He hides that fact, however, and acts stubbornly in an effort to extract as much as he can. He takes the ledgers to his lord's supervisor to press his claims and so brings shame on his lord. The members of the lord's household, lulled by how convenient things have been, believe the retainer to be a man of decency. They have entrusted anything and everything to him, including the accounts for all income and expenditure. As a result, they have no clear idea of the depth of their debt. What the vassal stole from them becomes an additional debt and a cause of their suffering. Moreover, they are put to shame and succumb completely to the plotting of their servant. The situation is soon beyond repair.[11]

There are many *rōnin* these days who specialize in swindling warrior houses by making a profit from the business of lending. They take up residence in the household of some warrior with a substantial fief and then, though they are not even retainers, insist that they have a special relationship with the household. They assume management of the warrior's finances, collecting a profit for themselves in the process. Warrior houses are enticed by a moment's convenience, and before long they have their hands bitten. Many are those who sink into the depths with no hope of swimming.

In general, lending and borrowing should not enter the relationship between lord and vassal. Nothing is so damaging as when the Way of lord and vassal is lost in disputes engendered by the quest for profit. However, in this present age, as I have previously stated, even the shogunate makes loans to its vassals for profit; daimyo take their cue from this to profit from their own vassals. It even happens that, as described above, vassals make loans to their lords and then press them mercilessly for repayment. One has to acknowledge that the Way of lord and vassal has hit rock bottom.

The Causes and Consequences of Warrior Impoverishment

Warriors are impoverished and unable to make ends meet because the world as a whole has become ever more profligate. Everything has become costly, and, since the Way of lending and borrowing is prevalent everywhere, a warrior easily incurs unforeseen debts, and interest is laid upon interest. A warrior who wants to keep his finances in order for the foreseeable future stands no chance unless he distances himself from the world at large and maintains a modest and frugal lifestyle. But if he does so, relatives and housemen will all accuse him of parsimony; others too will despise him for it, so it will not happen without a steely determination. Imagine there is perchance a man of wisdom, who pays no heed to the insults of either those around him or the world at large; he establishes the strictest regimen in order to assert order in his household.

---

11. For an example of the doings of such a "fixer" that resonates with Buyō's account here, see Katsu, *Musui's Story*, and Ōguchi, "Reality."

Even if there existed such a man, on his death his descendants would not devote themselves to the path he established and would quickly resort to the ways of the world as they are today. His successors would use for their pleasure all that their forefathers expended immense effort to acquire and save. All matters would become much more convenient, and relatives and housemen would rejoice and sing the current lord's praises. They forget that the source of these riches has now been exhausted, and they abandon their forefathers' strict laws. All this comes to pass because the world as a whole is ever more profligate, and the Way of lending and borrowing prevails everywhere.

Everywhere military families of greater and lesser status are destitute. Small-scale bannermen are in particularly bad shape. Without a second thought, they will sell off the armor handed down from their ancestors and the weapons their forefathers deployed in the lord's service, for which he granted them fiefs. Other valuable heirlooms are also dispensed with. They pawn without a second thought gifts bestowed by their lord, or they even sell them. They no longer ride on horseback when going to and from guard duty or traveling elsewhere; they leave behind their spear bearers; they forgo their escort of retainers and footmen. As for their outfits, they pawn clothing at the end of the season, using the money to redeem the set they need for the new season; or again they borrow for the moment ready-made items from traveling salesmen, who sell on credit. In this way, they make do. In extreme cases, they head for guard duty wearing outfits that they have conned the pawnbroker into temporarily restoring to them. Once they have come back from guard duty, they return the outfits directly to the pawnbroker. Their servants mock them for this; they make sport of their master, saying he wears formal robes taken in and out of pawn into guard duty and back out again; they taunt the household for its extreme poverty.[12]

In this way, bannermen of this sort are never properly equipped, so they are unable to uphold the standards of the house. The lord's authority inevitably declines, and the behavior of wives, children, and dependent

---

12. The original contains a triple pun on the characters for "up" and "down," which here denote the formal robes (*kamishimo*), those robes' repeated pawning and retrieval, and the master's going "up" to the castle for guard duty and returning home again.

relatives collapses. Retainers take advantage. The lord does not hand over the rice stipend or cash allowance to which the retainer is entitled and has to apologize each and every time the retainer comes to prompt him to pay up. As a result, the lord feels uneasy whenever he asks his vassal to perform some task or other, and lord and vassal end up as equal partners. Some retainers may become intimate with the lord's wife or daughter, involving them in all manner of improper or outrageous behavior. Or the bannerman may turn to a townsfolk servant, say, who has gained access to the house, and seek his aid in sorting out the family's financial difficulties. Before he knows it, the townsman is acting as if he were the lord's friend, and the lord ends up as the recipient of the most disrespectful behavior—or else he is taken for a ride.

The house's fief has yielded nothing in years; the farmers not only despise the fief holder for his fief's meager size but also, having been cheated by him, they become disobedient and pay no heed to his troubles. They refuse to respond to summonses, feigning sickness. They make the excuse that they are stupid and dumb and cannot tell black from white, so that they cannot possibly understand what the fief holder wants of them. However often they are summoned, they mock their master and do not deign to reply. On the rare occasion that they do respond to a summons, they act as though they are in the presence of an equal partner and show not a glimmer of awe or respect. They strut about and pay no heed to what the fief holder tells them. If they are ordered into confinement, they flee without a by-your-leave. The fief holder has no retainers to take care of such matters and no means of punishing the farmers. He always loses to the farmers, who pay him less than his due and willfully subtract deductions from their yearly land taxes.

Shogunal land and daimyo holdings were traditionally subject to repeated surveys that ensured that the yield increased and the land taxes submitted steadily grew. However, smaller holdings tend not to be surveyed anew. Farmers disguise fields as wasteland or the like, and the dues they pay have only decreased. Moreover, farmers, well aware of the finances and the habits of the fief holder, have grown arrogant. They have no respect for the small-scale fief holder and do not hesitate to report him to his supervisor; they may even submit a direct complaint to the supervisor when he passes by in his palanquin. Even if it is a matter of no importance, they turn up en masse at the fief holder's residence to complain. They appear in droves in their straw rain capes and straw hats, with hoes and scythes in hand; such disturbances may result in the shogunate's punishing the fief holder. Fief holders' loss of authority has its origins in their poor management of their financial affairs and their general incompetence, but that is not the whole story.

The fact is that minor fief holders have lost all means of punishing farmers. Minor bannerman fief holders can expel farmers from the village or arrest them and hand them over to the shogunal magistrate's office. These are the weightiest punishments [that a fief holder of this scale can levy]. Farmers have not the slightest fear, however, of being expelled from the village, and it is not in any way possible to implement mass village expulsions. Given the relationship between fief holders and farmers, it would be awkward for the former to hand the latter over to the magistrate's office [as it would show him to be unable to properly manage his holding]. Even were he to do so, there is little chance that the magistrate would issue a judgment with the desired effect. The latter's only consideration would be to smooth things over as quietly as possible. The bannerman's position is never upheld, since, whatever the matter, the magistrate invariably urges the fief holder to accept something improper in order to bring about a smooth resolution. The farmers who have defied him end up victorious. Beyond that, arresting farmers and handing them over to the magistrate's office would not be a feasible option, since the chief of the bannerman's unit or his supervisor most likely would stop him [to keep the shame from rubbing off on them].

In brief, there is no possibility of punishment, irrespective of the nature of the wrongdoing. If, by chance, a fief holder were to cut down an offending farmer, what would happen today is that the rumor would spread that the fief holder had lost his mind, resulting in a permanent blemish on him. Further, the farmers would hold a grudge and become more recalcitrant than ever. This is all the more reason why no fief holder ever takes such action. In the case of minor fief holders, farmers are thus not in the least intimidated; they pursue their headstrong ways to the utmost and brandish all manner of untruths to dupe the holder of the fief. As a consequence, warrior authority withers, and instead of collecting sufficient land taxes from the farmers, bannermen have to depend on their aid [by borrowing from the farmers]. There thus prevails an outrageous state of affairs in which bannermen always have to scrounge for loans for their daily livelihood.

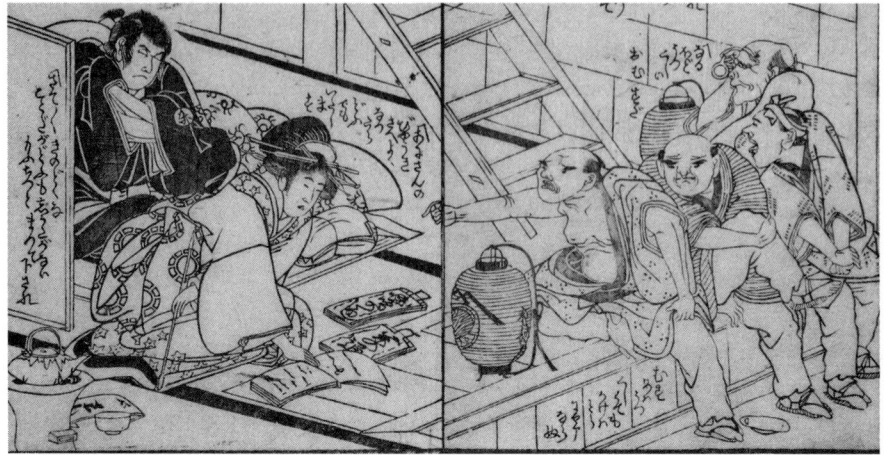

Bill collectors press an impecunious lower-ranking warrior on the day for settling outstanding debts. *Katakiuchi yozue no taka* (1802). Waseda University Library.

Samurai of still lower status occupy a realm where they muddle through depending on the mercy of those around them. Their rice stipends have already been taken over by the designated rice agents, leaving them without the wherewithal to make ends meet. As a result, they are in no position to make a choice between right and wrong; all they can do is try to meet the immediate exigency. Without any consideration of the consequences, they pride themselves on their ability to raise a loan. They pledge their storehouses or residences as security. They borrow from loan sharks, from blind moneylenders, or from lenders who insist on repayment in daily installments. Every three months when they re-sign the contract, the interest balloons. They pay service charges at rates of 10 to 20 percent and before long have forfeited half of the original loan.[13] Again, they might borrow expensive cloth or other goods and sell them on cheaply elsewhere. Or they lease swords, clothes, bedding, mosquito

---

13. See chapter 4, pp. 130–31, and chapter 5, p. 179, for further discussion of these various sorts of loan arrangements. Buyō expresses outrage over interest rates and sees the compounding of interest as something nefarious, but the rates and practices he describes were generally accepted as legitimate. For the first century of the Edo period, the shogunate did not officially limit interest rates. In 1736, it tried to specify that interest rates should not be higher than 15 percent annually, but in 1790 the town magistrates agreed among themselves to treat rates up to 30 percent as not actionable. See Wigmore, *Law and Justice*, 3A:259.

nets, and such and pawn them, but the moneys all disappear on rental costs and interest on the pawn.¹⁴ They end up spending what is left of their stipend and any other income on the interest. Interest piles on interest, and they pay off one set of expenses by incurring others. All this is destined to be the booty of the greediest and most immoral of lowly scoundrels.

Mismanagement of Warrior Households and the Adoption of Heirs

Today, the clever and the stupid, the upright and the immoral, all in the end yield to corruption. Some who have not yet come of age may be poised to fulfill their promise, but before their time has come, they embark upon the path of prodigality and dissolution; they end up incapable of carrying on the house. Many retire at an early age, handing over the house to their infantile sons, who are incapable of offering proper service to the lord. Or else they may set aside their own son, adopting an heir from a family with a different surname.¹⁵ Having retired while still in their prime, they proceed to engage with the impetuosity of youth in all manner of immoral activities. They live to a ripe old age, but all they do is cause trouble for the household.

When arranging for adoption of an heir, the qualities of the person to be adopted are accorded secondary importance; nor is there any concern for the pedigree of the family from which he hails. What matters is that he comes with an abundant dowry. If then the adopting family divorces him, it will never return the cash or clothing or furniture he brought.¹⁶ Some people will arrange for adoption many times over. Indeed, adopted

---

14. It would seem that at least in some cases the "lease" of goods was nominal—simply a device for charging additional interest for what was then used as security on the loan. For an example, see ibid., pp. 248–51.

15. Although adoption of heirs of a different surname was widespread in Edo society, many Confucian scholars, echoing notions that derived originally from Chinese social and religious norms, inveighed against it. The premise underlying the objection was that ancestral spirits would not be able to respond to rites performed by someone not of patrilineal blood descent. See McMullen, "Non-Agnatic Adoption."

16. In principle, return of the dowry and personal possessions was a condition stipulated in case of the divorce of a wife or adopted son.

sons have a vital role to play as successors to the family's forebears and, especially, in the house's performance of service to the shogunate. Families should educate an adopted offspring as they would their own and hand over control of the household only once they have assured themselves about his conduct. But nowadays, it is securing a large dowry that matters; the family future is of no consequence. Sometimes there may be suitable candidates for adoption among relatives of the same surname or a perfectly decent candidate among male dependents. However, in such cases there is no hope of a dowry, so the otherwise suitable candidate is disqualified on the baseless charge that he is sickly. This in turn means that the family bloodline is extinguished. The family head would sooner have the support of the financial resources of someone of another surname.

So, people may talk of the forging of parent–child bonds, but in such cases the parent lacks sincerity, and his authority is weak. Feeling that the abundant dowry he brought is something to boast of, the adoptee is deaf to the moral instruction of his adoptive parents. His adoptive father might take exception to his behavior and wish to dissolve the adoption. However, since the father has already made use of a sizable portion of the dowry, he is unable to return it [and thus dissolution is not an option]. Willy-nilly he lets things stand as they are; the adoptee then takes advantage of the adoptive parent's vulnerability and behaves with still more haughtiness. It may happen too that the parent condemns the child for his poor behavior; the child meanwhile reviles the parent for his lack of sincerity and honesty, and so the family is in a perennial state of discord. Such discord is often the result of both parties' having entered into the parent–child bond out of greed. Since parent and child are both motivated by greed, the parent is reluctant to hand over the household, while the adopted son takes what measures he can to lay hands on it. They end up engaged in a mental battle over the household. On the other hand, there are people who, precisely to avoid such battles, arrange to hand over the household from the start in return for the payment of a substantial sum, which they refer to as the "rate" for a house of that size. They further agree that the parent will be allocated a portion of the house head's stipend as a retirement allowance. Of course, the parent is surrendering his household in what is, in reality, a sales transaction.

In this way, even the headship of bannermen households is effectively sold. As a result, at present it is common for inappropriate people to be adopted into great warrior houses, including the sons of people employed in lower-ranking posts in the shogunal financial offices or as intendants in rural areas.[17] Even the children of people not engaged in military matters, such as shogunal physicians and members of the shogun's personal entourage, may be taken on as the heir. On the other hand, if a great house has become impoverished by entrusting its financial affairs to officials and vassals, it cannot find suitable adoptive matches for its noninheriting sons, no matter how grand it is. Rather, steered by these vassals, such sons can find a place only with houses of smaller scale, or else they finish their days as a dependent of the heir. It is all the more difficult to find an adoptive match for the child of a small-scale house. Regardless of whether they are of fine character, talented, and of potential use in government service, they sink without a trace. While still dependent on the house head, they may inadvertently be drawn into an instance of untoward behavior, which will leave its mark. The slightest incident is a prompt for vassals and relatives to gossip. No one will offer a second chance or help to arrange an adoption. Such a person then remains a dependent for the rest of his days. Otherwise, if the financial support that his family provides is too paltry to sustain him, he leaves home and heads elsewhere. He may seek the help of well-to-do commoners in urban or rural areas or turn to a temple. He may have the appearance of a long-term guest, but in reality he does the work of the lowliest servant. There are many who end their days in this situation.

Among shogunal housemen, some give over their position in return for a certain sum, determined by the going rate, which is called "the price of a guard-unit post." Here, again, there is no concern for the caliber of the person. Personal retainers of shogunal officials or subordinates of intendants who have become rich by some means or other put out large sums of money to purchase a certain house's post [by being adopted as the heir]. Some save up a sizable fortune, bid farewell to their hereditary lord, and temporarily become *rōnin*. They then use their savings to purchase a position as shogunal houseman. Others do the same thing: the sons of unpedigreed townspeople; those who greedily collect immoral amounts of interest by lending money at extortionate rates; the sons of blind moneylenders; and people from distant parts who have performed

---

17. Intendants (*daikan*) were the lowest rung of the warrior bureaucracy responsible for overseeing the administration of the shogunate's rural lands. They came under the jurisdiction of the finance magistrate (*kanjō bugyō*).

evil deeds in their own localities and, unable to live there any longer, turn their backs on their parents and head for Edo. Among those who obtain such shogunal housemen posts, are there not men who, having incurred the displeasure of the domain or fief holder who was their original lord, were released from his service with a ban on taking up service elsewhere? There are also bound to be monks laicized for having breached Buddhist precepts, or their children. There may even be pariahs and outcasts and their ilk. The reason for this is that the only thing held to matter is money, and not the caliber of the person.

Among shogunal housemen, too, are men who, serving as supervising officers and the like, are the successors to a military house of mounted rank and, as such, receive a proper stipend.[18] In this day and age, though, these people pay no attention to military matters. After all, since they obtained the position with the shogunate by purchasing a house headship, they do everything with a mercantile spirit. They do not maintain the number of retainers consonant with their status. They work their rota of four or five days a month, and for the rest they devote themselves to *haikai* poetry, tea, Noh dancing, koto, samisen, and other entertainments. They find all sorts of ways to make a profit, beginning with acting as an intermediary in arranging loans for others. The younger among them get bored with their easy job and begin to hang out with ne'er-do-wells; they go out at night to pursue pleasure, sometimes not returning home for four or five days as they indulge in profligacy. They become proficient at betting, love to fight, and generally behave as though they were lowlier than the lowliest.

Trends Toward Frivolity and the Decay of Warrior Customs

Those praised today as fine fellows and lauded for their scholarly accomplishments are those who are outwardly accommodating, avoid argu-

---

18. In general, shogunal housemen were not of mounted rank, but supervising officers (*yoriki*) were granted this privilege and hereditary stipends. The term Buyō uses, *ikki* (literally, "one mounted warrior"), originally referred to the number of men one mounted warrior would be expected to field as his military obligation. According to the author of *Jikata hanreiroku*, a late Edo guide to local administration, at his time this would correspond to a stipend level of two hundred *koku* and the obligation to field five retainers. See Ōishi, *Jikata hanreiroku*, 1:33.

mentation in their dealings with others, take great care to be polite in greetings and in taking their leave, and are concerned not to ruffle feathers in discriminating wrong from right. The realm is at peace, and so it is indeed appropriate to handle all matters with moderation. And of course etiquette should be properly observed. This behavior thus befits the times. However, such attitudes have grown ever more ingrained, and today the essence of what matters has been lost. Polish takes precedence over substance, so that people hesitate to act upon what in their hearts they had determined to do. People do not speak their minds; they are concerned only to protect their flanks. They adjust to the mood of the moment and use words that do not come from the heart. In extreme cases, someone might ask them whether a white object is black, and they will answer, "It indeed appears to be black!" Today, the custom everywhere prevails of acting without sincerity. Since this is now the environment in which people grow up, such behavior is the norm. Many warriors are indistinguishable from nobility or monks or women; they are incapable of discriminating clearly right from wrong or good from evil; they look only for superficial solutions. They may excel at comportment, arranging their *hakama* elegantly,[19] but no sooner do they face some incident than they panic and are of no use to anybody.

The discussion up to this point has concerned the habits of warriors determined to behave in a manner appropriate to their position; that is to say, those who are better than average. I will now turn to those of lesser quality, who have not the slightest clue about the Way of the civil and military arts. Even if by some chance one of this sort should catch an occasional glimmer of that Way, he will not be able to keep his mind on his duty, and so he is as good as clueless.

First of all, the passions of this latter sort today, as I have said, are samisen and other entertainments; these are their obsessions. These men do not *look* like warriors. Today, a fine fellow of this type is one with a pale complexion and a seductive elegance about him, who looks just like a woman. He keeps both his swords short but wears garments with long sleeves and hems. With his showy robes of fashionable stripes or small patterns and his scarlet undergarments, arranged fashionably to display the different layers, he decks himself out like a woman. In truth

---

19. A divided culotte-like skirt worn over kimono, *hakama* were a standard item of warrior public dress.

A high-ranking lord ignores his senior retainers' remonstrances. The lord (to the right), dressed informally, with pipe in hand and a relaxed posture, exemplifies the "feminized" type of warrior Buyō condemns. His retainers wear standard warrior garb of *hakama* with a winged, vest-like overgarment. *Ichi fuji ni taka katajike nasubi* (1788). National Diet Library Digital Collection.

he has not even a woman's mettle. Men of his ilk tie narrow belts high on their waists [so as to make them look long-legged] and have a distaste for [the proper male attire of] *hakama*; they sport the finest footwear, purses, and pouches, and their pipes and tobacco cases are of the most exquisite gold and silver. Or they favor imported goods and adopt the style of Kabuki actors and other lowlife entertainers. Wearing kimono patterned in the manner favored by prostitutes, they steep themselves in pleasures of the flesh, become addicted to visiting the brothel districts, or avidly pursue an illicit affair.

This age of ours is one in which women are in the ascendancy. The taste for luxury has increased enormously, and given the large numbers who devote themselves to singing and samisen, the extravagance with which women now clothe and feed themselves is extraordinary. For example, in arranging a marriage, it has become the established custom that the daughter of a house holding a fief worth one hundred *koku* cannot be sent off for even the equivalent of a year's tax income. Since such standards of splendor permeate all aspects of life, fecklessness prevails, and this leads to a tendency for illicit affairs to occur.

Illicit affairs are hardly rare in warrior houses. Recently they have been dealt with in the most perfunctory fashion, and moral disarray is the result. Nowadays, if such an affair is exposed, it is not the perpetrator but the wronged one who is made to feel shame. The perpetrator is the one who has behaved outrageously, but since this is an age in which fecklessness holds sway, he acts as if he had in fact done something to boast about. And if the wronged party is of some standing, he will dread the consequences of being put to shame. Thus, the current practice is to try to settle the matter quietly so as to ensure no rumor leaks out. As a result, the Way of the woman falls ever more into disarray. By rights, of course, when this sort of immoral behavior takes place, the wronged party should administer a beating or even cut down the guilty party. Recently, however, no one ever does such a thing; their concern is that such a response would leave a lasting blemish on the house.

This is not all. Warriors are slow to hand over wrongdoers and good-for-nothings to the shogunal authorities. Townspeople submit petitions or complaints directly to the shogunal government without any problem, but bannermen and shogunal housemen have to take the matter first to their unit chief or supervisor. Rear vassals must go through their lord,[20] and this process adds complications. Those acting as intermediaries often regard the matter as trouble for themselves and urge the wronged party just to forbear. Townspeople especially make a huge fuss over the slightest thing and devise all sorts of stratagems to bring lawsuits. Warriors, however, have no recourse to this sort of falsehood or exaggeration; they do their best to maintain a certain reserve. Thus, when the officials hearing the case look into the warrior's understated position, they conclude that he is the one at fault. Pressed by the officials' view, the warrior has no choice but to abandon his complaint. On the surface, it is made to seem he is being forgiving and merciful, but in reality he has yielded to the bravado of the other side.

Although some warriors may hold firmly to principle and insist on the rightness of their case, people today admire an intermediary who convinces them it would be in their interest not to pursue the issue and who manages to bring matters to a conclusion without causing a storm. Such intermediaries hold it to be an accomplishment to force the party in ques-

---

20. As samurai who served a daimyo or bannerman, rear vassals (*baishin*) were not directly under shogunal authority.

tion to keep quiet, even if this means departing from the Way of the warrior. Such an attitude does nothing to uphold the Way of the warrior; it rather undermines it. It comes about because people do not act out of sincerity but regard it as troublesome to become involved in others' affairs. This is the source of the disarray in the manner proper to the warrior.

In this day and age, no warrior who confronts behavior of the sort mentioned will ever cut down the offender; they will never seek action by the shogunal government. Since it is deemed inappropriate for men who wear two swords to mete out beatings, a warrior can take no such action. If he encounters some unacceptable, disrespectful behavior, he must first guard against losing his temper. He cannot reprove rudeness or poor manners; he fears rather for the consequences and pretends to see and hear nothing. As though avoiding fire, he takes pains to distance himself from trouble. Those oblivious of their own place have no fear of the warrior; they spot the slightest chance and take advantage, deceiving him. They also take advantage of their superiors' womenfolk, enthralling them and leading them astray. It even happens at times that wives and daughters will be violated by a vassal or a ne'er-do-well. The woman might have been lured out of her home, but when the warrior at length tracks her down, he seeks to keep the entire matter under wraps so that no one else gets to hear of it and ends up offering the seducer money to keep his distance. Anyway, warriors are bitten by the very subordinates whom they have fed; never do they get a satisfactory solution. Indeed, their efforts are all devoted to ensuring that there are no regrettable aftereffects.

In principle, it is craven for a warrior to beat a servant and shows his incompetence, for it is a clear sign of ineptness that one of sufficient status to wear two swords does not use them. The warrior ends up no different from the lowliest of the low. But in this age, when it is not easy for a warrior [to cut down a misbehaving servant], it is essential that he at least give the offender a beating and drive him away. In the old days, if someone tried to trick a warrior, the offender would be cut down immediately. Warriors were thus feared. Nowadays, though, were a warrior to cut down someone merely for tricking him, the argument would be that he was in the wrong to become involved with such a lowlife. The world at large would not approve of his action, and so craven have the shogunate's judgments become that the norm is to patch up all matters quietly, regardless of right or wrong. Townspeople, idlers, and even farmers mock the warrior, and it is nowadays not uncommon for the warrior to succumb to their intrigues. The warrior's hands have been tied in this way perhaps because the shogunate has sidelined the military Way and placed the circumspect ways of Confucianism at the center. Awe constrains me from saying more here about these matters.

Weakness Toward Warrior Servants

Trysts and affairs [between a woman of a warrior household] and a servant are greatly tabooed among warriors. They merit capital punishment; the man and woman alike should be cut down on the spot. After all, such behavior is the ultimate betrayal of one's lord. In recent years, however, there has been greater laxity about this, and men can save their necks with the payment of a fine; or they can return their wages and be dismissed with a ban on taking up service in a warrior household elsewhere.[21] Even such measures as this are now almost never enforced. It is rare to issue a ban on service elsewhere, and in the situation where the lord should exact repayment of wages, he finds instead reasons not to do so; in the end, the repayment is not made. Even if the wrongdoer is ordered to repay his wages, his guarantor may refuse to do so, making it difficult to collect them. If the lord protests to the shogunal authorities about the laxness in repayment, the case may drag on inconclusively, and he will have no choice but to endure the situation, wrong though it may be.

Even in the unusual instance where the lord issues a ban on the servant's taking up service in another warrior household, the ban is rarely observed. Other houses should check on the situation before employing the person in question, but since that would likely be a source of trouble, they pretend to see and hear nothing. If the servant comes to apologize, his former lord is swift to grant a pardon. If someone inquires [about the servant] with his former lord, no reply is given. Even if there has been some problem, the lord speaks as though nothing is amiss. This may be an act of compassion toward the erstwhile servant, but it is a deception toward the warrior who is about to employ that servant. Nowadays, servants in warrior houses are dealt with in too lenient a fashion, so they

---

21. The practice was to pay wages in advance. A pledge was routinely included in contracts to the effect that the guarantor would repay those wages if the servant was dismissed or was found guilty of some misdemeanor.

take advantage. They cease to perform their duties and even become involved in illicit relations with women of the household.

If a servant is ill-mannered, rude, insincere, or unfaithful, the lord must be able to exercise the authority to cut him down on the spot. The system of demanding the repayment of wages instead is based on a calculation of profit; it has no place in the relationship between lord and vassal. Such a way of thinking does not befit the moral principle underlying the relation between lord and vassal. This is why the practice of repayment itself has become lax and we have ended up where we are. Those in a position to cut down a misbehaving servant do not even demand the repayment of his wages, so servants cease to serve. The lord's methods have become ever more tolerant as he gives ever more care to how he treats his servants. The servants, though, duly take advantage, since they view a lord as someone to be duped. Whatever wrongdoing they engage in, they are at most dismissed from service. The result is that they become increasingly headstrong; being two-faced is part and parcel of their service. The master's dignity diminishes year by year; the servant's ambition swells month by month. Service to a warrior household comes to be seen as something to be performed with the minimum of effort; or it is decided that service will be performed only on a fixed number of days. Although the servant never works sufficiently to accomplish his duties, he becomes ever more negligent. His wages increase, even as his workload decreases; it is not even one-tenth of what it used to be. This is how it has come to pass that farmers, too, dispense with the effort of cultivating their land and instead take up easy service in a military household. As a result, land goes to ruin and the city population of idlers increases.

It is essential that the etiquette between lord and vassal be most strictly observed. The lord must have the authority to determine whether his servants live or die. But it has become difficult to punish servants, and the results are everywhere to be seen. The etiquette obtaining between lord and vassal is being steadily undermined, starting from the bottom with the behavior of servants. The more senior retainers and footmen are no different. Even if their lord admonishes them, they know the limits of his authority and make light of him, showing no fear. Obsequious and frivolous, they lavishly scatter compliments, seeking to dupe their lord. They wear the finest clothes and mouth fine words, but there is no sincerity to their service. There is not a trace of warrior frugality about them. In the end, this world is one that prizes superficial decoration; there is no longer any place for real sincerity.

Embezzlement and Bribery

Among rear vassals—high and low alike—it is standard practice to steal things from their lord; they are in the habit of cheating him whenever there are expenditures for weddings or funerals. As a consequence vassals dislike "external" posts such as a guard unit or those dealing with administrative affairs, because such tricks are difficult to pull. Rather, they prefer positions related to financial matters, where it is possible to make a gain on the side. I hear that in ages past men used to think it an honor to hold an external post, and that no one wanted to handle financial matters since these were seen as craven. I am sure this was, indeed, the case.

In ages past, there was a taboo about samurai handling gold, silver, and copper coins, and few samurai were willing to count money. How admirable an attitude! Nowadays, the warrior sets aside the blessings bestowed on him by birth and is driven by material desires no less than any commoner. And, to cap it all, he seeks to skim a share from his lord's expenditures, aspiring to the perquisites to be had from holding a post concerned with financial matters. What "perquisites" means, in fact, is the warrior taking bribes for all transactions he handles.

Bribery is prevalent in this day. People refer to a "senior official's assessment of talent," meaning that such officials never make a genuine assessment of a person's suitability for a post; they practice favoritism, taking as their benchmark the person who suits their own interests rather than those of the lord. Upright samurai do not bow and scrape or offer bribes, so they are never the object of such favoritism. The cunning, deceitful ones fawn to deceive people and end up getting the favors. Senior officials nowadays, being generally themselves frivolous and lacking in dignity, keep those who are upright and honest at a distance, associating themselves instead with fawners. They turn their backs on the good and employ only the evil, and before you know it, you have a team of senior and junior officials who are all self-seeking bribe takers. They will think about their cut of the profit when purchasing goods from the merchants who frequent their lord's residence. They also record all manner of costs in the ledger, and so claim for them, deceiving their lord. They rejoice when their lord incurs significant expenses and secretly smile to learn of a death or the succession of a new house head, of a marriage or the adoption of an heir, of shogunal requests for assistance, or of the burning of the lord's residence. The reason is that expenditure in all these cases is an opportunity for them to work their greedy ways to their heart's content. They turn to their own advantage the confusion resulting from the disarray in their lord's finances.

Households whose financial affairs are in good order have no such confusion to be exploited, and officials are not able to make an illicit profit. Officials in charge of financial affairs in a house where disarray obtains, however, oversee all manner of expenditures every day; as a result, the family of such an official lives in splendor, and whenever he goes out he does so in an extravagant style inappropriate to his station. Lesser officials follow suit and help themselves to anything and everything: brushes, ink, paper, oil, candles, cakes, condiments, charcoal and firewood, and vegetables. Thus, even a samurai who gets rations of no more than a few *koku* lives comfortably off the profit from side gains and can employ a manservant or maid.

Townspeople and artisans who frequent a samurai residence first make gifts to everyone, from the gate guard to the live-in foot soldiers, runners, and servants. They also send over a portion of the profit from the transaction, calling it a gratuity; they take special care to offer sizable bribes to the officials in charge. Or perhaps they will invite them to the pleasure quarters to enjoy illicit pleasures of the flesh; or they might treat them at a restaurant and nurture the intimacy that comes from sharing the same table. When construction jobs and other work are put out to tender, in principle the officials gather bids from various parties, investigate the range of prices, and put out the order on that basis. The investigations are to all appearances strict, but, in fact, the merchants and the artisans are all in cahoots with one another. Calling it an "encouragement," they do all they can to arrange in advance who will get the tender, on the promise that the lucky person will pay a cut from his profits to the guild. The samurai official in charge expects to get his own cut and so turns a blind eye to these machinations. When it comes to purchasing goods, he will raise various objections to ensure that the deal does not go through unless there is a cut for the mediating official. This applies regardless of how good the items' quality or how reasonably priced, or of whether or not they are to the lord's liking.

Nowadays people refer to these tricks as "the perquisites of office," and they are a common practice. Even if, by some slim chance, an upright official should appear, he will be unable to do his work if he distances himself from the behavior of his fellows. And since such matters are beyond the lord's purview, there is little point in a single individual's striving to be faithful. Should he interfere in the dealings of his subordinates to ensure matters are dealt with properly, they would definitely be resentful and impede any such attempts by putting obstacles in the way. Moreover, what matters is not the lord but currying favor with one's fellows. For the fact is that, before the lord ever learns what is really afoot, these fellows will slander the upright official to the domain elders,[22] bringing him down with sly insinuations. Or should an upright official try to issue sumptuary regulations to gain control over expenses, he will, as I have said, run up against the dissolute lord, who typically hates to feel constrained. One's fellow officials are even worse; lord and entourage alike will be filled with resentment.

As a result, all are loath to exercise authority and are far too indulgent. It is the human condition to slide toward vice, so that even a man who has been appointed on account of his steadfastness will, in due course, change his views and begin to do wrong. Toward his lord, he will begin bending the facts so that all seems well, and he will make sure never to betray his fellows. In the end, he will become as selfish and as addicted to luxury as the others.

Those financial officers whose lord's affairs are in disarray are particularly arrogant. In the name of "balancing the budget" or "ensuring cash flows," they spend every day out and about. They ignore the usual curfew for returning to the compound and come and go freely, day and night. They ride in fine palanquins, equipped with the best swords and outfits, so that they look for all the world as though they were rich; they convene all their meetings in the pleasure quarters. Of course, such officials charge the office with the expenditure needed for all matters private and public, internal and external; calculation is their business. Even when it comes to matters of military preparedness, they reduce them to calculations of profit. They heedlessly let damaged military equipment go as it is. Should the shogunate charge the daimyo with carrying

---

22. The elders (*karō*) were the highest-ranking officials in a daimyo domain, comparable to the senior councilors in the shogunate.

out some task, they manage it in the most perfunctory way possible. When it comes to the presentation of customary gifts, they skillfully make up some tale to get around the fact that they fail to follow precedent. They make a great fuss out of minor things, insisting, say, that this year their domain's harvest was poor. If it is a matter of submitting various requests [for loans], they are good at building a persuasive case, but they care nothing for failing to repay money borrowed [from the shogunate]. They are adept at getting the better of the shogunate, one way or another.

By contrast, when it comes to entertainment—their specialty—they spend money with no concern for the cost; it is all in the name of "socializing with the money masters." This yields only the most minimal effect in sorting out the lord's matters; it is entirely a question of using the excuse of the lord's needs for the purpose of personal indulgence. They will set up houses for their concubines and embark on the sort of pleasure outings that not even their lord can afford. When it comes to women and wine, they get intoxicated on fine sake and consume only fine foods with the rarest of tastes; they spend ten times more on extravagance than what their own stipend of 100 or 200 *koku* could buy them.[23]

Among the domain elders, those who deal with the lord's financial matters are the most arrogant. Everything has to be done specially; they frequent pleasure quarters and other places that are unbecoming for persons of their status. They indulge their desires, and since they are in cahoots with the financial officers in all things, neither the elders nor the financial officers have the slightest concern for the dissipation of the lord's finances. Toward the offices in charge of ordinary administrative affairs, they insist on extraordinary measures of thrift, and they readily reduce allocations for retainers, calling those cuts a "loan" from the retainers' stipends or rations. Yet they themselves squander vast amounts of cash and indulge themselves without limit.

The Plight of Those Without Access to the "Perquisites of Office"

In contrast to those who work with the lord's financial affairs, those samurai who have ordinary administrative duties are destitute. One of

---

23. A stipend of 100 to 200 *koku* would in principle yield the holder an actual income of approximately 30 to 60 *koku*.

the evil practices of the day is that the number of duties is growing all the time. In this age of extravagance, both clothing and other things [needed for official duties] become more and more expensive. Those with ordinary administrative duties have no unofficial perquisites and so cannot perform their duties or, indeed, keep up with their everyday expenses. As a result, there is now a thriving business in taking advantage of their destitution, with blind moneylenders, loan sharks, and lenders who insist on daily repayments all in on the act. The only concern of these warriors is to get through the day, and they are delighted to borrow cash at high rates of interest, with no thought for future difficulties. It is a case of anything to tide them over.

They then get pressed to pay excessive interest and end up unable to perform their duties. Some stay at home, feigning illness; others are reported to their lord's Edo representative, or to the shogunal inspectors, for failure to repay their loans on time. When this becomes publicly known, they may be confined to their residence and forced to yield headship of the house. Depending on the issue at stake, they may be dismissed from service, or expelled immediately from their lord's compound. Some, who cannot bear the humiliation, flee. Among some warrior houses, to have the lord's name reported to the town magistrates creates a major commotion and leads to severe censure.

Townspeople who live in Edo take the magistrates very lightly; they never suffer any repercussions [from lodging a suit against a warrior house]. A warrior, on the other hand, whether the matter is major or minor, will be held accountable by his lord [in addition to the magistrate]. So, a samurai dreads more than anything having his defaulting on debt repayments reported to the magistrate. He will come up with the interest and pay with apologies, even if it means going without food for the day. In extreme cases, it may mean his stripping his aging father and mother and wife and children of their clothing [and pawning these items]. If a samurai is unable to make good the debt, in most cases he will suffer a reduction in status. Lenders see opportunities here and work their way into warrior houses. How painful to see loan sharks do such damage to warriors' status!

Among the warriors of the various houses, those who are stationed permanently in Edo tend to be destitute. This is because customs in the shogun's castle town are extravagant and expenditure on everything is high. Moreover, because samurai stationed permanently in Edo adopt the current habit of indulging in what is extravagant and fashionable, they have little physical strength and are hardly fit for military purposes. Indulgence makes men spineless. The provinces have yet to see samurai indulgence extend this far, and there is at least some attention there to military preparedness. It is a good idea to have samurai live in the provinces and the countryside; it will benefit their lords and themselves, too.

Mismanagement of Concubines

The practices warriors today engage in when they take concubines are not proper; the whole matter is handled in an extremely insincere manner. To begin with, warriors do not pay due heed to the woman's family background; they delight in vulgar and unrefined women. They set about it as though they were buying a prostitute, and they change concubines periodically. Without pity, they dismiss a woman they have employed for several years and who has given them children. Some houses have the custom of dismissing a woman as soon as she has given birth. Immediately after the birth, she will be sent back to her parents or guarantor and told that, while she is free to marry whom she wishes, she is no longer welcome on the premises. They say that when a concubine bears the lord's child, she will become headstrong and difficult to control. The practice of cutting ties is born from calculation: if the woman were to be allowed to visit after her dismissal, the relationship between mother and child would necessitate providing her with substantive means of support, and that would cost money. The moral principle underlying the relationship between mother and child is utterly lost.

Neither does the woman serving as a concubine have any understanding of the circumspection proper to her relationship with the lord or of the true feelings of a mother toward her child. Her only thought is to make a temporary sale of her body; she has no regard for the house and no intention of acting with sincerity. She is likely to take advantage of the favor she is shown to get her hands on clothes, hair ornaments, and personal accoutrements to set herself up in style. Or she might skillfully upset the lord to just the right degree so as to get herself dismissed. She will have no qualms about leaving that house only to move in with a neighbor. Or she might seek service with close relatives of her former lord; or again, making use of the trousseau of material goods she has accumulated, she may marry a man of good background. Or perhaps out of a propensity for profligacy—so typical of this age—she might become an entertainer, a waitress in a drinking place, or a kept woman seeking to live in splendor by deceiving men. Some sink to the levels of prostitute and streetwalker. Others become the wives of townspeople or idlers. They might become wives of the low sorts such as hairdressers or steeplejacks;[24] or they might have a child with such a person so that a child born of a daimyo has for a brother a slum dweller.

It is said that the womb is something borrowed, but things should not be this way. If the woman is indeed the mother of the [daimyo's] child, she should be looked after properly for life. The [present wrong state of affairs comes about because the daimyo's] retainers do not deal properly with the matter. Again, the lord should continue taking care of a concubine whom he has favored and whose womb "he has borrowed." Instead, once the woman is dismissed, he directs all his attention to his new concubine and refuses to see the previous one again. This behavior is callous in the extreme. As a result, mother and child are separated, and in some cases the child is unaware whether his true mother is alive or dead, so he spends his life ignorant of whether to mourn or not.

Descendants should inherit their ancestors' bloodline and establish a reputation for their house. They should make themselves useful to many and treasure the military Way. Depending on the pedigree of their house, they may one day serve as shogunal proxy or be charged with some important shogunal office. To become the mother of such a descendant is no light matter, and it is essential that her background be properly checked; at the very least, a woman taken on as a concubine should be the daughter of a samurai house. As the Way of matrimony has its origin in the harmony of Heaven and Earth and is the foundation of human morality, traditionally it was treated as of the utmost importance. I am told that people of the soil in the provinces still retain the old ways and take care to select the bloodline and the qualities of the father and mother prior to sealing a marriage arrangement. People might thus be expected to take the utmost care, but daimyo and major bannermen behave worse even than farmers; they have no regard for pedigree. They choose a concubine on the basis of the woman's appearance; even then they dislike elegant women of refined beauty and prefer women with the style of a baseborn prostitute.

24. For more on steeplejacks (*tobi no mono*), see chapter 5, pp. 185–86.

Women with the style of a prostitute have all been raised in the houses of townspeople or in the backstreets. They have no pedigree, no sense of ancestry, no manners; they know nothing of what is appropriate. All they know is *jōruri* story chants, the samisen, the stringed instrument called the *kokyū*,²⁵ and danced dramas: all of them lascivious arts. They know how to captivate a respectable man, but that is all, and they are vulgar in the extreme. As a result, there are among today's daimyo men who, perhaps because they resemble their real mothers, sport the facial features of the lowliest of the baseborn. Their profiles are weak, their eyes amorous and flaccid, and they do not look like warriors. When one asks who their birth mother is, it turns out just as one would expect: she is some lowly woman. Definitely their hearts are no less vulgar than their appearance. When a concubine is so vulgar, she will at some later time behave badly and cause problems that do damage to her child's reputation—even if the father recognizes her as the child's real mother. Such a mother has no concern for divine retribution, knows nothing of rectitude or of shame. Carried away in her vanity, and ignorant of all but licentiousness, she becomes ever more dissolute.

The modern-day method of employing a concubine is thus entirely inappropriate. The overriding consideration is lust, as if one were infatuated with a prostitute. As a result, the women who find favor entirely lack sincerity; such a woman's only desire is to draw the lord into a pool of prodigality, and she sees floating in that pool as her entire purpose in life. A Chinese poem says, "Disorder does not come down from Heaven;—/ It is produced by the woman."²⁶ Is there not a moral here that demands the greatest caution? Because the women's quarters are in disorder day and night, and because the lord lives with such women as his companions, he himself becomes vulgar. He becomes fickle and prodigal. He forgets his duties and all shame and regards anything that gives pleasure to women as good.

Such a lord typically finds his governmental responsibilities distasteful, retires at a young age, and loses himself in infatuation for his concubines. He rejoices in spawning children that are no longer of any use

---

25. *Jōruri* is a collective name for various forms of story chants to the accompaniment of samisen music. The *kokyū* (Ch. *erhu*) is a two-stringed "knee fiddle" played with a bow.

26. A poem from the *Book of Odes*; see Legge, *Chinese Classics*, 4:561.

[since he has already passed on the headship to his heir]. He gets carried away with selfish greed and may take control over all his own house's money and valuables or borrow money elsewhere. He causes problems for his successors and creates difficulties for the entire retainer band. He has no regard for the affairs of the house and hesitates for not a moment about heading off somewhere every day to amuse himself with tea, poetry, or painting. He cavorts with pleasure-seekers and frequents bustling places of entertainment to indulge in dissolution to his heart's content.

Those who have taken retirement should exert control over their own bodies and minds; they should remain frugal in all things and use their leisured status to consider what might benefit the house. They should have consideration not only for household affairs but also for all the people in their fief, even the lowliest; they should devote themselves to making good whatever may be lacking in the current lord's governance.

Warriors are charged with governing the state, but they have quite turned their backs on this charge; they desire only those things that will wreak ruin on the realm. As for the tiny minority of samurai who are upstanding, how many of them are truly devoted to governing the state? The Divine Lord so dreaded the samurai's assuming courtly ways that he said Edo was too close to Kyoto. Astute as he was, he saw the world heading for doom. He foresaw how, in an age of peace, men would give themselves over to extravagance and bring the realm to ruin. How could one not be in awe before the astuteness of the Divine Lord's premonitions? The courtly ways he despised are deemed the height of refinement for today's warrior. The situation defies description. Eight or nine out of every ten are unworthy of the name of warrior and incapable of defending themselves in combat. The military Way that was laid with great care at the start of Tokugawa rule is now 70 or 80 percent lost. How regrettable! The foundations of the state are bereft of support; the civil and military Ways are in steep decline. I shall discuss elsewhere how they may be restored through reforms.

Chapter 2

FARMERS

The people are the basis for the country; they are the root, the foundation that sustains the realm and the state.[1] Warriors entrust themselves to their lord, and the lord is assisted by his retainers; both are able to maintain their house's honor by receiving the people's tribute in taxes. Monks and priests totally depend on support from the world as a whole, while townspeople, idlers, and various craftsmen all survive by living off others. In contrast, the people follow the seasons set by Heaven, cultivate their crops according to the basic conditions of the soil, and do not depend in the least on the benefice of others. Existing between Heaven and Earth, they expend their physical strength in hard work; as the lowliest of the low, they eat rough food, wear the poor man's garb of padded cotton, and deal with the humble. In summer, they roast under the hot sun and suffer along with oxen and horses. In winter, bitter cold afflicts them in the midst of frost and snow. Most of what they get goes to pay tribute; they always have to obey the lord's or fief holder's rules, work at corvée labor, and provide various required levies and services. In reality, they are responsible for practically everything in this world, because they produce not only the five grains and other foods but also all the goods of use to the country. To sum up, they nurture everyone. They are the ones who produce wealth, the source of the world's prosperity. It is thanks to their labor that others can take pride in today's orderly rule and enjoy peaceful lives. The reason why we enjoy the effects of peace year by year, season by season, day by day, every instant, is because the humble people work hard at their occupation. Truly the farmers are the country's foundation

---

1. By "people" (*tami*), as noted, Buyō means farmers.

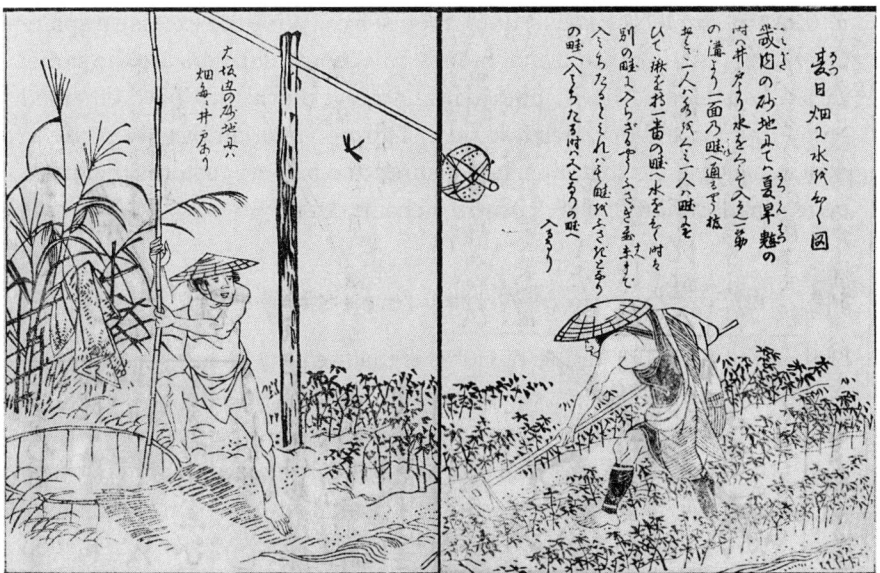

Farmers irrigating dry-crop fields. *Nōgu benri ron* (1822). National Diet Library Digital Collection.

and the world's treasure. Therefore, the crucial matter in ruling the realm is to ensure that the people lead secure lives.

As peaceful conditions have continued, however, evil customs have arisen that cause more and more harm to the people, making it impossible for them to live quietly and securely. Among such evil customs, first is the tremendous expansion in luxury throughout the realm. In addition, townspeople and idlers are all too numerous, and they relentlessly pursue the Way of profit and interest. The cost of luxury for those above and below and the competition for profit in worldly affairs all end up as loss for the people. The people have to bear much additional suffering owing to the evil customs brought by peace, and since the pursuit of luxury and profit expands day by day and month by month, they are not able to overcome its effects. This is already striking at the root of their existence. Right now it is beyond their capacity to cope with the problems caused by this age of order and peace.

It would be difficult to cope with this burden even if it were shared equally among all the farmers, but recently the farmers' customs too have changed, so that six or seven out of every ten evade this burden, and four or five are left to take it upon themselves. With the excessive splendor characteristic of our age of orderly rule, not all farmers are the same; various distortions have appeared, and great disparities have emerged between high and low, rich and poor. This polarization has given rise to deplorable customs that must be censured and piteous customs that must be rectified; conditions are truly in a chaotic state.

The Extravagance of Wealthy Farmers and Its Bad Effects

The first of these deplorable customs is that wealthy farmers have forgotten their status. They set themselves up in the same luxury as people of high status who live in cities, and their houses are as different from olden times as night and day. They embellish them with stately gates, entryways, polished horizontal timbers, formal sitting rooms with an alcove, and decorative shelves. They arrange their sitting rooms and such with exquisite taste. Some offer what they call a gratuity to the shogunate to be officially recognized as praiseworthy; they receive permission to use a surname, carry two swords, and flaunt their authority. Others present loans to daimyo and fief holders, and through this merit they too are granted the use of surnames, the right to swords, and a retainer's stipend. They brandish their authority in their locality and oppress ordinary farmers. Others disdain small-scale fief holders, curry favor with imperial abbots and others of court rank, and through bribes of money become purveyors [to the shogunate or a daimyo] or even acquire status equivalent to retainers. They overawe the ignorant people and do whatever suits their interests.

The village officials and all the other families with a surplus leave the cultivation of crops to their male and female servants, while they themselves wear beautiful clothes, imitate warrior ceremonies and rites for their marriages, adoptions, celebrations, and memorial services, and invite people to elaborate banquets.[2] They keep *rōnin* and the like on a regular basis so they can practice martial arts unsuitable to their status and seek out teachers so they can devote themselves to Chinese poetry and prose. They write in the Ming writing style, learn Japanese and

---

2. Such village officials (*mura yakunin*), it should be kept in mind, were themselves of farmer status and part of the village organization rather than warrior officials overseeing village administration from outside.

Chinese painting and calligraphy, or employ tea ceremony teachers, teachers of *waka* and *haikai* poetry, and musicians so that they can study the performing arts and make these people their partners in pleasure. They bring back a beautiful woman from the city, make her a concubine, and hold drinking parties every day. Or they slip off to town to amuse themselves, and while having wife and concubine in the countryside, also keep a woman in the city. Some stay in the brothel district, flirt with a prostitute, and make her pregnant.

Others go to Edo on official business, including lawsuits and other services rendered for their lord or fief holders, but they treat such business as secondary and instead pursue their own pleasure. Their hearts seized by the town's bustle, they are delighted when the official settlement to the suit is drawn out while they waste great sums of money in entertainment day after day. They wedge such expenses into dues assessed against the village's yield and disguise their expenditure in the entertainment district as a part of the annual land tax and village costs, which are then levied on small-scale farmers. Since the small-scale farmers cannot accompany the village officials to ascertain what they are doing in Edo, they cannot check the officials' claims. Because the village officials have means to discourage them from the beginning through intimidation, the small-scale farmers are not able to say one word of complaint, even if proof of wrongdoing becomes clearly known, and so the matter is just left as is.

The village officials' duty is to do a good job in taking care of the small-scale farmers, but nowadays they do not concern themselves with the farmers' hardships. They do not care if a farmer goes bankrupt; they do not concern themselves if parents, wives, and children end up scattered one from another; instead they take everything coming to them without mercy. For these reasons, in recent years levies for village costs have increased tremendously everywhere, sometimes to the extent that they come to more than the annual land tax, and the small-scale farmers' hardships have doubled compared with what they were before.

Generally speaking, the wealth noted above originates from what is squeezed out of small-scale farmers; it is not acquired from someplace else. Furthermore, since such people do not work the fields themselves, this is not a surplus that is wrung out of their own flesh and bones. Through various devices and stratagems, they work their greed and injustice against the ignorant and gather up the land's abundance. They lend money at high interest with land as a collateral, and even though the loan is for just a small amount, the interest piles up year by year until finally they make that land their own or take control of the borrower's livelihood. They become wealthy with the surplus accumulated through preying on the weak. Later they carry it off to other places where they entertain themselves in splendor. Such men are criminals against the land; they are great thieves.

If we pursue the theme of luxury further, we see that the sons of farmers without a surplus, and also the wives and daughters of the poor, covet and try to emulate the ways of the rich. Out of feelings of jealousy and resentment against the wealth that they cannot achieve, they become determined to show off, so they neglect the tasks they should be doing and instead of spending their evenings braiding straw, making straw sandals, spinning thread, or weaving, they imitate whatever is currently fashionable. Aping the ways of the prosperous city and disliking the homespun woven by their daughters, they buy the products of other provinces without any regard for what is appropriate to their status. Men even go to a hairdresser to have their pate shaved and their hair arranged. They do not look like farmers or poor people at all, but just like city folk.

People of this sort enjoy drinking parties and entertainment, form youth groups that waste too many goods on shrine festivals and the like, and do whatever they can to make themselves look beautiful. Seeing whatever astonishes others to be good, they put on an enormous show. Crazed by their hot blood, they think dissipation second to none to be a great deed, and they scorn those unable to indulge in it as worthless. The rare honest lad they trick, swindle, and lure, pulling him into the Way of luxury, or perhaps even dragging him into bad ways by encouraging him to gamble so as to cheat him out of money.

Troublemakers and the Problems They Cause

Once their behavior has deteriorated to this point, it is impossible for such people to return to being simple and sturdy farmers. Many of them further ruin themselves by making gambling their profession, and, driven by evil intentions to seize the goods of others, they become what are called troublemakers. They start fights and quarrels, intimidate the weak, or else speculate that a person has concealed a bad deed and resort to blackmail. Thinking his parents' honesty a dismal thing, such a man forgets how important is the task of nurturing his parents. In the end he runs away from home and loiters in places where he does not belong. He may steal another man's wife or have illicit relations with his daughter, and the most degenerate and immoral will commit the crime of rape. Not only that, but lying that the woman has agreed to marry him, he will sit down in her parents' house and refuse to budge so as to force them to give up their daughter. He may call at her house with fake porters to take the woman and her belongings away,[3] or he may extract consolation money or a payment to settle the matter privately and then send her back. In other cases, such a man may hate the thought of giving a woman back without anything to show for it, and he will deprive her of her virginity first, so as to prevent her from being given as a bride to another house. Another may entice the girl to move to a different place, where he makes her into a prostitute.

A man of this kind engages in all sorts of other evil deeds as well. He abandons his aging parents, leaves his proper place of residence, and becomes an unregistered wanderer. Forgetting his base status, he shows no deference to people of high rank and status and becomes bold and fearless. He gambles, forces people to sell him goods, to buy his goods, or to make loans; or he stays at a brothel, knowing full well that he has no money, and eats and drinks his fill without paying for it. When pressed for payment, he starts a quarrel or deliberately sets himself up to be hit so that he can falsely claim injury and extort a payoff; in this manner he gets through the world doing as he pleases. Once things have ended up like this, he is unable to pursue an ordinary occupation in the city or find work as a live-in servant [because he lacks the proper papers], so he becomes totally caught up in evil deeds and swaggers back and forth between city and countryside.

These sorts of mischief-makers often go elsewhere to commit their evil deeds. In the past when this happened and the authorities punished them, their home village would be ascertained, their family and the village officials would be summoned, and these would suffer too. For that reason, miscreants would be scolded or threatened at the slightest sign

---

3. Porters (*nikatsuginin*) hired by the bridegroom played an important role in wedding festivities. On the day of the wedding, the bridegroom would call at the bride's house, accompanied by porters and his relatives, to receive her and transport her clothes and belongings to his house.

of misbehavior lest they become, as the saying has it, the type to put the rope around their parents' necks. Neighbors would admonish them, and the village officials would try to prevent them from going elsewhere and keep them under control lest they misbehave.

Nowadays, to avoid troublesome procedures for both places, a wrongdoer is commonly treated as being unregistered, even if his name has not been erased from the village register at his family's request, and even if his parents have not formally expelled him from the household. This means that the village officials are not involved, no rope is thrown around the parents' necks, the relatives do not incur blame or threats, and no one has to trouble himself about what the mischief-maker may be doing elsewhere. The mischief-maker, for his part, becomes all the more bold, knowing that no matter what he does, his village will not be involved and he will not cause trouble for his parents. In the end he comes to think that if he is willing to gamble his life, he can profit from doing evil, and should he get away with it, the profit will be even greater. Thus, he becomes a menace to the world.

If villagers take so little care about mischief-makers on the village register, they are all the more nonchalant about giving troublemakers who come in from outside a place to stay. Even if a troublemaker is captured by the authorities, the claim is made that he was captured on the road, and the affair ends without the slightest repercussions for the person who offered him lodging. This person can thus safely put up troublemakers from other places and become an instructor in evil for the young. How merciful, people say, for the shogunal authorities not to blame relatives or punish people who provide lodging for troublemakers. People also say that with so many troublemakers in today's world, to investigate each one's home village would take too much effort. Is it better to extend blame to the parents, as happened in the past, or to treat people still officially registered as if they were unregistered, as is currently done? Although the pluses and minuses have yet to be thoroughly considered, the way things are today is not right. Is this not owing to laxity in institutions of regulation, especially given that as things are today troublemakers easily come and go?

In the shogun's capital too, there are many troublemakers who survive without occupation or funds among those in the meanest houses, backstreet tenements, or places where unregistered wastrels freeload in others' houses. Few among them were born here; most come from various provinces. These unregistered people and troublemakers who have swarmed out of the provinces got their start as noted above. Since it is easy right now for unregistered persons and troublemakers from the provinces to roam about at will, they have no qualms about leaving their place of birth, and they do not fear being formally expelled from their household. Even if they are banished from their village, forbidden entry into their domain, or sent into exile, rather than regret what the future might bring, they are delighted. Furthermore, since the label of unregistered person or troublemaker strikes fear into those they pass, they travel widely in complete freedom. Should they be put in prison, it only makes them bolder; should a [punitive] tattoo or some other mark be carved on their body,[4] their rank as a troublemaker goes up, and it goes up another step should they kill someone. All are assets in the competition to survive.

In recent years, this proliferation of unregistered persons and troublemakers has spread across the provinces, and since human sentiment naturally tends to move in a bad direction, many sons of warriors, farmers, artisans, and merchants fall away from [their family's occupation], and the post stations and villages are full of loitering good-for-nothings who disturb good people and disrupt the world's affairs. Because customs have deteriorated even in the villages and dishonest people have become prevalent everywhere, the countryside has steadily lost its uprightness, and everything is pushed in the direction of the frivolity found in flourishing cities. Especially along the Tōkaidō highway, but even in rural towns throughout the country, there are now unlicensed prostitutes and serving girls who double as prostitutes, and that leads to even worse misbehavior and unfiliality. This situation fosters unregistered wastrels and troublemakers; there are many fights and quarrels, as well as much illicit sex and adultery. Gambling and various other games of chance become popular; instances of night robbery, mugging, murder, and arson begin to occur. Some people give up humble farming to offer their houses for such activities; others make their living by acting as a go-between or mediator, or they open pawnshops, drinking holes, baths, and hairdressing shops.

This leads to the ruination of local customs. When that happens, only troublemakers and immorality flourish, and the people's original voca-

---

4. For a detailed analysis of the punishments visited on criminals by the shogunate, see Botsman, *Punishment and Power*. Tattooing was incorporated after 1720 into the standardized repertoire of punishments that displayed the regime's authority.

Troublemaker with farm youths gambling on a roadside outside the village. *Ehon hiyu bushi* (1789). National Diet Library Digital Collection.

tion gradually withers away. This is the terrible consequence of these despicable customs. They must be reformed. Indeed, the shogunate has always had laws that forbade townspeople and farmers from indulging in luxury: they are not allowed to wear silk except coarse pongee; they must not allow unlicensed prostitutes, engage in gambling, games of chance, and lotteries, or provide lodging to unregistered persons from other provinces. Such laws once had effect, but now they are breaking down. Deterioration is everywhere, and the shogun's laws are no longer enforced.

The Hardships of Small-Scale Farmers

The expenditures wasted on wealthy farmers' prideful extravagance, the money squandered by young punks and rakes, the abuses committed by the troublemakers floating in from other places, and the profits secretly extracted by various merchants and artisans do not come from some outside source; all of them come from the vital resources of the village, which depend on the small-scale farmers' labor. In this fashion the wealthy, young punks, and troublemakers as well as merchants and artisans all plunder the land of its abundance. Left behind are the small-scale farmers who keep to the old ways and the path of righteousness. They have to make up for this waste and take on more than their share of hardships because of these atrocities and immorality. They are to be pitied.

These small-scale farmers' circumstances are basically fragile. They know not the slightest leeway, they do not understand dissolution, and they are as naive as the day they were born. They involve themselves solely in the people's basic occupation and struggle to do their very best, but all that remains is appropriated by those gangs. Those who should be pitied in this world are precisely they. They must be saved.

It stands to reason that when one person enjoys paradise, another person has to suffer. Because there are so many idlers right now, suffering in their shadows are a great many people who year after year work their fingers to the bone. This is owing to the evil customs in our age of peace and tranquility. A one-*shō* container will always hold one *shō*. In no matter which village, the amount of land and the number of people is gauged to a nicety, so that if there are one hundred people there is land for one hundred people, and there is food for one hundred people without surplus or lack. Out of the rice and grains produced by those hundred people, that part of the harvest that is meant for the annual land tax and various duties is supposed to be sent out of the village, but if too much of what remains is taken away to other places as well, that in itself will cause a shortage. But what happens now is that wealthy houses squeeze [money] out of small-scale farmers without getting their own hands dirty, take it to other places, and waste it on their own entertainment. Or else, the young punks and degenerates steal from their parents or expropriate [wealth] from other people and take it to other places. What the merchants and artisans cajole out of the people through the interest they charge is also taken away to other places. This leaves great lack and great poverty within the village.

Generally speaking, in a village with one hundred people, all one hundred alike should work at agriculture without distinction, without negligence, without even one person not doing his share. But today wealthy men, degenerates, merchants, and artisans have appeared in the countryside. Out of every hundred, some fifty have become idlers who do not cultivate the fields, and furthermore, as noted above, they take village produce away to other places, so that the remaining fifty people not only have to break their backs in heavy labor but also are left short of everything, including food. At this time, fifty small-scale farmers suffer double hardships because they have to perform the backbreaking labor of one hundred without even sufficient food. In order to make up the deficiencies in what is available to eat, they have no other option but to engage in some sort of production of commercial goods and use this to bring back money from other places to buy food.

Engaging in the production of commercial goods requires extra painful toil and adds another hardship on top of the two others mentioned above. These three hardships arise from the change in customs and the polarization between rich and poor farmers. In the past, farmers never bought food. I have heard that in the past, when one hundred men worked equally as one hundred men, each made his own miso and stored up various grains as his own food supply. None purchased any goods. Since the hardships described above have become more severe over the years, poverty-stricken people tide themselves over by selling off their rice and other crops as soon as they have been harvested and then only barely manage to buy back [what they need to survive] by adding on ever more side jobs. When they sell their crops, the merchants take one profit by forcing them to sell at a low price and another by making them buy necessities back at a high price. [The farmers'] losses in such transactions constitute another hardship. Because fifty of the righteous small-scale farmers fall behind and suffer under the accumulated weight of these three or four types of hardships unheard of in the past, they find it harder and harder to endure and go off track in various ways. Some send their sons or daughters off to work, or they themselves go to other places to work, or they give themselves over to greed, and the number of righteous people decreases.

Indeed, this sort of behavior has become customary in the environs of the shogun's capital and nearby provinces and in all provinces with convenient circulation [of money and goods]. In short, because of this convenient circulation, the wealth noted above can appear, extravagant people can appear, degenerates can appear, and large numbers of merchants and artisans also appear. On the other hand, in other regions, especially peripheral areas where the lord's dominion is province-wide or in remote mountain areas where access is inconvenient and circulation is poor, you find poverty worse than that noted above.

The Corrupting Effects of Commerce and Calculation

Nothing is better, it is thought, than the convenient circulation [of money and goods] for bringing prosperity and helping people to supplement their resources, but that is not the case. As we have seen, it leads to polarization between rich and poor, luxury and destitution, and to the emergence of large numbers of profit seekers who ravage the people. Not only in this area around the shogun's capital but also in the neighborhoods of Kyoto, Osaka, and the castle towns of the various provinces, and also in places close to post stations and other places where townspeople live, farmers exchange vegetables and daikon for coins and sell even flowers and miscanthus grass. In these areas the people's original conscience is lost to an evil cleverness that swindles others and covets profits. People in places where expensive goods such as silk crepe and the like are manufactured become wise in the Way of greed. They plant mulberry, hemp, Asian pear, persimmons, indigo, cotton, safflower, medicinal plants such as *murasaki* root and various species of peony, arrowroot, lily root, potato, Chinese water chestnut, lotus root, and other things on wet and dry fields. They find the five grains repugnant and covet that which brings profit; they bargain about everything with a merchant's frame of mind; they are quick to put aside moral rectitude for the sake of making money; and they cleverly understand the ins and outs of how to do everything. Some travel far to other provinces to work out of greed. In other cases, profit seekers come in from other places, thus disrupting the census registers. Popular attitudes become disordered, and the people's occupation declines.

The Way of Heaven and the Ways of the gods, sages, and buddhas all agree that single-minded adherence to honesty is good. They also hold it good that the people's hearts and occupations be focused on a single thing. Now, however, the hearts and occupation of the people of the soil have changed. A devious intelligence attuned to the ins and outs of things has arisen, leading to a cleverness of speech and, particularly, an understanding of circulation and profit unsuitable to people of the soil. Some learn how to cheat those above them and deceive those of high status. Even in years when there is no great crop failure, they will complain of damage caused by wind and rain and come up with clever excuses. Or they will lavish hospitality on survey officials and give them bribes to have them deduct losses, or start a mass protest to intimidate their lord or fief holder into reducing the annual land tax.[5] Or they will

---

5. The early modern equivalent of today's demonstrations or protest marches, the largest such protests, known as "appeals by force" (*gōso*), mobilized tens of thousands of farmers behind demands for reductions in taxes or corvée labor burdens. See Walthall, *Social Protest*.

Farmers in an area near Edo growing Asian pears to be sold in the city. *Edo meisho zue* (1834). National Diet Library Digital Collection.

use bad rice to pay the land tax and keep the good rice to sell as they please. When they go to the magistrate's office or other governmental offices, they deliberately wear ragged clothing and make themselves look shabby, so that they can appear as rude people of the soil when they enumerate their hardships. They stubbornly press a point when it suits their argument; if they are caught in misbehavior, they act as though they do not understand because they are people of the soil and give all sorts of excuses. They argue for unnecessary construction of dikes to control rivers, irrigation canals, drainage ditches, and so forth, with an eye to charging needless expenses against the lord or fief holder. Claiming that it will benefit the soil, the village officials and wealthy landowners connive and twist those expenses to their own use, without giving a drop of the windfall to the small-scale farmers. In any case, they show no deference to those above, they do not understand how indebted they are, and they turn warrior administrative officials into people they can manipulate.

When such baseborn people of evil intelligence look up at honest and straightforward people of high status, they see them as stupid, as people easily deceived. Therefore, such wicked people take advantage of the honest officials and strip them completely naked. Even if an official knows about their guile and pursues a strict investigation, in the end will come a day when he has won the battle only to lose the war. In other words, when it concerns matters of profit and loss, he cannot beat the baseborn. For that reason, honest officials are useless in this world. Even the sagacious among them have only a general understanding of the difference between good and evil, truth and falsehood; they do not have a penetrating grasp. Because today's good and bad, true and false incorporate a deviousness rooted in greedy calculation, one cannot fully understand the situation if one does not understand that deviousness. Understanding the true motives of deviousness has been difficult both now and in the past, and in today's world, all things are rooted in deviousness. If you are not a devious person yourself, it is difficult to recognize each of these devious acts.

Therefore, we have come to an age when officials are of no use if they are not wicked. For that reason, the officials in today's world have to have hearts unsuitable to a samurai in order to accomplish their task. They have to understand the circulation of goods and finance like a merchant, know how to seize what belongs to others, thoroughly master various courses of action, and be well aware where cunning lurks. Unless officials have that knowledge, the people below will overwhelm them. For this reason, you have to make yourself a devious person first, and then you can recognize the deviousness that people perpetrate; but this is an exceptionally onerous task.

Because it is such hard work to strike against this sort of guile in those below, the easy course today is to give up trying to crush it, to leave it to its own devices, to take a bribe and let things go. Adopting that easy course is the way things are done today. Today, those who are lords or high-ranking officials have no direct knowledge of how things are. If a disturbance breaks out below, they proclaim that it is because the officials in charge took immoderate measures. In the present world the lowly have become devious and have no fear of those above. The lords and high-ranking officials think it troublesome to strictly investigate the entire crowd when those below riot, so that many such incidents end up being blamed on a blunder on the part of one or two officials. This is because both lord and retainer are weak-kneed.

If the authorities were strict in dealing with a riot even when an official's blunder was to blame for it, they would be able to impose their will, break it up, and settle the issue with resolution and bravery. If this is not done, the lower officials will not be able to maintain the dignity of their office, they will be unable to keep matters under control thereafter, and ultimately they will despise those above. In the past, when the Divine Lord was still based in Mikawa, the Ikkō adherents banded together and caused a serious disturbance because Suganuma Sadamitsu had rashly seized grain from Jōgūji temple in Sasaki. Yet Lord Ieyasu did not censure Sadamitsu.[6] Although it awes me to speak of such matters, a resolute, honest administration would have been impossible if Lord Ieyasu had not handled it this way. At present, higher authorities do not give lower officials' will due importance: instead they try to put all the blame on the person directly in charge. Therefore, lower officials fear the consequences of taking clear-cut action. Some simply retreat in a dishonorable manner, others accept bribes in accordance with the wishes of the lowly, and in the end they let things get off track. That is only to be expected.

Small-scale farmers basically have no artifice whatsoever, and because they have no understanding of profit and loss they do not get into quarrels. Throughout the year they are crushed by the leading farmers, and even if they are imposed on outrageously, they do not have the wherewithal to appeal to higher authority and explain their situation. No

---

6. The Mikawa uprising by Ikkō adherents (followers of the Honganji, or True Pure Land, sect of Buddhism) posed a serious challenge to Ieyasu. See the further discussion in chapter 3, note 25. According to some accounts, including Buyō here, it was sparked by Ieyasu's vassal Suganuma Sadamitsu's forcibly requisitioning grain for military purposes from the temple, which claimed immunity from interference by political authorities. Ieyasu later elevated Sadamitsu to daimyo status.

matter what sort of injustice they suffer, a lawsuit cannot be initiated without the ability to pay expenses. Should they go so far as to bring suit, they are not able to wait until the point when they would win. Thus, they accept a private settlement halfway through even if they have a winnable case because they have exhausted their assets during the time it takes for the court to come to a decision.[7] Anticipating this lack of resources, the opposing side will maneuver to drag out the case so that a suit that should have been won ends up being lost. Many also end up losing because they do not have the ability to offer the bribes so popular in today's world.

The chief reason for the neglect of the people's proper occupation in this world is their move toward greed and evil guile; this comes from the convenience of circulation, which has surely warped everything and has led to the world becoming polarized. Places with convenient circulation flourish, giving rise to guile, whereas in inconvenient areas where there is no circulation, the population has declined, with only waste fields and dilapidated houses remaining. Even in the Kantō, it is reported that there are villages with waste fields and dilapidated houses in over half of Hitachi and Shimotsuke provinces. Right now, the hardships of large and small daimyo with domains in those provinces, and especially of bannermen with small fiefs there, are immense. Even though the villages' putative yield remains the same as in former days, they cannot pay their annual land tax with the decline in households and nothing but waste fields. All of them are in arrears for over half or more of what they paid in the past, so that a lord of 10,000 *koku* cannot get the income one would expect from 5,000 *koku*, and a bannerman of 1,000 *koku* cannot get the income one would expect from 500 *koku*. Generally speaking, the land tax tends to be insufficient to cover a lord's needs even in places where it is collected in full. In recent years this happens all the time. The fief holders can no longer endure it, and so they oppress ever more heavily places where the population has declined. This causes hardships on top of hardships.

Additional hardships are caused by the corvée burdens levied by the shogunate for public works and for horses and porters serving the transportation system. Since this region has lots of traffic on the Nikkō highway, the highway to the far north, and the road to Nikkō taken by

7. For "private settlement" (*naisai*), see chapter 4, note 17.

imperial messengers,⁸ post stations and the assisting districts are supposed to perform post horse and porter duties. This too is divided up and assessed on each village's putative yield in such a way that in places where it is difficult to supply more than ten or twenty farmers, the allotment is for thirty or forty men, and in places that cannot supply five horses, the allotment is for ten or fifteen. As a consequence, it is said, villages are forced to supply the post stations with funds to hire laborers to perform this service. I have also heard that overall the expenses for men and horses at the post stations are more than double what they were in the past. Since this increases the weight of hardships all the more, people are unable to endure, and thus they keep scattering, leaving behind wasteland and dilapidated houses. This is to be expected.⁹

Farmers and Lawsuits

Since the handling of lawsuits is a matter that concerns the shogunate, I will summarize it with all due deference. First of all, it is not easy for farmers in the provinces to undertake a lawsuit; it is truly troublesome. In distant provinces it is difficult to bring even cases that are about

---

8. The Nikkō highway and the highway to the far north were two of the main "five highways" radiating from Edo; the two highways largely overlapped until Utsunomiya in Shimotsuke. As shown in map 3, the road to Nikkō taken by messengers sent every year from the imperial court to make offerings to Ieyasu's enshrined spirit at Nikkō branched off the Nakasendō at Kuragano near Takasaki and ran through Kōzuke and Shimotsuke provinces to join the Nikkō highway near its end point.

9. The post-station transport system involved three tiers of users. Shogunal officials and some major temples and nobles holding dispensations from the shogunate traveled for free; daimyo retinues traveling on alternate attendance paid fixed rates; and ordinary travelers paid "negotiable" rates that were generally about twice the fixed rates. In return for providing transport services, post stations were exempted from taxes, but because they could not support sufficient numbers of porters and packhorses to meet the demand for free and fixed-rate transport by shogunal officials and daimyo, they convinced the shogunate to require nearby villages (which were not similarly tax-exempt) to make up the lack by providing "assistance" (*sukegō*). As travel became more frequent, the areas forced to supply assistance expanded. The farther removed an assisting village was from the post station, the more time villagers had to spend in transit, increasing the burden on them.

matters of principle to a clear-cut conclusion. The townspeople and idlers of Edo, Kyoto, Osaka, and other prosperous places initiate lawsuits as part of their everyday lives and take even trifling matters to the magistrate's office to get a settlement.[10] People who have sufficient wherewithal to employ a clerk send him in their place, claiming that they are sick, or they hire what is called an advocate as their representative and leave the negotiations in the suit up to him.[11] They deceive the magistrate's office by pretending to be sick and then go out on private business or for entertainment rather than spending the day discreetly at home; they show not the slightest feeling of deference to the shogun's authority. Being skilled at negotiating at the magistrate's office, the advocate knows that if he presents the case in a certain manner, it will work in his favor and that if he pushes another way, things will fall into place for him. He deceives those above and despoils the opposing side. By putting on an appearance of make-believe deference to the investigating officials, he ingratiates himself with them. He correctly calculates how the case will develop, and although he uses expedients and falsehoods, he succeeds in carrying it off. In the end he confuses all by calling white black and wins his case.

Farmers in the Kantō provinces and especially the Edo environs have become comfortable about appearing in lawsuits, and because they are so accustomed to Edo, they have no fear of the magistrate's office and see straight through the officials. Having acquired the bad habit of going to Edo at every opportunity, they get into disputes on the slightest pretext and immediately take these to the Edo courts. Since they fully grasp the ins and outs of the procedures and understand how the matter will be concluded, they can assume an attitude of confidence. Farmers from far away places, in contrast, are not like that. They are afraid of Edo, let alone the magistrate's office. To go on a long journey and engage in a lawsuit

---

10. The term translated as "magistrate" here, *bugyō*, in fact encompassed a range of offices. Which magistrate one dealt with depended on one's status and locale. For Edo townspeople it would be the town magistrate (*machi bugyō*). Rural residents would bring suits to the finance magistrate (*kanjō bugyō*), who had jurisdiction over the administration of the shogun's lands.

11. The shogunate recognized "lawyers' inns" (*kujiyado*), which provided lodging to people from elsewhere who had come to Edo to bring a suit and assisted plaintiffs in preparing the necessary paperwork. In principle it prohibited "advocates" (*kujishi*), seeing them as taking advantage of the judicial system by encouraging people to bring suits over debts and other money matters.

from a distant area costs a tremendous amount. In addition, the innkeepers officially permitted to lodge farmers who are in Edo to file a suit take advantage of the ignorance of people from far away and swindle them by charging them for petty things.[12] Besides, the farmers fear the investigating officials, whom they take for honest men, and think it inexcusable to make a mistake in one word or even a syllable, or to raise objections. Having been raised in a faraway province where the customs vary and ideas are different, they are not accustomed to the officials, which means that they are not able to fully explain their views, and their anguish is enough to last a lifetime. The anxiety of waiting for days as the proceedings drag on exhausts their perseverance; they worry about conditions back home and grow weary from the multiple tasks that need doing, so that finally they have no choice but to accept a private settlement. They return home without having the right and wrong of the matter clarified, and the innumerable hindrances to cultivation and the considerable expense they have incurred in traveling great distances have all added up to no effect.

Sources and Consequences of the Disparity in Wealth in the Countryside

Here I will describe the situation of those people who live in distant provinces and remote regions, in whom evil desire has not given rise to guile, who have fallen behind the times, and who, pressed by poverty, destroy their own houses and ruin themselves. If such people land themselves in trouble with the wealthy, even the most trifling misfortune will become difficult to withstand. All the paddies and fields that they ought to be cultivating will be taken by the rich, and having lost their livelihood, they will have to move to another province. Generally speaking, small-scale farmers are in the same circumstances as people who survive from day to day in the cities, and no matter how hard they work, they will lack the wherewithal to endure. Various sorts of occupations are possible in the cities, making it easy to get by, but because farmers have only agriculture, they can do nothing but go to another province once they lose that. In all villages the wealthy end up owning the top-grade fields, whereas [the

---

12. The inns (*hyakushō yado*) to which Buyō refers here were one category of the above-mentioned *kujiyado*.

other farmers] own only low-grade fields where little grows. Furthermore, in some areas, those who have been driven to sell fields have to discount the putative yield on those fields by transferring the difference to their remaining fields in order to get a good price.[13]

In this way, the wealthy single-mindedly buy up good sites with a low putative yield, and the poor come to be assigned a large amount of yield on the bad fields remaining in their hands. Because the poor have to put out more than their fair share of the annual land tax and do more than they should in corvée labor, loss piles on losses. The families who have lost even their bad fields can only work as tenant farmers, and they exhaust themselves in laboring for the farmers who own land. Because they pay all the rice that they cultivate to the landlord [in rent], the only things left for them are husks, bran, and straw. Throughout the year they never get their head above water, nor do they have time to draw a breath.

People who do well thus become ever more prosperous. They buy up fields one after the other, set up their second and third sons as branch houses, and build fine residences. Those in declining circumstances, on the other hand, fall still further, until they have to leave their paddies and fields and sell their dwellings. With the family sunk in poverty, its members, young and old, men and women, end up scattered. In today's world the imbalance between rich and poor, between those who get ahead and those who fall behind, has become extreme. Around every wealthy person there are twenty or thirty impoverished farmers, and just as plants cannot grow alongside a big tree, farmers too cannot live in security alongside a great house. As a matter of course [small-scale farmers] will be swept away by the wealthy person's power, and many people will be stricken by poverty. Uprisings and conspiracies will definitely erupt where there are such extremes in the imbalance between rich and poor. Farmers' riots do not arise solely because of the daimyo's or fief holder's tyranny. In every case there is someone who has more than he

---

13. Since the putative yield was the basis for the tax assessment, fields deemed more productive were taxed at a higher rate than fields producing little. Buyō is suggesting that when farmers sold land, they negotiated not only its sale price but also the rate at which it would be taxed, with the understanding that the original owner would be responsible for paying the difference between the original tax rate and the rate negotiated with the buyer.

should in that area, and because he preys on the small-scale farmers, their pain spurs them to plot uprisings.

In villages where in the past one hundred people worked together, today fifty of them not only idle their time away but also despoil the small-scale farmers. Fifty small-scale farmers have to bear up under hardships that have quadrupled or quintupled, and their food supply does not suffice at all. In the time they can spare from cultivation, they transport goods for pay, or they work as day laborers or at some sort of cottage industry. But because they live far from the cities, work of this sort does not provide that much extra income, and they cannot free themselves from anxiety. In some cases they are unable to nurse their sick parents, and as a matter of course they cannot afford to provide them with medicine. The members of their household suffer from fleas and mosquitoes on summer nights, and in cold weather they rely on the meager light from the hearth to spin hemp or silk or to weave cloth for sale. In some cases they have had to take out an advance loan for the loom from merchants, who then set whatever low price they please for the goods offered in partial repayment for the loan. Those merchants may find fault with the product and extract all sorts of extra charges, so that no profit remains to the worker. All the work that they have endured night after night goes for naught, and it is just as though they worked in order to lose their capital. But in areas far from the cities there is no other way to acquire money, so they can do nothing but bring out their goods and have them priced. Even if they lose their capital and wear themselves out, they have no choice. In former days people could get by without producing commercial goods, but now conditions have arisen that ravage the people of the soil and cause this kind of suffering.

On land where people have to get by on agriculture alone without other enterprises, it has become even more difficult for them to endure. In some cases their parents are so old as to be useless, while their children are so young that they cannot help out with cultivation, nor are they yet old enough to be sent out as an apprentice. Then the only thing a husband and wife can do is work like crazy morning and night. Ignoring the cries of their nursing baby, they work at rough, poorly paid jobs. When they leave for the fields, they place the infant in a basket and leave him in the care of his older siblings during their absence, or they tie a crawling toddler to the roots of a tree or the handle of a hoe beside the paddy they are cultivating. Even when the child is tormented by a belly full of worms, they can give him no medicine; their manner of child raising is no different from that of a dog or cat. All they can do is wear themselves out with the harvest and the public works corvée.

In some places, a couple that is unable to support all the children they produce will kill some of them in the practice called thinning. This is heartless and cruel beyond words. However, the epitome of inhumanity lies elsewhere. It is not easy to raise a child, even if one does nothing more than a cat or dog would. If in the end [the cost of] trying to keep the baby alive might result in the house's destruction, the parents have no choice but to kill it. The criminal responsible for killing this child should be sought elsewhere. Small-scale farmers are commonly called "water-drinking farmers," but some, in fact, do not even have water to drink.[14]

Farmers with many dependents such as aged parents and children—those said to be burdened with many parasites—are likely to find their livelihood toppling. With only a tiny income, they are unable to eat even rough grains. As a matter of course they fall into arrears on their annual land tax; they sell off the small number of paddies and fields that they have not already sold, as well as their house plot, and even doing that, they are unable to pay the village officials their share of the village expenses. In some cases it is difficult for them to offer excuses to landlords and others in lieu of repaying their loans. Under pressure of obligation, they are forced to change their status [and become tenants] in order to make amends. In some cases they seek work elsewhere, leaving aged parents to fend for themselves or small children, who do not understand what is happening, dependent solely on their wife or parents. Or husband and wife may split up and entrust their children to others while they go off to seek work in cities such as Edo. In this way they are separated from the people's basic occupation and their place of birth and are led into bad habits. It is not an easy thing for parents and children and the whole family to end up scattered. Before that point, they have so exhausted themselves body and soul that they can do no more and are simply left with no other option.

---

14. The term "water-drinking farmers" (*mizunomi byakushō*) indicated their lack of other resources.

The Lure of the Cities

Farmers who move to the cities lose their bearings, and for two or three years all they can do is aimlessly eke out a meager existence. Having spent two or three years in such circumstances, they finally become used to the local customs and begin to commit misdeeds that make it even more difficult to return to their home in the countryside. What with one thing or another, they shift ever more to the ways of their current locale, and finally they put aside their native village's troubles. Up to then they had understood that honesty and integrity were good in all situations, but once they get on the wrong track, they become caught up in the customs of today's cities, where integrity is out of place. No matter how much they think to do better, there is no way that they will be able to abandon the easy life of the city and return to a place of unbearable hardship. For example, with the three *ryō* that you can make as a servant, you can buy eight or nine bales of rice on today's market. If you work as a tenant farmer back home, it is difficult to make even half of that. It is not difficult to obtain wages of three *ryō*, and it is easy on your body. For these reasons, people change their minds and begin to think of staying in the city. As noted before, aged parents, wives and children, and the feeble are the only ones remaining in the countryside, where they sink to the depths of hardship. Even though it is impossible to forget day or night how eagerly they await one's homecoming, the above logic is too strong, and it becomes impossible to return. This is entirely to be expected.

In comparison with that place of hardship, one of the splendors of the shogun's capital is that even someone who enters service as a mere samurai servant can depend on others for his dress, food, and dwelling and live a life free from constraint. In your native place, the village officials stand ready to push your head down. When you enter a senior farmer's front yard you must remove your footwear, and you are not allowed to use umbrellas and rain clogs within the village. Here in the city, someone who had been crushed by these constraints finds a place free of such hardships. Furthermore, you need not show any sign of deference to the daimyo and fief holders, who in the provinces are venerated like gods and buddhas, but can simply pass them on the road with an exchange of glances. Nothing is so strict as it is in the countryside; in the city there is no bigotry or narrow-mindedness; you can eat rice morning and night and drink good sake, sleep and sit on tatami mats, and enjoy prostitutes and courtesans without suffering discrimination because of your status; you can do what you like so long as you have the money to pay for it; and you can change your master as you please. Living a trouble-free life on your own, as the years go by you cease to think about your parents' worries back home, about their growing old and feeble, about the lamentations of your wife and children.

Even a servant who can barely make three *ryō* will not return home under these conditions. Those who leave their homes as young men and conduct themselves outrageously in the cities, or those who have a bit of quick-wittedness enabling them to work for a profit in accordance with the fashion of the times, are even less likely to return to their native place. People who from childhood were sent away to work as apprentices are accustomed to city ways from the time they first become aware of things. They may become addicted to luxury in the high spirits of their prime, or else they vigorously stride the path of profit. They learn to make a living by exploiting others, take coldhearted insincerity for cleverness, excel in the kind of guile that quickly grasps how matters stand, and become skilled in the use of twisted schemes to the point that the idea of returning home to nurse their parents becomes unthinkable.

In the countryside the old customs remain in all sorts of ways. People fight over whose lineage is older, take pride in their ancestors' genealogy, exaggerate matters of obligation or shame, and in general make much of such things. In comparison with this, customs in today's cities are more easygoing. Obligation, shame, lineage, truth, and falsehood are all unnecessary. The best of great deeds is simply to accumulate money; nothing excels this in our world in terms of achieving supremacy, and people put their knowledge of good and bad to work in the pursuit of greed. This is only to be expected.

Because of the conditions described above, people flow out of their homes to other provinces. In today's world, the townspeople populations of the three cities, as well as of provincial towns and post stations throughout the country, have naturally increased. Various sorts of idlers and troublemakers have appeared, and the farmers in isolated parts of the provinces have gradually declined. Generally speaking, there is too much convenient circulation in the world today; frivolous customs readily become prevalent, and because townspeople, idlers, and unregistered persons can then easily make a living, people also move easily. People leave the provinces to gather in cities with their sights on the townspeople's abundance. Although cities consequently flourish all the more, such things weaken the country's foundation.

It is generally not good to have too many people gather in cities. In the countryside of the various provinces and in isolated areas where people do not mix with those from other places, the old customs remain, people have consideration for their fellows and a strong sense of duty, and conditions are tranquil. When people come together from other places in the townsmen's blocks, particularly when they are good-for-nothings or ruffians, they treat everything lightly because no one knows where anyone else comes from. In today's interactions, all sense of duty is lost, and people seek to exploit others for their own benefit. This is the basis of the disorder in today's customs. Should too many people gather in country towns in the provinces as well, the situation will become very problematic. Where will this trend end?

As noted before, everything in this world has a set limit, just as a one-*shō* container always holds one *shō*. As there is a measurable limit to the grains and other goods that can be sent out from the provinces, there should also be a general limit to what comes into the city. If provinces send out grains and various products beyond that set limit, it will cause problems and corresponding shortages in the countryside, and this will give rise to ever greater poverty. Further, when masses of people come into a large city beyond what it can properly accommodate, there will be an insufficiency in various goods. For example, when 150 or 200 people squeeze into a place with a set limit of 100, as a matter of course the prices of all goods will rise because there is insufficient food and not enough profit to go around. In the intensifying deadlock as competition for profit increases, people are sure to commit unreasonable deeds and feed off one another. Because particularly here in the shogun's capital too many people have gathered in the past hundred years, the lower orders face a tight situation, and the wealthy are few. Many people have become impoverished, and each of them struggles to gain sufficient income. They feed off one another in various ways, and this gives rise to evil outrages.

Conditions have worsened year by year, although it may not be immediately apparent how bad the world has become. Many rich people amass paddies and fields or lend money to monopolize the land's abundance. Merchants and artisans emerge and make profits by engaging in activities inappropriate for the countryside. Sometimes officials come to threaten the people with the power of their authority, and because the situation in the countryside is often confused, there naturally are many things for the various government offices to look into. Officials occasionally come to make an on-the-spot investigation, and that is expensive. In many cases they do nothing but skim off their own share, which leads to further losses. If you borrow money in order to survive such losses, you are immediately overwhelmed by the interest, just as though you had drunk medicine that turned into poison. Debts finally end up destroying your life. What is worse, the people end up in such a state that they can no longer sustain their basic occupation. The Divine Lord established a strict system of rule; he suppressed extravagance by the state, reduced costs that plundered the people, and made it possible for people to live in peace and security. Now the system is crumbling, the people have no security, they move about too much, and they are robbed and preyed on beyond reason.

Nowadays, whatever a person's occupation, no one is really ignorant, humble, and unskilled at calculation. Those with even a little wit think about abandoning the people's occupation or changing to other lines of work. Although they may understand that by undertaking an unsavory job they may come to a bad end, they see abandoning the people's occupation as preferable. Things have gotten to such a state that to be a pariah or outcast in a city is seen as far better than enduring the people's occupation. As a consequence, those who can be considered the "true people" are gradually disappearing. At present, the number of people who remain in their native place is only about half of what it was before. They are the true people who sustain the state, do not change their occupation, preserve the old ways and obey the law, and sweat and labor in heat and cold, all while their just portion is wasted or expropriated in the various ways noted above. They sink into poverty without knowing extravagance or becoming greedy; they treat their native land as important; and in particular they have a deep-seated deference not only for the large and small daimyo but for all warriors. They commit themselves to agriculture so long as they have breath in their bodies, pay the annual land tax, perform various labor duties, and do many things beneficial for the state.

Seen from the eyes of townspeople, idlers, rakes, unregistered wastrels, and troublemakers, it is the utmost in stupidity and foolishness to live in such a humble, base, and constrained fashion, but from the state's or the realm's point of view, these old-fashioned humble people are truly treasures. Year after year they produce the prosperity [that others enjoy];

they are truly the people who in our age sustain the state and the realm. They exert themselves to the utmost morning and night in order to sustain the state, without giving the slightest consideration to anything else.

Nowadays, the heavy burdens that are caused by the splendid comfort enjoyed by those of high rank and status, plus the townspeople's and idlers' extravagance and dissolution, all fall on this segment of the world. It is the few remaining people who sustain the state who must pay the retribution for all the world's splendor with agony, sweat, and tears. The splendor of the cities all derives from the villages of the poor. What comes out of the villages of the poor becomes the world's abundance. While people in the cities grow fat and robust, the poor in distant provinces and remote regions exhaust themselves and weep tears of distress. When city men enjoy a harmonious life with their wives and concubines, in the countryside husband and wife must part. When food and drink are tasty in the cities, people of the soil starve.

Everything is like this. The cities and the remote countryside are like two sides of the same coin, front and back. The impoverished people work at the back. Is it not pitiful? They really endeavor to do their best. They really do their best to endure. Even though they should be pitied and appreciated, in this world no one pays them any attention.

Chapter 3

TEMPLE AND SHRINE PRIESTS

These days, because of the splendor of the times, monks know no hardship and enjoy the finest clothing, food, and housing, living lives of unequaled comfort. They have forgotten that they depend on the world for their nurture and are obliged to others for their well-being, and without exception they put on airs and behave arrogantly. As persons who left their households, monastics were originally solitary people. Being so unfortunate that they had no household of their own, they fled the world, cutting off all common attachments. Therefore a monastic should have no possessions and no desire for fame; he should follow a master and lead a humble life. He should go around with a begging bowl to receive alms in return for transferring merit for the benefit of others.[1] Or else he should live as a hermit, sewing his own clothes and carrying firewood and water to cook his own meals in his hut. There he should spend his days offering incense, flowers, and holy water, accumulating merit through the study of Buddhist doctrine and the practice of austerities, and seeking a state of no self and no desire. Or he should search for a wise master, traveling from province to province and in remote regions so as to gain instruction in the deepest meanings of the dharma. Or yet again, he should undergo training in a particular school, obtain a temple upon reaching a certain age, instruct the people in Buddhist teachings, and guide them to reach salvation in the next life.

---

1. Buyō refers here to *ekō*, practices of creating merit (positive karma) by various means and transferring it to a patron or a deceased person.

Priests holding a lottery at an Edo temple. The crowd outside the temple hall is pressing in to hear which lot has been drawn by the priest standing on the steps. The government sanctioned such lotteries on the premise that the funds raised would be used to build or preserve temple halls. *Tōto saijiki* (1838). National Diet Library Digital Collection.

The Corruption of Buddhist Clergy

As people who gather merit and acquire virtue through years of austerities and difficult practice, monastics have always been respected and treated well even by people of high status. At present, however, they merely pride themselves over the favors they receive, and they no longer go around with begging bowls or transfer merit to others. They are spared the effort to supply their own clothes and food; they are negligent in their study and practice; they do not travel to faraway lands; and they acquire temples before they reach the right age. In their arrogance, they ignore the laypeople, showing no desire to assist them, and they display more greed and deceitfulness than any layman. They dress in ornate clothing and are concerned solely to surround themselves with splendor. They use large timbers and stones to build temple halls and shrines, without thinking twice about the labor of the workers. They lavish gold and silver on Buddha canopies, fretwork, sacred cabinets, and draperies, squandering the world's resources on splendor. With frivolous flattery they hand out compliments, deceiving the laypeople so as to get them to agree to all kinds of selfish requests. They are quick to understand that women young and old and nuns have little wisdom and are easily charmed. Therefore, they preach to them about this-worldly benefits or scare them with talk about the next life and urge them to have rites performed or prayers said and to make donations and offerings. Taking advantage of others' goodwill toward them, they trick people into making offerings without giving anything in return. They ignore normal moral obligations, maintaining that they cannot take part because they have left the world; but when it suits them, they may plot to file a complaint on the basis of those same obligations. At times they engage in quarrels with laypeople or even sue them, using convoluted arguments and big words. They are more bigoted and obstinate than any layman and always put their own obligations last. When a matter is not to their liking, they use their unworldly status to force the other party to yield. In their dealings they are very selfish indeed.

These days, it is common for the position of chief priest of a temple to be secretly bought and sold. Age and virtue are of no relevance, and temple priestships are priced according to the size of the temple's property. The official monastic ranks used to be reserved for priests of great virtue and knowledge, but now they are traded for bribes, with no consideration for age or virtue. Therefore, monks who are clever in the way of greed and who have a talent for collecting money seek promotion early and acquire positions at the great temples. Priests of high rank are thus those who have put the dharma to one side and concentrated solely on making a profit.

Lesser monks are all the more driven by greed. They organize Buddha viewings,[2] hold sermons, and perform rites for feeding the hungry spirits,[3] but not to save the sentient beings; they do this only as a way to make a profit. For memorial services, funerals, and prayer ceremonies, they establish different grades and procedures, depending on the size of the donation. They organize lotteries, collect donations and offerings, and run confraternities with monthly fixed dues. They also plan credit associations and all sorts of other activities intended to further the circulation of money.[4] In the rare event that a notable or wise monk appears who edifies the people and attracts their faith, the bonzes flock together to capitalize on this and devise ways to gain a profit by selling this single virtuous person. They may have shaved heads and wear dharma garments, but underneath, they are as greedy as any boor. All they think about is how to live off the laypeople without putting themselves to any trouble.

These days, the Buddha Way has been corrupted by greed. The monks engage in fornication and meat eating, and they sneak around to enjoy all kinds of inappropriate pleasures. They pay no heed to their temple duties and leave the morning and evening sutra recitations, tea ceremonies, and merit-transferring rites to trainees. These trainee monks, too, are arrogant, and even while they call themselves "temple caretakers" or

---

2. *Kaichō* (literally, "opening the curtains") were occasions when a statue, relic, or other precious object that was usually kept hidden was put on display. At the time of such viewings, which became very popular in the Edo period, the temple grounds would be filled with booths selling various goods or staging all kinds of entertainments.

3. *Segaki* (feeding the hungry spirits) was a rite performed mainly around *obon*, the summer festival for the dead. Spirits who could not attain salvation because of bad karma or a lack of descendants were thought to cause all kinds of trouble. In this rite they were offered food, drink, and the benevolence of the Buddha so as to enable them to escape from their sorry state.

4. Members of such credit associations (*tanomoshi-kō, tsumikin-kō*) made regular contributions to form a shared fund, which was then paid out in rotation to one member of the association, decided by lots, bidding, consensus, or other means. As the organizer, the temple could expect to extract benefits from the arrangement.

"cloister representatives," they refuse to perform such religious duties. In the end these tasks end up being turned over to filthy menial monks, who, banging on gongs and clappers, conduct some sort of imitation of the rites. The offering of flowers and other things is of no concern to the chief priest and is left to the lowest hedge-priests. The chief priest does not serve the Buddha, and many days pass between each time he sees the face of the main Buddha image in his temple. He suits himself by leaving the temple to indulge in amusements even in the evening, staying overnight at other places. There he wastes money drinking fine sake and enjoying good food. Or he may keep a woman in another house that he calls his concubine's residence; he may even hide his woman within the very temple and have children with her. He lets others run a restaurant or a tea stand, taking a share in the profits, or he participates in gambling matches with dice and cards. When he returns to the temple he scolds the monks who have been on duty, and to divert attention from his own misbehavior, he blames them for running the temple badly or other things. Meanwhile the other monks take advantage of the chief priest's absence to steal donations made to the temple. They take coins from the offering box and spend them on drink and food, they gamble, and they abandon the temple they have been left in charge of to indulge themselves with whores in the brothels. Both the master and his subordinates misbehave and break the law.

If such misbehavior escalates, it can lead to the temple's ruin. Donations from other places and funds for the performance of permanent memorial services are embezzled,[5] temple buildings and landholdings are sold off, long-cherished temple paraphernalia such as statues and sutras are pawned, and objects donated by parishioners or left to the temple as mementos of deceased people are lost. The money is squandered on gambling, fornication, and other amusements, and in the end, even the position of chief priest is put up for sale.

Monastics have no wives and children and no families to take care of, and being independent, they can do as they like, free of all worries. If they commit an error that cannot be covered up, they simply retire. Even when they go into retirement, they commit various kinds of deceit and

---

5. Funds for permanent memorial services (*eitai kuyōryō*) were donations intended to continue to create revenue and thus cover the costs of regular ritual services for a deceased person, ideally for ages to come.

swindle their parishioners. After having collected money for a provision fund, they sell the temple—and even if they pass it on to a disciple, they contract debts without worrying about the problems these may cause, leaving it to their successor to suffer the consequences. They hand over the post of chief priest after first having made generous arrangements for themselves, and on top of that, they pester their successor, claiming that he has numerous obligations to his old master, even though there is no sign of any relationship between master and disciple in the true sense of the word. For these reasons, temples everywhere have lost their old and venerable treasures, such as Buddha statues and scriptures; their precincts are dilapidated; and their lands have been squandered away. Temples are burdened with debts incurred by generations of chief priests, and most of them are in trouble.

Even after they have retired, monks do not become frugal. They establish a dwelling in a town house or the house of a layman, or they set up a retirement house on the town outskirts and live a life of self-indulgence. They go out to the pleasure quarters at night and sleep in the morning, they keep women, and they play go, shogi, and games of chance. They use their retirement funds to make high-interest loans, and if it looks as if their evil deeds will come to light and an official investigation might be instigated, they flee and hide, visiting small temples in different provinces and going underground there. After a while they acquire a new temple, where they once more deceive the lay households who are their parishioners. Their free and easy way of life has no comparison in this world. In the past, if famous and wise monks ran away, it was because they disliked being treated with extravagance when they inspired faith in high-ranking people, or because they could no longer bear the pressure of crowds of people gathering around them. They were unhappy with the fact that all this upset the virtuous life that they had upheld in their quiet seclusion, or they grew tired of having to listen to the greedy desires of laypeople. They thus would simply disappear and withdraw to a mountain forest or a distant valley to concentrate on the dharma. The monks of this age are different. They flee because they have given people trouble and committed too many crimes. Among the chief priests of our time there are few who perform their duties to the end, and many retire because of excessive offenses.

This is how it is even with monks who are chief priests of a temple; when it comes to lower-ranking trainee monks or monks who wander around from one province to another, things are even worse. Petty thefts, fraud, robbery, and absconding are by no means rare. Monks have always maintained that they have fled the world and that they are "long-sleeved worthies" to whom conventional rules do not apply.[6] The laypeople, too, have of old had the habit to look the other way and close their ears, never blaming or punishing [the monks]. Therefore, monks reckon that it is nobody's business how they behave, and they act without concern for shame or reputation. Their way to make a living is the easiest in the world. The four classes of warriors, farmers, artisans, and merchants, and all others as well, have to depend on their own efforts to secure clothing, food, and housing; only monks are exempt from this. Wherever they roam there are plenty of temples, and they are never short of a place to live. It is said that because monastics have left their households, they have no home in any of the Three Worlds of past, present, and future—but these days, these so-called house-leavers can pick and choose between any number of homes. And when it becomes inconvenient for them to have a home, they give it up and act with complete freedom.

Temple Income, Ranks, and Perquisites

Temple income came to be as good as fixed as, together with the establishment of a lasting peace, the funds parishioners are expected to provide to their temples became largely set both in the towns and in the countryside. A warrior's house stipend is not fixed, because it depends on the year's harvest in his domain and on the price of rice. The same applies to farmers. Townspeople's income also varies with their success in trade and with the rise and fall of prices and therefore is not fixed. Such matters do not affect temple income, which is as if set in stone. If monks are particularly greedy, they can moreover extort more money from the people by organizing Buddha viewings and sermons, collecting donations and offerings, and performing rites and prayer ceremonies. However much they take in, it will not result in a reduction of their fixed income. This is a business that has no need for investment capital, and there is no other business quite like it. Because temples

---

6. "Long-sleeved people" (*nagasode no mono*) was a term for nonwarriors such as nobles, priests, scholars, and the like, whose unpractical long dangling sleeves stood in contrast with the style of dress worn by active warriors.

both in the towns and in the country have an income that is as good as fixed, novices and trainee monks grow accustomed to this regular revenue and are raised to be indolent. They undergo no hardship or austere training, nor do they engage in profound studies; they have no knowledge about the dharma, and to make things even worse, they are unremittingly self-indulgent. This is because the world has become too splendorous.

Such misbehavior should be stopped by the head temple or the liaison temple,[7] but liaison temples, too, have a high income and much authority; therefore, they are all the more given to luxury and covert debauchery and are in no position to chastise others. Moreover, for some reason there is no census register of monastics, so keeping them all properly under control is virtually impossible. The teachings and precepts of the Buddha Way are stuck in the [wrongheaded] notion that it is a good thing to ignore sins and to refrain from cutting down those who deserve to be cut down; thus, there is no one who corrects wrongdoers. Further, whatever a monastic may do, it will have no consequences for his secular relatives, so that he has nothing to fear. Therefore, few monks are true to the Way, while an ever-growing number are neglectful to the extreme. When among men, they display their authority and dwell in luxury, disdaining even men of high status; when retiring from the world, they behave like boors and tramps. From start to finish, they live off the state and swindle the realm at their whim.

Temples with official connections, such as imperial cloisters, imperial prayer temples, other official prayer temples, head temples, and liaison temples, have special ranks and tasks.[8] These temples are richly decorated both on the inside and the outside, and they employ large

---

7. There were three main levels of temples: national head temples (*honzan*), which oversaw all temples of their sect in western or eastern Japan; liaison temples (*furegashira*); and branch temples (*matsuji*). Liaison temples, which were usually located in Edo or a domain castle town, served as a conduit for the shogunate and daimyo to transmit instructions (*fure*) to temples within the sect. Although they were not originally part of the sect's internal organizational structure, head temples also found them a convenient channel for exercising influence over branch temples.

8. Imperial cloisters (*miya monzeki*), headed by imperial princes, were the highest ranking among all temples. Imperial prayer temples (*chokuganjo*) performed rituals and prayers for the health of the emperor and the protection of the

numbers of people. They are covered in illustrious crests of chrysanthemum, paulownia, and hollyhock leaf, radiating authority.[9] Sliding doors and screens close off their main sanctuaries and entrance halls, hiding their Buddha images from view. This prevents ordinary people from worshipping and gives a general impression of inaccessibility, showing a lack of interest in saving the people. Such temples station special guards to serve as watchmen, and these scold and threaten visitors who fail to follow the right procedures. This is not how things should be in the Buddha Way. These temples make a great show of authority even in their outward appearance; on the inside, their sumptuousness is extraordinary. They must rank highest in the world when it comes to displaying lavishness from morning to night.

When priests from temples of this kind perform ceremonies in front of the Buddha, such as funerary services, rites of transferring merit, and memorial rites, they do so with a great show of dignity; yet there is little reverence for the Buddha in their incense burning and sutra reciting. Rather than expressing faith [the lavishness of the procedures] serves to underline the dignity of the priests themselves. When it comes to their parishioners, priests often fail to perform the funerals and memorial services of small-scale warriors or rear vassals in person, passing them on to stand-in priests instead. Should a parishioner make a special request to have the priest perform the rite in person, even this involves a fee of gratitude. There should be no difference between high and low ranks in the Buddha Way, and salvation should not depend on fees of gratitude. When priests of this sort meet with parishioners of lesser rank, they make a grand display of authority. They sit in a higher place than their parishioners and look down upon them with a condescending air, more stern and commanding than a warrior. By rights, the parishioners are the patrons on whom the priest and the temple depend; but this is certainly not how they are treated.

When priests of this sort go on a journey, they take along vast amounts of traveling attire. They travel in palanquins with vermilion wickerwork

---

realm. Official prayer temples (*kiganjo*) performed a similar function for the shogunate or a daimyo.

9. These crests were used by the imperial house, high-ranking noble and warrior houses, and the Tokugawa house, respectively. For a temple to use such crests indicated a special connection with these houses.

and wear garments of gold brocade, and they select the best quality of folding parasols and luggage boxes.[10] They are accompanied by a procession of men-at-arms and footmen similar to those of warrior houses—these days, high-ranking priests' processions are in fact grander than those of warriors. Those who travel back and forth to distant provinces are especially extravagant. Flaunting their status as representatives of a temple holding a vermilion seal, they force all passers-by to stop.[11] Showing no consideration for the exertions of the coolies and horses supplied by the post stations, the priests have them carry large loads of long-handled equipment and the like. They arrogantly proceed right down the middle of the road, blind to the inconvenience that they cause others. In their haughty pride, they appear as though they would not hesitate to kick away any person unlucky enough to stumble in front of their train.

When monks who reside within one of the imperial cloisters or other special temples travel, even on personal business, they carry prominently the placard showing the temple's prerogative to freely requisition post-station coolies and horses.[12] They themselves ride in a palanquin or on horseback, showing no concern whatsoever for the burden imposed on the coolies and horses. Their passage is even more imposing than that of a mounted warrior, and they intimidate people. They have truly lost all sense of gentleness, humility, and charity. Even a chief priest of a great temple with a high court rank and large stipend should refrain from a boastful display of authority and intimidation. He should not slander the laws of the state and should be especially careful to show respect to warriors, who are the state's guardians. He should not set himself above warriors. Even the lowest samurai puts his life on the line for the state, and this makes him the equal of the wisest and most virtuous of priests; therefore, no priest should be disdainful or fail to treat him with propriety.

These days, moreover, imperial cloisters, head temples, and liaison temples lend out money to branch temples and other parties under the

---

10. "Luggage boxes" (*hasamibako*) were square boxes attached to a pole and carried over one shoulder.

11. Direct grants of landholdings issued by the shogun to warriors, court nobles, and religious institutions carried vermilion seals. The temple or shrine receiving such a vermilion-seal grant (*shuinchi*) was able to collect taxes for the institution's use from the farmers who worked the land.

12. The shogunate issued such prerogatives to certain temples and nobles in addition to officials traveling on shogunal business. See chapter 2, note 9.

name of "temple hall funds" or "preservation funds," charging exorbitant interest in return. In fact, the original amount of such funds is very small. The temple takes in money from rich townspeople and farmers, lends it out, and shares the profits with the original owners.[13] This is a lowly, mean business, very different from the elevated stature such temples always insist on. Since the branch temples are under the control of the higher-level temples, the latter are free to squeeze and extract interest from them. It is as though parents robbed their own children. Alternatively, a great temple may lend only the name of such a fund to a townsman or farmer, charging a fee in return. The townsman or farmer then exploits the authority attached to the temple's name to lend out money at high interest. Temples and shrines with vermilion-seal land grants or with long-standing official status similarly lend out money under the name of "august tomb fund," "memorial service fund," or "tea ceremony fund," taking interest from the poor. The priests say that this interest will be used to cover the costs of honoring the gods and buddhas, but in fact only a small fraction of the money is spent on such things, while most of it goes into their own pockets to pay for their luxurious way of living. To collect interest in this manner is against the Way of the buddhas and the gods. What would accord with the hearts of the buddhas and the gods would be to give assistance to the poor and help them. It goes against the Way of the buddhas and the gods even to take back what one has lent; to take interest on top of a loan is outrageous.

If a loan falls into arrears or the payment of interest is overdue, the priests of such temples fly into a rage and marshal all kinds of accusations. If the other party is a warrior, they become rude and use harsh words to cast shame over him. If their adversary is a townsman or a farmer, they use foul language and scold him, or they arrange for the town or village officials to keep strict watch over him [so he will not abscond], stirring up trouble and putting pressure on him. They behave like those demons called *asura*, or like "hungry spirits with means."[14] If

---

13. "Entitled" funds of this sort, in theory set up to cover some temple need, could be expected to receive special protection from the authorities. As mentioned in chapter 1, note 6, this meant that loans made from them would be readily collectible. Such funds were thus an attractive investment for wealthy commoners.

14. Those who live lives full of greed and desire may be reborn as hungry spirits. There are many kinds of hungry spirits, depending on the karma they carry; some cannot partake of any food, while others do. These latter are known as "hun-

they cannot put enough pressure on their victim on their own, they appeal to the shogunal authorities and file a lawsuit. Like merciless devils, they never give up until they get what they are after. Is that the kind of behavior that would please the buddhas and the gods? When money has been collected by stripping the fat from the bones of the poor, even if some is offered to the spirit of the noble deceased for memorial or merit-transferring services, would that spirit welcome such offerings? What impiety!

Temples' Involvement in Prostitution and Other Irregular Practices

Vermilion-seal lands and other areas near the gates of temples and shrines have come to be called "places of evil."[15] Their grounds reek of the business of fornication; they are full of "hells" offering illicit prostitutes and serve as hideaways for kept women.[16] Packed with taverns serving fish and fowl and tea stands put together of rush mats, they also offer other kinds of amusements, such as theater plays, pantomimes, jugglers, and storytellers—all conspiring to deceive people and steal their money. Even in the provinces, these vermilion-seal lands are nests of gamblers, troublemakers, thieves, and murderers.

The first principle of the Buddha Way is to shun women, and places such as Mount Hiei and Mount Kōya are off-limits to women.[17] Even so, priests install large numbers of women in their temple precincts; and even worse, a great deal of prostitution takes place. This is completely unacceptable. A place that should be pure is turned into a place of utmost impurity. Among the monks who live in these places, not a single one has a true heart; all have the hearts of bandits, and even novices and temple apprentices fall into wicked ways from a young age. They learn how to be troublemakers and follow their masters' example by behaving

---

gry spirits with means" (*uzai gaki*). In daily parlance, this Buddhist term was used for misers who lived austere lives while hoarding large amounts of money.

15. "Places of evil" (*aku-basho*) referred originally to recognized brothel districts such as the Yoshiwara but came to be applied more widely as well to theaters and other entertainment areas.

16. "Hell" (*jigoku*) was a popular slang term for an illicit brothel.

17. Mount Hiei, northeast of Kyoto, and Mount Kōya, south of Nara, served as major centers of, respectively, the Tendai and Shingon sects.

just as wantonly; therefore, all monastics have become troublemakers. Really, there are no words to describe the misconduct of today's priests, both in the cities and in the countryside.

In the vicinity of the shogunal castle such matters are investigated from time to time, so that there is some outward discretion and things are not so obviously visible. As one travels out from this city of Edo, however, one finds that monks are hardly controlled at all. Daimyo do not have the means to suppress the monks, and they harass laypeople at will, as arrogant as though the entire district were theirs. In the villages, since temples must impress their seals on the registers of religious affiliation each year, the monks act as if no official business can be conducted without them. Therefore, farmers fear and revere the monks, causing them to puff themselves up even more. Monks interfere even in lawsuits and conflicts, and while they maintain that they are intervening in order to bring matters to a harmonious solution, they are in fact partial toward one or the other party for reasons that have to do with their own desires. "Pushing from behind" and "offering aid," they cause even insignificant cases to develop into large conflicts. In the process, they use their authority to engage in fornication and other grossly unlawful acts.

In Edo, of course, and in the eight Kantō provinces, people readily undertake lawsuits. As already mentioned, even farmers are familiar with the handling of suits, and they have a general understanding of rectitude and the severity of crimes and punishments. Even if matters are left to be settled among equals, they can judge quite readily what is right and wrong. In the distant provinces, however, lawsuits are known only from ancestral tales, and people have no idea about how to judge rectitude and justice. Things have always simply been settled locally; they have no understanding of justice and reckon that the wisest way of dealing with things is to smooth them over amicably. To them, the talk of monks, who are knowledgeable and worldly-wise, sounds reasonable, and they listen carefully to them. Buoyed by this, the monks can easily show favoritism and arrange things in a one-sided manner, thereby ensuring that the weak and poor lose and the evil and rich win. If someone wins over his fear and defies a monk's words, or reproaches him in disgust over his misbehavior, the monk will carry a grudge against that person and take revenge. He may refuse to stamp his temple registration at the time of the religious survey; or he may fail to send over the necessary documents when someone in the household is to be married or adopted into a house elsewhere.[18] When there is a death in the household, he may draw out the preparations for the funeral, for example by feigning illness, or he may shame the family by slandering the deceased as a sinner and refusing to perform the rites intended to secure the deceased's salvation. Whether they are right or wrong, monastics have of old always been treated with reverence both in the cities and in the countryside. Especially in the distant provinces and in rural places, people have placed all their trust in them, and when dealing with unadorned rustics, monks have been able to act with complete freedom.

It has recently become fashionable for temples in villages around the country to give bribes to the court regent houses and other noble families so as to gain permission to enshrine these families' ancestral tablets and brand the temple an "official prayer temple" or the "repository of the ancestral tablets" of one noble house or another. The monks adorn cabinets, draperies, and curtains in the temple with the family crests of these nobles and in that way add to the temple's own prestige. By selling their ancestral tablets, the court regents and nobles have for a long time further fueled priestly arrogance and thus caused trouble for layfolk. This is an inhumane and unfortunate way to act. Monks buy nobles' prestige and use it to harass the simple folks. This is truly a gross insolence: they deceive the Buddha, sell the dharma, and steal authority. They are in truth the greatest enemies of the state in our age.

Another fashion of our times, which is spreading both in the cities and in the countryside, is to erect grand halls and shrines and apply for court rank. It is said that in the ancient Engi era [901–923], Buddha halls and pagodas were not to be larger than seven *ken* square. Also, there were limitations as to how many people per province and district could be allowed to leave the world and become monastics in any given year, and permission was not given lightly. It was a measure that reduced the outlay of the state, prevented the people from falling into poverty, and set clear limits on the extravagance of the Buddha Way. Today no such limit exists, and the size of Buddha halls and pagodas is

---

18. When someone married or was adopted into a household in another locale, the village officials were supposed to forward the temple registry documents to their counterparts in the other locale so that the person's temple affiliation could be changed to that of his or her new household. On the oppressive aspects of the so-called *danka* parish system, see Hur, *Death and Social Order*.

enormous, as is the extravagance of their adornment. In villages everywhere temple construction has the highest priority. No building is larger than the temple—there is not even another building of the same order. What about such splendor, which exceeds that of all the temple's parishioners?

The money monks use to erect such Buddha halls and pagodas or to further their own careers by securing court rank is not something that people have willingly contributed for the good purpose of edifying the populace. Monks urge people to make donations and offerings, bringing strong pressure to bear on those who are reluctant to do so. They do not care whether such a donation will cause people trouble with their lands or even ruin their house; they simply apportion out the shares each has to pay and take what they need. As mentioned above, they squeeze the lifeblood out of the people by all possible methods of greed—credit associations, loans, and extortionate interest—and use the proceeds to build Buddha halls and shrines and to enhance their own careers. On their vermilion-seal lands they have begun organizing lotteries, which invite large crowds of people to travel the road of greed. They make people rob one another, and from this battle between the greedy they extract a profit that is used to build Buddha halls and shrines. In today's world, the buddhas and the gods have become generals on the battleground of avarice. These temples with vermilion-seal land were originally built with the help of donations gathered from the provinces. Now, they can no longer collect sufficient funds through donations, and, as is said, nothing beats a lottery.

As for donation-gathering tours sanctioned by the authorities, in these days of luxury [high-ranking monks] do not go on these rounds personally. They send so-called temple caretakers in their place, or they appoint contractors and "money masters," who use various tricks to inspire awe and fear and take people's money in that way. Colluding with one another, these caretakers and contractors start doing their own private deals on the side. Because they wallow in drink and women day and night, the people they visit on their rounds see through their pretenses to what they truly are. They inspire no faith, and confronted with their ugly conduct, people cease to make donations. If the monks would make these rounds themselves, traveling lightly, and if they would give excellent dharma sermons with a mind to edify the people and in that way inspire a sincere wish to erect a Buddha hall or a shrine, surely the people would willingly make donations, and their endeavor would succeed. In that case, they would not even need the sanction of the authorities.

In medieval times, monks who erected Buddha halls and pagodas did not use sanctioned donation tours, credit associations or loans, and least of all lotteries. They achieved their aim thanks to the faith of the people. Even when they did travel around to beg for donations, they personally donned straw sandals and brought out their walking sticks, spreading salvation among the people and collecting offerings in return. Halls and shrines that are founded by way of such physical exertions must be good places to live in for the buddhas and the gods. The gods and buddhas will hardly be pleased, however, by the splendor that is thrown up these days with the help of impure money. It is doubtful whether the halls and shrines of our times are indeed dwelling places of gods and buddhas at all.

These days, those who preach the Way of the gods and buddhas are all bandits. Śākyamuni Buddha set forth his teachings to help people order their lives and assist the world. But in the end, in place of his dharma of no self, no greed, purity, and no defilement, the vices banned by the precepts—desire, anger, sexual misconduct, slander, and drunkenness—have now become the norm. The dharma is as sullied as mud; there is not a single spot of purity left in it, and it has turned into a Way for stealing from the people and damaging the state. If Śākyamuni were to appear in the world today, he would be shocked. He would punish the monks and put a stop to the whole of Buddhism. Those monks are lucky indeed that Śākyamuni or Bodhidharma has not yet put in an appearance.

It is most peculiar that this state of affairs has not incurred some form of punishment. The gods must have returned to Heaven and the buddhas to their Pure Lands; the Way of correspondence between this world and the other must have come to an end, causing divine rewards and punishments to cease altogether.[19] Have all monks fallen into hell and become sheer sinners? Seeing how evil the world has become, it is only to be expected that there are no longer any devout and upright monks and that the dharma has been cast aside.

---

19. Buyō uses the term *yūmei no michi*, an allusion to the notion that the spiritual forces of the other world respond to people's behavior in this world with rewards and punishments.

The Evils of the Honganji Sect

A place that has lost even the last shred of the Buddha Way is the Honganji sect.[20] In medieval times, Hōnen preached chanting the name of Amida Buddha, Nichiren proselytized chanting the title of the Lotus Sutra, and other learned monks founded yet other sects.[21] One claimed his method would lead people to buddhahood; others said their own was assuredly the means to generate the greatest merit. They thus confused the masses and caused competition for people's hearts to emerge within the single dharma of Śākyamuni. Their crimes are not few, but at least they all abstained from breaking the monastic precepts. They set up strict rules for the time after their own karma [had run out], did not seek court rank and title, did not desire temple income, and disliked luxury and splendor. Because people naturally drift toward laziness when their finances are secure, these learned monks shunned stable temple incomes. Knowing what was best for the dharma and for the monastic community, each instituted his own rules and guidelines, stipulating that even in these latter days of the dharma, a monk's property should be limited to three robes and a begging bowl and that he should always abide by the Way of poverty, observe the precepts, and devote himself to the study and practice of Buddhist teachings.

In all sects, the rules laid down by the founding patriarchs are strict. Only the patriarch of Honganji, Shinran, was different. First of all, he allowed fornication and alcohol. In his sect, no particularly profound study was necessary—there is no dharma method other than that of the three Amida sutras—and he had a wife and children and lived in stable comfort.[22] He truly turned his back on the teaching of Śākyamuni and deviated greatly from the dharma. On the other hand, as noted above, the monks of all sects have now become corrupt and have abandoned the

---

20. This sect, which Buyō refers to here by the name of its head temple, is commonly known today as the True Pure Land sect (Jōdo Shinshū). Regarding its name, see also note 23.

21. Hōnen (1133–1212) is known as the founder of the Pure Land (Jōdo) sect and Nichiren (1222–1282) as that of the Lotus (Hokke) sect, also referred to as the Nichiren sect.

22. A follower of Hōnen, Shinran (1173–1262) went beyond his master in emphasizing total reliance on Amida's saving grace and in his break with existing monastic practices such as celibacy.

precepts. Compared with them, should one perhaps prefer a sect that has been in breach of the dharma from the very outset? Things that brand the monks of other sects as the greatest sinners and criminals under Heaven are in fact quite normal in this sect—a curious matter indeed.

The monks of the Honganji sect have wives, children, and dependents. They pass on their inheritance to their children and grandchildren, who grow up in the temple where they are born, have no teacher other than their father, and do not engage in any form of study or practice. They know nothing about the hardships of this world and do not foster any disciples. Even if they were to excel at their studies or in their practice, their achievements would not lead to a promotion to a larger temple, nor would they rise in rank. It is difficult for one with the status of a disciple to become a temple holder; it is those who never move who are guaranteed a life of stable comfort. Because they [are expected to] have a household with a wife and children, nobody reprimands them for their lust. In truth, even among businesses that do not need capital, they enjoy lives of great comfort.

Even more puzzling is the fact that the lay followers of this sect do not resent these comfortable, lazy monks in the least. They treat them with greater devotion than is shown to any monk who is firm in his abidance by the precepts. They surrender themselves to the teachings of this sect with extraordinary dedication. Thousands, tens of thousands, even millions of them are united in their rejection of prayer rituals and in their single-minded dedication to Amida alone. In that respect, this sect stands out from all others; its followers are so strongly united that they do not even intermarry with members of other sects. They call their sect the "True" Pure Land sect, and they boast that theirs is the sect of paradise, outshining the rival Pure Land sect in the strength of its faith.[23] They call Honganji the "August Head Temple" or the "August Imperial Cloister" and grant it more respect even than they do the holder of the domain or fief where they reside.[24] People who are unable to pay their annual

---

23. The Honganji sect (known also in the Edo period as the Ikkō, "Single-minded," sect) asked the shogunate for permission to change its name to Jōdo Shinshū (True Pure Land) in 1774, but upon protests from the Jōdo (Pure Land) sect, this request was rejected. It officially adopted the name Jōdo Shinshū only in 1946.

24. The Eastern and Western Honganji were ranked as *jun-monzeki* or *waki-monzeki*, temples that were not *monzeki* in the narrow sense (that is, temples

land taxes to the daimyo or fief holder, and who refuse to contribute to extraordinary levies, make handsome donations to this August Head Temple without stint. Even misers who close their purses for their own parents and children and who would rather suffer from hunger and thirst than use money for food and drink make special offerings to the so-called August Imperial Cloister. This is truly a sect that treats the people with extreme greed.

As a result, the two Honganji temples in Kyoto are grand on a scale that is not easily rivaled by the headquarters of any other sect. It is said that the double-roofed main hall is thirty-seven *ken* square and has ninety-two pillars along its front façade. Each is three *shaku* in diameter and is made of fine-grained timber of the best-quality zelkova wood. With these pillars lined up like a string of jewels, the effect is superb beyond words. In addition, there are the founder's hall, the guests' quarters, the bell tower, the monks' quarters, the outer gate, the encircling wall, and the inner gate—all richly decorated from one corner to the other and constructed with a quantity of timbers unequalled, it is said, anywhere in Japan. When people see all this splendor they are overwhelmed and exclaim that even if all castle towers in the realm, including that of the shogun's castle in Edo, were to be rebuilt, one would need only half this amount of timber. They may well be right.

The stream of offerings from followers in the provinces never wanes even for a day. Valuables of all conceivable kinds spout upward like water from a fountain, and the monks live in a state of magnificent luxury and comfort that is unrivaled in the whole of Japan. The head temples of other sects never receive offerings directly from laypeople living in the provinces. To maintain the temple they depend on their own temple income, combined with gratitude payments from their branch temples. Even if they enjoy splendor and luxury, they are no match for Honganji. Honganji receives monetary donations from each and every one of its lay households throughout the country, even those in the most rustic and remote corners. The head temple itself exacts these donations. The head temple also distributes the Buddha images that laypeople enshrine in their family altars, as well as printed materials produced by the sect such as hymns and scriptures. Moreover, the head temple gives aged laymen

---

headed by imperial princes or scions of regent lineages) but were treated as "virtual" *monzeki* by the authorities.

and laywomen permission to shave their heads, and when they receive such permission, people send gratitude offerings. All these forms of income amount to a huge sum. Other head temples do not have such arrangements.

Nor is this all. Even daily necessities such as brushes, ink, paper, rice, grains, oil, candles, tea, sake, soy sauce, charcoal, firewood, vegetables, and pickles are delivered by large numbers of lay groups organized into confraternities for this purpose. It is said that whatever the quantity, these confraternities supply such items as and when they are required. Apart from this, there are both regular deliveries of goods and additional deliveries for special occasions, with the result that the Honganji head temples overflow with an abundance of materials that not even the lord of a great province can match. In line with this example, other temples of this sect, down to the most minor branch temples, are all extremely rich because they mimic the head temple in collecting goods from their parishioners, and because they organize confraternities to supply them with daily necessities. This kind of system does not exist in other sects.

The fact that its priests are united [with their parishioners] in this manner is of great advantage to the Honganji sect, but the result is that [these parishioners] give second priority to the holder of the domain or fief in which they live and pay no heed even to their relatives. At times, this can be harmful to the state and an obstacle to military vigilance. Lord Ieyasu himself was troubled by uprisings of Honganji followers when he was still in Mikawa.[25] At that time, such uprisings occurred not only in Mikawa but in many provinces, causing military leaders great trouble. Even prominent warriors were taken in by this sect's teachings and joined the uprisings; not a few lost their sense of loyalty and duty. Among all Buddhist sects, this one in particular teaches that this life is temporary while the afterlife is eternal. Therefore, those who are misled by such teachings tend to lose their sense of duty and readily commit evil

25. At the time he was still a relatively minor daimyo, Tokugawa Ieyasu struggled to impose his authority on Honganji followers in his original base of western Mikawa. The fact that many Tokugawa retainers sided with the temples' efforts to preserve their autonomy was a major obstacle to his attempt to extend control over the temples and the province as a whole. After a military campaign in 1563–1564, Ieyasu eradicated the sect from his territory by demolishing all Honganji temples, forcing their followers to convert, and expelling those who refused to do so.

acts in this present world. It will not do for such teachings to spread too widely among the people. It is particularly bad if warriors have faith in this sect. Such warriors are wont to commit acts of betrayal against their own lord. I hear that in the early days of Tokugawa rule, orders were sent to all daimyo and lesser Tokugawa vassals to the effect that this sect must be shunned.[26]

A certain person says, "In various provinces, the population has decreased because people follow the practice of 'thinning' their children. However, in provinces where the Honganji sect is widespread, people are firm in their faith, and no such inclination toward cruelty is seen. Quite to the contrary, the population has increased, and it is said that in those regions there are no useless sorts, nor do people fall into poverty. That is why the population is large in the five home provinces, in Ōmi, Iga, Ise, Mino, Owari, and Mikawa, in Wakasa, Echizen, Kaga, Noto, Etchū, and Echigo, and in Kii and Harima. This is because Honganji stresses the importance of descendants continuing the bloodline, even in the case of monks, and because families are united in upholding their faith. This is a sect that accords fully with the Way of the divine country of Japan."[27] This sounds reasonable enough and might be granted if it were said about Shinto. This sect, however, belongs to the Way of the Buddha, and yet it offends against the Way of the Buddha. What is more, it also creates trouble for the state, and it goes to extreme lengths in its greedy exploitation of the people. Therefore, it is the vilest sect of all.

Today, there are two vile enemies that undermine the great Way of the realm. The first is the Honganji sect. As I have already explained, this sect has lost Śākyamuni's teaching and utterly destroyed the dharma. It is said that Hōnen, the founder's teacher, broke with him out of abhorrence for his violation of the precepts. Today, Honganji followers revere this same founder as "Saint Shinran." The other enemy is prostitution. The Way pertaining to the union of man and woman is linked to the harmony between Heaven and Earth; it is a crucial element of human

---

26. Perhaps Buyō reached this conclusion from the fact that although the shogunate issued laws to regulate other sects (starting with the Kogi Shingon sect in the Kantō in 1609), no such recognition was given to the Ikkō (Honganji), Nichiren, and Jishū sects during Ieyasu's lifetime.

27. Fabian Drixler (*Mabiki*, p. 28) suggests that there was some truth to this notion that infanticide was less common in areas where the Honganji sect was strong.

morality. It should not be reduced to the greedy realm of buying and selling.

It is probably difficult even for the state itself to put a stop to these two evils—the Honganji sect and prostitution. It is frightful how difficult it is to maintain the Way of good over a long period, and how easily that Way becomes empty and hollow. Consider how the Ways of Shinto, Confucianism, and Buddhism are being cast aside. Consider, too, how the laws are crumbling. Once the Way of evil has gained a foothold, it will grow as time passes and nobody will be able to stop it. Such are all matters in the realm, large and small. Of course, Buddhism would be of supreme value to the state if it would act in accord with Śākyamuni's teachings; but as it is today, it is a great threat that corrupts the state, leads the people astray, and brings no benefit.

The Corruption of the Sōtō Sect of Zen

Monastics of all sects break not only the laws of the state but also the regulations of their own sects. Relying neither on age nor merit but only on greed, they defile their court ranks, tarnish the priestly positions in the big temples, and altogether act heedlessly. Let me give a few examples.

The regulations of the Sōtō sect of Zen, laid down by the Divine Lord, state that one cannot become a senior monk unless one has practiced the dharma for twenty years since first participating in a retreat, and that one cannot become an abbot and acquire one's own temple with less than twenty-five years of practice.[28] The Divine Lord must have laid down these regulations after discussions with virtuous monks of that sect. At these retreats, monks face one another and exchange questions and answers about the meaning of the dharma. This serves to test who is in front and who behind. At these sessions, the monks used to ask unexpected questions and correct misunderstandings. But today, they secretly show one another the points they will raise prior to the session. It is no longer an examination, as it was before. It is like a performance of

---

28. Buyō refers here to the two codes issued in 1615 to the head temples Eiheiji and Sōjiji; these applied to all Sōtō temples under their jurisdiction. See Williams, "Purple Robe Incident," for an analysis of this passage in *Seji kenbunroku* and the institutional realities behind it.

set pieces in sword or spear practice, not a real contest. Today, monks do not exert themselves in practice nor do they train their mental powers, and so they can no longer deal with a serious contest.

Not only have retreat sessions become purely formal but also monks no longer care to wait for twenty years or to strain themselves with any dharma practice. They become senior monks simply by paying a bribe of ten *ryō*. To acquire a temple, so I hear, they send these ten *ryō* to Kyoto. Stating falsely that they have completed twenty years of practice, they pay five of the *ryō* to the head temple to obtain an authentication of their statement. They then proceed to the Kajūji house, to which they pay the remaining five *ryō*, and with its recommendation, they readily obtain an imperial edict allowing them to become a senior monk and thereby qualify for promotion to the rank of grand abbot.[29]

Thus, the retreat is false, the dharma practice is false, and the number of years of practice is also false. Both the head temple and the Kajūji house know that these are all false, but both nevertheless readily give permission so long they are paid five *ryō*. If the monks would really undergo the years of training specified in the regulations, they could not hold their own temple until they are at least forty. These days, however, neither merit nor age are of any consequence, and through the kind of machinations described above, monks acquire temples while they are still youngsters. Moreover, those who are unable to raise enough money for bribes are denied promotion to the title of grand abbot even if they have practiced the dharma as stipulated and acquired merit in that way. What is one to think of such a state of affairs?

If monks would acquire their temples according to the regulations, after reaching the age of forty or more, their behavior would likely be good and they would not fall into error. As things are, however, they become grand abbots without engaging in the stipulated number of years of dharma practice by simply paying money collected through greed. Because they come to hold their own temple at a young age, they do nothing but engage in unsavory deeds and are all the more ready to discard the

---

29. The Kajūji, a prominent noble family, had secured a sinecure whereby they acted as intermediaries for obtaining priestly appointments that formally were awarded by the emperor. It appears that the actual sum needed to cover the costs of securing abbotship permission was around forty *ryō* rather than ten, as Buyō suggests. For details, see Tamamuro, *Edo jidai no Sōtōshū*, p. 85.

dharma and concentrate on making a profit, and gradually they fall into evil ways. Thus, they violate the dharma, the rules of their own founder, and, most important, the laws of the land. Moreover, as they accumulate more money by evil means, they move on to better temples, proportionate to the power of their wealth. They become chief priests of great temples or of temples with vermilion-seal lands, thereby securing large official fiefs.

The overall head temple of the Sōtō sect is Eiheiji in Echizen province. It is said that he who wishes to become chief priest of this head temple must raise a sum of at least 2,000 *ryō*. One thousand *ryō* is needed for the various expenses incurred when entering the cloister, while another 1,000 *ryō* is needed to cover the costs of paying one's respects to the imperial court, including gratitude payments and such.[30] Recently, a change of head priest took place there. A certain monk of that sect whose years of dharma practice and merit qualified him to be chief priest failed to be appointed because he was unable to collect enough money. Instead, a monk appeared from Ōshū [in the far north]. He was unlearned and impious to the extreme, but he was wise in the ways of the world and skilled at deceiving people; he thus raised those 2,000 *ryō* by means of various stratagems and secured entrance to the cloister. This is how it is even with the position of chief priest of the highest head temple. It goes without saying that positions at lower temples are also bought for a price based on each temple's rank and the number of parishioners.

Circumstances differ slightly from one sect to another, but they are all similar. Nowadays, court ranks and senior titles are not awarded in recognition of great achievement in learning or great merit in practicing a sect's dharma. If one only makes a gratitude payment, imperial appointment is granted without hesitation. Court ranks have become entirely a commodity sold by the court, and they do not deserve the world's reverent respect. Because all sects can freely buy ranks and appointments for money, the dharma rules of the patriarchs and the laws of the shogunate are ignored in the interest of immoral profiteering. These days, the chief priests and high-ranking monks of the head temples, the liaison temples, and the other great temples of the various sects are by no means wise

---

30. This amount is quite accurate; Tamamuro, *Edo jidai no Sōtōshū*, p. 92, concludes that an Eiheiji abbot appointed in 1822 paid in excess of 2,270 *ryō*. See Williams, "Purple Robe Incident," p. 38.

men of great virtue. They are ringleaders in a world of greed and immorality. They are the greatest villains of the state.

The Way of the buddhas and gods is meant to restrain human desire, to purify people's minds, and to protect the state through compassion. However, the millions of temple and shrine priests in the provinces and in the villages lead lives of overweening pride, placing themselves above the farmers and the warriors as they wallow in luxury and indolence. None in the world are as dedicated to greed, immorality, lawlessness, and inhumanity as they are. They turn the gods and buddhas into chiefs of evil and soil the state with their wickedness. One wishes for prompt reforms. If millions of evildoers are left to conduct their business as they do today, surely neither the Way of Heaven nor the buddhas and gods will continue to overlook this state of affairs. Is it not certain to bring great disaster to the realm? It is a most fearsome matter. If only this evil is reformed and the law restored, the Way of Heaven and the buddhas and gods will once again illuminate us, shower us with their compassion, and resume their protection of the realm and state. Then, this evil world will be transformed into a good world where the seven misfortunes will instantly disappear and the seven fortunes materialize,[31] and our land will indeed become a Pure Land where all the sentient beings are filled with faith. Will not the buddhas and gods as well as all the myriad things of the world then be as one, united in emptiness, with all in a state of peace and harmony? I pray for such reforms from the bottom of my heart.

---

31. This is a common Buddhist phrase, found in the sutra *Ninnō-kyō* and, for example, in Nichiren's *Risshō ankoku ron*. Lists of the seven misfortunes and fortunes vary among sources.

Chapter 4

THE BLIND

Many in the world suffer defects in their five extremities, but the first among cripples are the blind. Despised by Heaven, they are ignorant of the brightness of the sun, moon, and stars and are unable to see the faces of their father and mother. No creatures among the birds and beasts, or even among fish, reptiles, and insects, lack eyes, and none among them are blind. Yet for some reason there are many blind people among humans. Perhaps this is because of the fickleness of human disposition.

When we examine the disposition of the blind, we find that they are invariably stubborn, selfish, and, most notably, cruel. They are driven by the desire to deceive and swindle people and are completely unable to take an interest in others' concerns. They do not believe in others' sincerity and suspect all honesty to be a deceit designed to trick—for ill-doers assume others to be like them. Have they become so suspicious and selfish because they cannot see? I cannot believe that this is the case. Normal people who are cruel and stubborn also lose their eyesight when they reach middle age. Thus, it would seem that these are people whose disposition has lost all integrity and who have suffered Heaven's ultimate punishment as a result.

It therefore defies belief that the blind can obtain official rank and appointments.[1] People who, unable to receive the light of the sun and moon, are inferior even to birds, beasts, fish, and reptiles, are received in audi-

---

1. See "Buyō Inshi and His Times," pp. 19–20. Buyō refers here to the arrangements whereby members of the blind guild (Tōdōza) obtained sanction from the imperial court for titles and rank within the guild. Such titles and rank did not mean, however, that members of the guild were appointed to government offices.

Two blindmen (*zatō*) hounding a debtor. *Ehon azuma miyage* (1790). Waseda University Library.

ence by the emperor and share sake with him.[2] Cripples who have suffered the ultimate heavenly punishment for their fickleness attend audiences with the shogun and receive gifts. These are truly disgraceful scenes to behold. How is it that persons who are of no use to the state and of no benefit to others, who waste the resources of the world and are a true burden, reach high rank, receive the favor of the realm and the state, and live in extreme comfort?

The Blind and Money Lending

When the present Tokugawa reign began, the blind were granted the boons of benevolent government. They were allowed to make a living by receiving donations of rice and coins from households throughout the land, from daimyo on down, whenever these houses conduct marriages

---

2. This refers to a ceremony called *tenpai*, where worthies receive sake from the emperor as a sign of appreciation for their services to the realm. Buyō is exaggerating or, at least, using *tenpai* in a more abstract sense to refer to the honor of receiving court rank.

and funerals. These gifts are known as "distributions" because they are meant to be distributed to all the members of the blind guild.[3] This arrangement is indeed an expression of the shogunate's benevolent compassion. The blind thus were allowed to go begging for alms from the warrior houses as well as the houses of farmers and townspeople. Others visited daimyo and high-ranking bannermen to perform music or give massage and acupuncture treatments, for which they received recompense. Some were allowed to obtain title and rank from the court and attained the ranks of *kōtō* or *kengyō*.[4] In the Kan'ei years [1624–1644], however, a blindman called Sugiyama, who was highly skilled in acupuncture, found himself treating the third shogun, Lord Iemitsu, and received extraordinary favors.[5] He was given a high status and his son was taken into shogunal service as a bannerman. Since that time, members of the blind guild have improved their standing and gained in authority. Holders of the titles of *kengyō* and *kōtō* were treated as having audience-rank status. Despite being cripples, they have come to imagine themselves the equals of bannermen and brag of their status and look down on ordinary people. Thanks to the merits of this one Sugiyama, those blind persons who made their way through life depending on the largesse of farmers and townspeople have quite by accident won the beneficence of the authorities, and now they have come to despise those same farmers and townspeople. Thus, the world is turned upside down.

To obtain rank and title for one's accomplishments in music or acupuncture can perhaps be said to be justifiable. However, the *zatō* of today are different.[6] First of all they lend what they call their "rank funds" to

---

3. Such distributions (*haitō*) were in effect an alms-giving mechanism whereby the blind guild established a regular relationship with town neighborhoods and higher levels of authority and acted as a channel for distributing the alms received from these entities. See Groemer, "Guild of the Blind," pp. 363–65.

4. *Kōtō* and *kengyō* were ranks of high status within the blind guild. These titles derive from Buddhist temple and imperial court hierarchies, where they denoted specific functions. In the context of the Tōdōza, however, they merely indicated ranks.

5. In fact, Iemitsu's acupuncturist was called Yamakawa Jōkan; Sugiyama Wa'ichi (1610–1694), who established acupuncture as an important occupation for the blind and received lavish honors from the shogunate, was in the service of the fifth shogun, Tsunayoshi.

6. *Zatō* was the lowest rank within the blind guild; it became virtually synonymous with "blindman."

the poor at high interest.[7] They take 10 or 20 percent interest, plus another 10 or 20 percent in so-called service charges. When they lend out a certain sum, they subtract the interest and the service charges from the basic amount. They make the contract as being for a deposit without interest. If a borrower fails to meet the deadline for repayment, they use the authority of that deposit contract to collect the loan.[8] They extort money through all sorts of other greedy and dishonest practices as well. For instance, they make loans for a term of only three or four months, and if someone proves unable to repay within that period, they rewrite the contract into a new loan. Every time they do this they levy new service charges. By charging "added months," they turn one month's interest into that of two or three,[9] or they require repayment in monthly or daily installments. Thus, borrowers are dragged down by interest payments, service charges, and "added months," and within a year, the cost of their original loan has doubled.

When the blind use such greedy and dishonest practices to attain their rank and position, they see this as quite in line with today's normal custom. Nowadays, when a blind person enters the association of *zatō* it will cost him 10 *ryō* to acquire the lowest grade. After this, the amount steadily increases. The position of *kōtō* costs 500 *ryō* and that of *kengyō* 1,000 *ryō*. In today's world, all things depend on money. If only one puts out the stipulated amount, there is no need to advance step by step through all the guild's 16 ranks and 72 gradations; one can obtain the rank of *kōtō* in one go, or that of *kengyō* overnight. That is why the blind

---

7. On these rank funds (*kankin*), see "Buyō Inshi and His Times," p. 20.

8. For interest rates, see chapter 1, note 13. The shogunate held as a general policy that disputes over money loans should be a matter for the parties concerned rather than for official adjudication. This principle underlay the periodic "edicts ordering the parties to resolve matters on their own" (*aitai sumashi rei*), but it also led lenders to seek various ways to forestall such an eventuality. The practices Buyō describes here are a case in point. Because shogunal courts were more likely to enforce repayment of a "deposit" than the collection of interest, disguising a loan as a contract in this way was a safeguard for the lender.

9. When the contract was rewritten, the outstanding interest would be added to the original principle. "Added months" (*tsuki odori*) was a widespread practice whereby the interest due in the final month of the old contract would be reallocated as a further charge to the first month of the new one. The shogunate issued repeated warnings against the practice, but with little effect. See Kitahara, *Edo no fudasashi*, pp. 53–54.

always act with greed and dishonesty, and why they regard the robbing of others as an admirable skill. A *kengyō* of my acquaintance began his career by loaning out a mere 2 *bu* of gold. Within 10 years he had become a *kengyō*, and after 15 years there were 2 *kōtō* among his apprentices—and in addition he had outstanding loans of 5,000 *ryō*. The same goes for all the others. If there is a blind person somewhere who is not greedy and dishonest, he will fall behind. They say that there are 300 or 400 *kōtō* in Japan today, and 120 to 130 *kengyō*. Out of those 120 to 130, some 80 live in Edo. This goes to show the splendor of this city, and it demonstrates the extent to which the Way of robbery thrives here.

Of course, there are today also blind persons who teach the koto, samisen, or *kokyū*,[10] or who only practice acupuncture. It is not easy to amass a great fortune by pursuing those arts, though. To be sure, the arts of amusement thrive in our time and the income to be made from pupils is considerable. The teachers take special high fees for certifying their pupils as being "registered performers," "certified performers," or "fully initiated performers." In addition, they ingratiate themselves with persons of high status and rank, men of leisure, and the rich and serve as their companions in play. They receive clothing and money from them and gain fortunes such as a sighted person could never earn by honest work. Even so, their earnings cannot be compared to the profits made by money lending.

Moreover, to reach the point where one can instruct others in the arts requires great effort, teaching itself takes much energy, and innate talent naturally varies in degree. The Way of the moneylender, however, requires no particular training and the question of talent is irrelevant. It is enough to let loose one's greed and dishonesty and to indulge in one's own desire without any concern for others; anyone can do it. Therefore, eight or nine out of ten blind people put the arts to the side and gravitate toward money lending.

Blind people from the provinces who have come to the city looking for prosperity, dressed in dirty rags and with no more than their blindman's stick to their name, may work hard for a while as masseurs and acupuncturists, but as soon as they have saved a small amount of capital, even they begin to lend it out. They stop doing hard work and turn bad. [Instead of working garb] they begin to wear the kind of robes worn by a man of

---

10. A *kokyū*, as mentioned, is a two-stringed "knee fiddle" played with a bow.

leisure, they scold and threaten people, and they rob the world. At present in Edo there are more than 3,700 such persons, it is said. In addition, there are many blind people who do not join the *zatō* association and who are not registered in the books of the guild superintendent's office.[11] Some 3,000 of those 3,700 are moneylenders, evil people full of greed and dishonesty. One might expect that those who have risen to the rank of *kōtō* or *kengyō* would no longer desire money, but in fact their greed never ends.

The Cruelty and Arrogance of the Blind

In general, the blind are cripples also when it comes to human feelings. They are insensitive to the situation of those who are cornered by poverty, and they refuse to compromise if even a penny they are owed is missing. When sighted people meet face-to-face, they naturally feel empathy for each other. They cannot simply hold to reason and press their own advantage regardless. Because the blind lack the sense of empathy that comes from seeing another's face, they will not give an inch as regards their own reasoning, and they do not hesitate to heap shame on others. It is most convenient for them not to be able to see.

Let me give a few examples of their lack of feelings, their greed, and their cruel dishonesty. When a warrior debtor lags behind with his payments, they will go right into his entrance hall and state their claims there and then in a loud voice, without any concern for appearances. This is known as a "sitting-firm claim" or an "insistent claim." If the debtor is a townsman, they will revile him and shower him with abuse while making sure that the neighbors hear it all. Since it is the debtor who is in the wrong, he can say nothing in return, however the lender may berate him. If he talks back he will only cause the lender to become even more vehement, so he has no choice but to nod and bow. He cannot tie up the lender even if the latter makes a scene. The lender takes that into calculation in presenting his case as forcefully as possible. If the debtor so much as touches the lender, the lender will make an immense fuss and accuse

---

11. The *sōroku*, or superintendent of the blind, was a person of *kengyō* rank who controlled the blind in Edo and the eight Kantō provinces. His counterpart in Kyoto, who had jurisdiction over the blind in the rest of the country, was called the *sō-kengyō*.

him of causing bodily harm. The lender will trumpet his official guild status and make a complaint.

To be sure, not only the blind but all the usurers and dealers in daily-installment loans that flourish so today behave in this way,[12] using all sorts of means to browbeat their debtors. But those who are sighted possess at least some degree of human feeling, and they are not quite so bad; they leave some room for compromise. The blind, however, make no allowances for saving one's face. Concerned for his reputation, the debtor will pay up even if he has to skip a meal or strip the clothes from the aged or the small children in his household [so as to pawn them]. If nothing works and the debtor fails to pay, the lender will file a complaint with someone with influence over the debtor just as if he were a thief or a swindler: the debtor's supervisor if he is a warrior, or his landlord if he is a townsman.[13]

For a rear vassal, in particular, an affair of this kind is sure to bring shame if it reaches the ears of his domain's Edo representative, inspectors, or especially the domain elders. Indeed, since everyone regards the rank funds lent out by the blind as something special, it may well lead to his being placed on restricted service or even, depending on the house customs, dismissal. Among the weak of heart, some cannot bear the shame and abscond. In such cases the debtor's family, too, will fall permanently into dire straits.[14] Of course, it is a very dangerous matter to borrow such troublesome money, but sometimes one has no other choice and ends up doing so despite knowing that loans of this kind are poisonous. Such may happen if a person who is already impoverished confronts a pressing need—for example, he may have to care for his parents or find himself unable to equip himself properly to perform his service for his lord. Even townspeople who are barely scraping by may fall ill or suffer other calamities and have to borrow money when their capital runs out and they are unable to carry out the day's business. Nowadays, many

---

12. Such loans (*hinashizeni*) obliged the borrower to repay part of the loan every day.

13. House owners were responsible for keeping a supervisory eye on their tenants. In Buyō's time, about 70 percent of Edo's commoner population were renters.

14. If a warrior absconded, the lord he served would likely terminate the relationship, which would mean that the warrior's family would be left without any means of support.

among both warriors and townspeople are poor. As a result, there are many moneylenders, and the numbers of *kōtō* and *kengyō*, with their special talent for cruel dishonesty, have increased greatly. From these examples we can know [just how unfeeling and greedy the blind are].

The blind of today engage in acts of greed and dishonesty, feast off tens of thousands of people, rise to the high ranks of *kōtō* and *kengyō*, and pride themselves on their luxury and comfortable lives of ease. Having attained a status equivalent to audience rank, they arrange matches for themselves and their daughters with bannermen of good family and indulge in the pleasures of life with their wives and concubines. They have apprentices and hire clerks, turn their sons into shogunal housemen, or adopt a son if they have none of their own. In many cases, they purchase for these sons positions as supervising officers. Among shogunal housemen, such an officer has the rank of a mounted samurai, and to acquire such a position is no light matter.[15] When these *kengyō* and *kōtō* go out in public, they go by palanquin, accompanied by men-at-arms and footmen and by retainers holding long pikes and spears and staffs decorated with silver. This makes for an imposing procession. It is beyond the pale for a monastic official, let alone a blind person, to be attended by samurai carrying spears in this manner. This is appropriate only for those who carry out the work of the realm and the state and who may be called upon to perform military tasks. In what way do these blind persons make themselves useful to the state, let alone perform military tasks? Will they wave those spears about "blindly" in case of a military emergency? A sickening thought indeed.

Surely it would be enough for the blind to make do by begging for alms from households that are holding weddings and funerals, as stipulated in the regulations issued at the beginning of the Tokugawa reign. On the other hand, the present manner in which the blind collect alms from townspeople door to door throughout the land is extremely improper. Using their shogunal authorization as a shield, they have become

---

15. The position of supervising officer (*yoriki*) marked the dividing line between those positions held by hereditary vassals and those held by retainers who were not in principle regarded as hereditary (although many of the latter in fact succeeded to positions held by their fathers). As such, it was a symbolic marker of status, and Buyō refers to it in several places as a position for warriors of "mounted rank" (*ikki*); see chapter 1, note 18.

haughty and arrogant. When they reckon that the alms they receive are insufficient, they loudly complain and demand more. If they do not get what they want, they come back time and again, or they gather a large gang and cause trouble until they succeed in extorting an additional sum. It is the day's custom among the baseborn that those who have an official authorization of even the flimsiest kind use it to intimidate and rob others. If those *zatō* would ask for compassion with true sincerity, visiting houses to offer congratulations at happy occasions and condolences at unhappy ones, people would surely give them a suitable amount as alms, since everybody knows that this is based on an established shogunal ruling. It is because they extract donations as if they were taking what belongs to them that people become resentful.

LAWSUITS

In today's world, lawsuits are so numerous that they may well come to ten times what was typical in the Genroku-Kyōhō period [1688–1736]. The reasons for lawsuits, too, are quite different from what they were a hundred years ago. In the past people used to argue fiercely over disputes having to do with moral obligations, but people today care nothing for matters of moral principle. All they fight over is profit, loss, and greed. But people today, as I have said above, are profoundly knowledgeable when it comes to perpetrating wrong, and they cunningly conceal their own desires twice, thrice over. Consequently, it is difficult to quickly sort out good from bad and right from wrong, and investigating a case takes time and effort.

Lord Ōoka Tadasuke, the town magistrate in the Kyōhō period [1716–1736], is famous today as a wise person.[16] From what I have heard about his approach to handling lawsuits, the people of that time were not yet so

---

16. Noted as one of the most able administrators of the Tokugawa period, Ōoka Tadasuke (1677–1751) played a key part in various aspects of popular governance under the eighth shogun, Yoshimune, and served as town magistrate from 1717 to 1736. He also figures as the hero of *Tales of Ōoka's Decisions* (*Ōoka seidan*), a widely circulated Edo-period work that describes him as resolving knotty judicial cases with a Solomon-like wisdom. The latter stories are largely legendary (many draw from Chinese collections of tales of wise judges), but Buyō's image of Ōoka and the kinds of cases he dealt with perhaps derives as much from them as from more historical sources.

driven by desire. It was only about that time that cases growing out of desire began to occur. Cases revolving around moral obligation thus made up the major part of those Ōoka dealt with, and such cases were easy to judge. Even when the matter concerned greed or machinations, the deviousness was quite elementary, and so it was easy to sort out right from wrong. And since people were not so stubborn in the pursuit of their desires, it seems that black and white instantly became apparent if only the judge raised his voice and scolded the parties loudly. Since people held authority in great awe and deep inside still had much uprightness, they were quick to confess.

From the time the current house came to rule the realm until the Genroku-Kyōhō period, it seems that down even to the most lowly, people understood moral obligation, they deemed desires to be shameful, and they did not make a point of trying to trick others. Starting in that period people began to be devious in the pursuit of greed, and in the one hundred years since then, the taste for luxury has steadily increased and people have grown ever more greedy. As a consequence, people have become ever more practiced in deceit, until, as at present, they mutually cheat and plot to trick one another.

As for lawsuits at the present time, people try to steal from others as much as their own skills allow, and they turn to lawsuits to achieve what they cannot obtain by relying solely on their own skills. Thus, from the very start, the plaintiff prepares a statement of the case that is full of lies, saying whatever he pleases to make an immense fuss out of something slight. The defendant does likewise, making up his own lies to answer the charges brought by the plaintiff. Today, this has become the usual way of doing things, and although these lies become apparent at the hearing where the two parties confront each other, the judge does not castigate them for perpetrating such deceit. Because lawsuits have become so numerous, were the judges to scold the parties about such details, they would not be able to take care of them all. But since the judges then let such deceptions go, those who become parties to a lawsuit are convinced that to lie is the best strategy, and they do their best to brazen through. As a consequence, those who come out on top at the time of the hearing are the strongest wrongdoers and those who are most skilled at telling a good story.

Since people have become ever more cunning, they grasp the direction in which the trial is developing and can see the intent behind the investigating officials' questions. Not being at all in awe of authority, they merely seek to bend it to their own ends. And since matters of desire that in the past would have been thought shameful are today seen as something ordinary, they are not in the least embarrassed about them. Instead, they stubbornly hold their ground and skillfully devise all sorts of fabrications. As a consequence, it becomes difficult to tell what is true and what is false. It even happens that in a case of adultery, duplicity lies more with the husband than the adulterer, while in cases of cheating or deception, the true plotter may be the one seemingly cheated rather than the purported cheater. The trial is thus difficult to handle, and in some instances a wrong decision is handed down.

Private Settlements

Under these circumstances, today even lawsuits that appear to concern moral principle, in the vast majority of instances boil down to being about loans and debts and profit and loss. When things are sorted out, one finds that one was wrong in one's initial impression that this party was good and that party bad. Since ultimately each side is driven by greed in equal measure, it is impossible to make a clear distinction between good and bad or to make a decision in favor of one or the other. In many instances, part way through the hearings, the presiding officials thus urge the parties to come to a private settlement.[17] This is the common custom in the world today.

When things come to a private settlement, the two parties—plaintiff and defendant—come together and discuss the matter at issue them-

---

17. "Private settlement" (*naisai*) was a formal procedure whereby once the parties had reached an agreement with the court's encouragement, the court would endorse the settlement, giving it legal force. Looking upon disputes over economic issues to be fundamentally a "private" matter between the parties concerned, the shogunate frequently sought to have them reach a private settlement rather than carry a suit through to judgment by the court. Government-endorsed private settlements of this sort differed from private resolutions (*aitai, jidan*) that the parties reached on their own, on occasion at the court's direction, and which did not have legal standing should a further suit ensue. The measures known as "edicts ordering the parties to resolve matters on their own," which the shogunate issued periodically to clear courts of a backlog of pending cases, essentially relegated these cases to the latter category of matters to be resolved solely by the parties concerned.

selves face-to-face. In this situation the one who is more clever and whose desire is the more intense has the advantage, while the one whose greed is more shallow and who is less devious loses out. Although the headmen and members of the five-household group [of the respective parties] or a go-between take part in the proceedings,[18] they let the stubborn and selfish one, who digs in his heels and refuses to compromise, get his way. Prevailing upon the good-natured or timid party to be understanding, they wear him down with various arguments and resolve the matter by convincing him to put up with the situation. Thus, the cunning calculate just how the suit and the private settlement will take shape, and in the end the one whose greed is stronger wins the day.

One hundred years ago the authorities would not have allowed such unreasonable behavior to pass, and the go-betweens, too, would have despised such evil and would not have given in to stubbornness. At the present time, though, those above and below are alike lacking in sincerity and readily give in. Consequently, those who employ stubbornness and glibness to the full always win. And once they have won, all the world praises them as clever and skillful, so that stubbornness and glibness grow ever more rampant.

At present, even matters that come to a lawsuit cannot be easily resolved in court; most end up in a private settlement, without the right of the matter being resolved. Beyond that, since the hearings take an inordinate amount of time, the parties cannot easily set aside their regular work and cover the expenses of going to court. In current practice, the costs attendant on being involved in a lawsuit are great. You have to provide the headman, monthly representative of the five-household group, and such who accompany you to the magistrate's office with an allowance for lunch, and then, on the way back, it is customary to invite them to stop at a restaurant and to entertain them with drink and food. Once the suit is finished, all those concerned have to be thanked, whether you have won or lost. Should you win the suit and gain a substantial benefit, you have to be lavish with your thanks, whether spontaneously or not. Whichever, the costs will be great. And, as I said above, if it comes to a private settlement, the end result will depend solely on the relative skill

---

18. "Five-household groups" were neighborhood units organized around the principle of collective responsibility. See "Buyō Inshi and His Times," p. 16.

of the two parties. Since there is thus no point in going to court, people do not easily decide to bring suit.

If nevertheless, despite all this, you end up in the single situation out of a thousand where there is no choice but to bring a suit, the cost will be great and so will be the time required. Further, in the end the moral principle of the matter will not be clarified. Consequently, many lowly people do not resort to an official hearing and simply try to settle the matter among themselves. But then the results are even more scandalous. Thus, in the world today moral obligations steadily disintegrate. When people do resort to the courts, it turns out that the officials in charge of the investigation have to deal with far too many cases for them to manage, and when the right and wrong of the matter cannot be decided immediately, expenses pile up. Since the matter is not one that calls for a rigorous trial but is simply one of mutual greed, in the officials' eyes the only choice is to get the parties to reach a private settlement. While the negotiations for the private settlement are going on, the officials are kept busy trying to sweet-talk and cajole the parties just as if they were the intermediaries between them. They thus grow tired of the matter, and even if there are errors in what is worked out as the private settlement, they pretend not to have seen or heard and just let things go as they are. Compared with how matters were handled in the old days, it is a weak-kneed approach indeed.

Warriors' Disadvantage

At present, the practice of private settlement is not applied in lawsuits involving warriors. Since the old standards are applied, without twisting or bending moral obligation or changing a single word or phrase, should a warrior become involved in a lawsuit, he ends by losing his status. Even if it concerns a minor matter that could have been easily resolved, it inevitably turns into a lifelong blemish. In the case of townspeople and farmers, even if they engage in deception, they are simply scolded, and the matter ends there. And because they are directed in various ways to reach a private settlement, no one is declared in the wrong, and the matter is settled on the spot. For warriors, who give priority to moral obligation and despise expediency, the present state of affairs is most disadvantageous, while for the lower classes, who give priority to expediency and are not bothered by shame, it is highly beneficial. In the past someone [of lowly status] would never sue a warrior and bring him to court. Even today, it is said, this never happens in the provinces. Of course, if a warrior abuses a townsman or farmer, he may come under investigation from above, but never do those below sue warriors. This is how it should be. In Edo, on the other hand, it is easy to bring a suit against a warrior. Consequently, people do so without hesitation, making a big fuss out of something small.

Warriors are supposed to be not in the least lacking in their attention to rectitude and proper etiquette in their relations with others, not in the least caught up in greed. The reverse applies to townspeople; they are not expected to know anything of rectitude and etiquette, while avarice goes with what they are. When a warrior puts out his elbows and insists that something is a matter of rectitude, none of them will agree; rather they will say, "Now that is being obstinate, so out of touch with the times!" and put him to shame. The greedy calculation of profit dear to townspeople is regarded as splendid and is taken for granted even when it is blatant for all to see.

Take an instance where the warrior is at fault in a matter that bears on [the townsman's] avarice, while the townsman is at fault in failing to respect proper etiquette and moral obligation. Fault lies with each in equal measure. But even if the warrior complains vociferously about the townsman's failure to respect proper etiquette and moral obligation, the officials will simply say, "There is reason in what you say, but since he is a townsman, he can hardly be expected to have any sense of etiquette or moral principle. And since he has apologized, you should put up with it and let the matter go." When things are put to the warrior in this way, there is nothing he can do, and if he continues to stand his ground, he will just seem obstinate and mean-spirited, so he gives up and overlooks what happened. Even if a warrior is humiliated to the point of damaging his reputation, that humiliation cannot be weighed on a scale or calculated in terms of monetary value. If he will simply endure the humiliation, everything will be settled on the spot without any lingering problems. How sad to be a samurai, saddled with the burden of pride! In these circumstances, officials simply urge the warrior to put up with humiliation and try to settle the matter without any winner or loser. This is the common practice today. In the past, would not the moral obligation and reputation of the warrior have carried the day? Certainly, moral obligation and reputation are a samurai's essential capital. How wretched to lose that capital without paying heed to the cost!

Since the townsman's calculations are based on profit, the amounts involved are all clear, and it is impossible to force him to give up even the slightest sum. The only way to get him to give up his claim would be to prevail upon him to do so as an act of charity. There is no other way. But how could a warrior ask for charity from a townsman? The officials cannot persuade him to seek charity, and indeed it is not something that the townsman would readily grant. Should he in fact go so far as to do so, truly the warrior's fortune will have run out; he will be obliged to the townsman forever, generation after generation unto eternity. Townspeople have a solid capital that does not disappear and stands solid wherever they go. Everyone today simply recognizes this as a matter of course.

Given this situation, should a warrior be treated with disrespect and a failure to recognize moral obligation, officials will not take action to help him recover his damaged reputation. By and large they will simply ignore the matter. On the other hand, since they cannot ignore the avaricious calculations that are the townsman's concern, they accept the latter's assertions. Thus, in a situation where each is equally at fault, the warrior is sure to lose and the townsman to win. On nine points out of ten, the warrior may have the better argument, but when the remaining point has to do with avarice, on exactly that point he will lose. In matters that involve even a slight profit, a townsman may well bring about the downfall of a warrior to whom he has long been greatly obliged. The warrior may have shown him a great benefice in the past, but its legacy will not suffice to compensate for his liability, and thus he will lose. At present, government officials care nothing for what in the past was held to be moral obligation or a debt of gratitude, not only when it comes to lawsuits involving warriors [but in other matters as well]. It seems that they reach a decision solely on the basis of the calculation of profit and loss.

Townspeople who seek to undertake some profitable activity in exchange for the payment of compensatory fees to the government, or who submit a request to a government office regarding some other project, will offer bribes to the officials concerned or send presents to the official's retainer who mediates on their behalf. Then, if what they are trying to do does not work out well, they harbor a grudge. They press in various ways those involved or shame them, or they bring a suit in which they claim they have been cheated and turn the retainer to whom they are indebted into a common criminal. Simply because the person to whom they made the request was not able to work things out, they put aside the obligation they owe him, ignore the fact that they were the ones who made the original request, and plot revenge against him—the audacity of it is beyond words!

As regards the relative culpability of the two, the townsman who tried to make use of the retainer and aimed to get an immense profit solely for himself by cheating the world at large is a greedy criminal. The retainer who accepted the bribe and tried to arrange things is a petty miscreant who took advantage of the opportunity. But because he is of a status where not the smallest bribe or act of avarice is acceptable, the retainer is damaged for life. The townsman who is the main perpetrator, on the other hand, gets off quite lightly. Since the matter is brought to formal trial, the retainer cannot say a single false word; he cannot even make an exaggerated claim. If the townsman is found lying, on the other hand, it will only be a matter of being scolded on the spot, and depending on the situation, he may gain by exaggerating his case. [Unless those judging the case] take the warrior's disadvantage and the townsman's advantage into account, it will not be possible [to reach a proper decision]. It is indeed most dismaying that at the present time, rectitude, reputation, and shame—the attributes proper to the warrior—carry no weight at all, while avarice and deception—the attributes of the townsman—win out every time.

The concern for rectitude and reputation and distaste for shame fundamental to the warrior are of great importance to the state. Without them one is not a warrior and cannot be of use to the state. To bend and compromise about this point is to lose the state's core framework. But now, people have ceased to care about even extreme instances of disrespect, denial of moral obligation, loss of reputation, and shame. Should there be warriors with a proper understanding of things, they will not be able to gain a hearing from those in government. Instead, since they are supposed to act as a model for the people of the world, they will simply put up with the situation and try to keep the matter from being generally known. As warriors grow weak in spirit, they frequently lose face. When townspeople meet with the slightest mistreatment or the slightest loss, they will immediately challenge the warriors, spurred on by avarice. Might it not come to their even bringing the warriors down?

Problems in the Handling of Lawsuits and Investigations

At the present time, bribes are a standard accompaniment to the hearing of a lawsuit. Consequently lowly people mistrust those above, and when the case they present results in their receiving a scolding, they are sure that it is because the officials have received a bribe from the other side and are showing that side favor. Unaware of their own faults, they harbor doubts about the officials and enmity toward the other party and become all the more recalcitrant. The scolding they receive fails to correct their behavior, and they become even more stubborn. So long as bribery exists, people will harbor doubts and resentment toward those above and revile the officials. Officials suffer a loss of authority, correct principles are obscured, and evildoers grow ever more rampant.

Lowly people become aroused over a slight matter of moral obligation, or, unable to stand a slight loss, will not listen when officials try to persuade them to understand the situation. The officials then scold and berate them and do not pay any attention to their complaint. However slight the issue or loss, it is important for the person concerned. Thus, the officials should just listen carefully to what the person has to say. Even if the investigating officials think the matter is minor, for lowly persons it is major. Because it is something major for them, they have put all their efforts into bringing the suit. Officials should put themselves in the plaintiff's position and listen to what they have to say. It is not proper for one who serves as a judge to disregard small details because it is tiresome to look into them. A concern for rectitude and scrupulousness shows more in minor matters than major. One needs to put much effort into dealing with the lowborn and obtuse and listen to them patiently and calmly. The officials hearing the matter must set aside their personal interests and make a concerted effort to investigate what such people have to say, taking into account the good and bad in their hearts, their degree of intelligence, their wealth or poverty and status, where the principle of the matter lies, and where things have become entangled.

In presenting their cases, some people are skillful, while others are clumsy; some are bold and others timid; some are pleasant in manner, while others are awkward in appearance and pretentious in manner. Officials do not need to make a particular effort in dealing with those who present their case logically and express themselves skillfully, or with those who are personable. In dealing, however, with those who are not good at expressing themselves or not personable, or who are full of trepidation and do not explain their situation sufficiently, one has to devote special attention to make sure that nothing has been overlooked or failed to be heard. And since there are good people who do not look the part, one should not come to hasty conclusions.

At present, lawsuits take a great deal of time and trouble and are costly; moreover, because of bribes, the right of the matter is not clarified. Therefore, people throughout the world today feel that it is better to solve things below, by themselves, and that if they go to the government, they will only suffer a loss. Even if they are robbed or cheated, they keep the matter to themselves, and if they come across a thief, an arsonist, a mugger, or a murderer who is lying low, they pretend to know nothing of it. Or else they hide him or help him flee elsewhere. This happens because people dislike getting involved with the government and shun the cost. It is also because those above and below alike no longer feel antipathy toward evil. At the present time, not a few murderers and other lawbreakers have managed to flee into hiding or otherwise escape being brought to justice. Not only do they escape being brought to justice, but also such people without fail end up becoming troublemakers who roam the provinces, doing as they please. At the present time, there has been an immense increase in the number of troublemakers throughout the provinces. Of course, thieves who break into houses, muggers, murderers, and the like are the object of thorough investigation, and those associated with the suspect are ordered to undertake a fixed-term search. But although officials may order a fixed-term search, the recipients of the warrant do not make the least effort to track down the miscreant, and once the term is up, he is simply placed on permanent search.[19] The officials responsible for the search have to

---

19. If the suspect in a crime was not captured immediately, the relevant government office would issue a warrant for his arrest to his family and the village officials or block officials of the area where he was registered as living. Typically, the warrant would be for a fixed term (*higiri tazune*) of thirty days. At the end of the thirty-day period, those assigned to conduct the search had to report its current state to the office, which would renew the warrant. If at the end of six such periods the suspect had still not been located, those who had failed to find him would be fined or reprimanded, and he would be listed as on permanent search (*nagatazune*). The same procedures were applied to absconders, who had not necessarily otherwise committed a crime, but in the latter part of the Edo period,

146   PART 2: MATTERS OF THE WORLD

deal with the new problems that constantly arise, and so they just let the matter slide as an event of the past.

Since the investigative offices of even the shogunal government are in this state, the investigations conducted by daimyo and other fief holders are all the more lax, and they let many miscreants escape. I have heard it said that in the past it was impossible for someone who had committed a serious crime to stay hidden and remain undetected. At that time, for any case as serious as murder, it was customary for the shogunal government to circulate a description of the suspect. And once the person being hunted was found in such-and-such province and place, a second order would be circulated, canceling the first and announcing that there was no need to search further. There were no instances, it is said, where such a search did not turn up the criminal. There is a saying that one cannot escape Heaven's net, and in fear and trembling people referred to a shogunal government search as "Heaven's net."[20]

At the present time, notices are sent out only for particularly heinous crimes such as the murder of one's master or parent, and no description of those who have committed other crimes is circulated. According to what a certain old-timer has said, even in the case of the murder of a master or parent, often notices are not sent out, and it is rare to have a search canceled because the culprit has been found. As this suggests, at present it is quite easy to escape Heaven's net, and wrongdoers go through the world as they like, committing all sorts of offenses. Even in the provinces and countryside, the old rules grow more lax and laws crumble. People do not care if unregistered persons and troublemakers from elsewhere come to stay, and even if they know that the shogunal government is seeking someone as a criminal, they ignore the matter. Troublemakers of this sort take the lead in organizing lotteries, games of chance, and gambling, and then move on to night thefts and muggings. In the past, troublemakers did not roam freely through the countryside, but now people have ceased to detest evil; quite to the contrary, many

---

after the initial six months' search, these were frequently simply removed from the religious and household registers. This relegated absconders to the category of "unregistered persons" but reduced the liability of their families and neighbors for any crimes they might commit.

20. The saying derives from *Laozi* 73: "The net of Heaven is cast wide. Though the mesh is not fine, yet nothing ever slips through" (Lau, *Lao Tzu*, p. 135).

have come to like troublemakers and their evil doings, so that others of the same sort readily gather from elsewhere and take over the locale.

Investigative officials see misdeeds as not affecting them and thus show no indignation because they have no true understanding of the fundamental meaning of government. One who does not feel even angrier than the person directly affected and does not take punitive action is not worthy of the name "official." The basic function of the magistrate is to search out and punish as many thieves, arsonists, and murderers as he can. It is the utmost dereliction of duty to think only of getting through each day without trouble. Today, though, both those above and below dislike the severe laws of old and prefer the weak-kneed present-day style.

Chapter 5

TOWNSPEOPLE

Merchants are people with no steady livelihood and without a steady mind. Their status is low to the extreme, and they are inferior to warrior houses, farmers, and all others. They make a living by stealing a profit from the process of buying and selling. In the course of more than two hundred years of peaceful government, the profits that they have embezzled have accumulated to such an extent that nowadays the financial means of townspeople have become vast. There is a limit to the financial capacity of warriors, who offer their lives for the state. Farmers pay a large proportion of their harvest, won by hard work in cold and hot weather, in the annual land tax; they perform corvée labor, produce various kinds of goods, mingle with soil and excrement, and suffer all the hardships of this world. An artisan can earn only so much in a day's wages, and it is impossible for him to exceed that limit. For a merchant there is no such limit. His earnings depend solely on the profit he gains and on the extent of his greed. He is not affected by wind, flood, or drought; he pays no annual land tax; and he has no service obligations. Surely, he enjoys the greatest freedom of any in our world.

Favored by the system, merchants are free to move their goods to any province or city and to increase their wealth by bargaining wherever they want. Edo has thus become awash with merchants over the more than two hundred years that have passed since the Divine Lord established it as his seat. Since the beginning of Tokugawa rule, the number of people, households, and blocks has increased also in Kyoto and Osaka, where merchant prosperity is beyond words. Merchants thrive also in the castle towns in the provinces and in all corners of the country. They handle all goods with complete freedom and keep daimyo and fief holders in the

A shop owner (right) has his clerks calculate debits and credits after the close of business for the day. *Genkin saru ga mochi* (1783). National Diet Library Digital Collection.

hollow of their hand. Their splendor and extravagance increase every day and month that passes; it is easy for all to see that nowadays they have exceeded the farmers and sit on top of the world.

First of all, all warriors of Japan, from daimyo great and small down to the lowest samurai, gather in Edo, where they spend gold, silver, rice, and copper cash. Because of this abundance, the Way of commerce thrives to such an extent that nowadays it puts the warrior houses in the shade. In expediting all matters, merchant ways are more effective than military might, and merchants do their bargaining throughout the country from the comfort of their homes. It is the way of our world that townspeople have come to handle all shogunal needs, from money exchange and the management of rice payments to the shogunate down to the supply of all kinds of goods. Even matters of military importance such as the hiring of men-at-arms and foot soldiers, travel preparations, and the purveyance of military, equestrian, and other goods can be arranged only by townspeople. As a result, townspeople have become even more conceited. All warrior houses, temples and shrines, and farmers, together with everybody else in the land, are dependent on the townspeople, who rob them for profit. Because these ever more arrogant merchants steal all the surplus in the world, down to the tiniest crumb, warrior houses, farmers, and others are all in straits. Because of this tendency of our time, townspeople have in recent years become haughty, scorning warriors and looking down on farmers; their arrogance goes beyond all bounds.

While the townspeople have grown conceited in our age, there are two tendencies among them, one that inspires abhorrence and another that arouses pity. The latter is the imbalance between the poor and the rich. But let me first give a rough description of the matters that are to be abhorred.

Shogunal Purveyors and Wholesalers

Townspeople who are shogunal purveyors, such as those who handle bills of exchange on behalf of the shogunate, the shipping of shogunal rice and other products from shogunal lands, or the purveyance of other goods to the shogunate, without exception lead lives of luxury.[1] When they do personal business they pretend it is official, and when they travel they label even goods that they trade privately as shogunal purveyances. Referring to their right to carry swords on the road, even the overseers of their goods trains travel in palanquins, using more men and horses from the post stations than they are entitled to and thus causing harm to the farmers. They see no difference between the authority of the shogunal government and the authority of their own wealth, and because even great and small daimyo employ them to solve their problems and treat them with the greatest respect, they grow ever more arrogant. A shogunal purveyor of my acquaintance who is stationed in Kyoto travels to Edo every year; because he does not like to drink a different kind of water on the road, he carries all his water with him from Kyoto. Such extravagant behavior would not be possible for a daimyo holding less than a hundred thousand *koku*. This is how it is in all matters.

When these merchants make loans, they bring their status as shogunal purveyors into play and set the same conditions for these loans as if

---

1. As Buyō notes, large merchants of various kinds who were recognized as purveyors to the shogunate (*goyōtashi*) had a central role not only in supplying goods but also in the management of shogunal fiscal affairs. From the 1790s, for example, a group of such purveyors was designated to manage the investment of newly established government loan and relief funds.

they were lending on behalf of the shogunate; here too they act out their greediness by relying on both their private and their public influence. They think lightly of others, make no allowances whatsoever, and demand huge profits. In all matters they abuse their official capacity in this same manner. They mark their chests, their luggage boxes, their lanterns, and even their wrapping cloths with the shogunal crest. Even when they take their wives, concubines, and clerks out for a pleasure excursion, they use goods marked with that august crest.

These shogunal purveyors leave all their official business to their clerks, and they know nothing at all about their own trade. They make it their business to engage in various pastimes and to visit the amusement quarters. They keep concubines in lodgings here and there, use the best clothes and eat the best food, and steep themselves in extravagance. When warriors are dissolute, the shogunate will reprimand and punish them, and on occasion it will order those warriors who are rich to carry out various tasks. Moreover, a rich warrior will not be praised but rather rebuked for his selfishness and vulgarity. No one, however, will reprimand a townsman for debauchery, whether he is a shogunal purveyor or not, and nobody will begrudge him, however high his piles of gold, silver, and jewels may reach. Compared with warriors, they have a much easier time of it.

Because the shogunal government makes no attempt to control these townspeople, nobody points a finger at those shogunal purveyors or at any other rich townspeople. Therefore, they fear nobody in the world. They exhaust themselves in dissolution, and they constantly go out, spending the night elsewhere and absenting themselves from their residences for days at a time. The clerks who accompany them become equally dissipated. Both master and servant make light of the services they perform for the shogunate and forget the gratitude that they owe for the favorable treatment they are receiving.

With both master and servant going to extremes in outrageous behavior, all control both inside and outside [the household] is lost. The purveyor incurs debts that are beyond his position, or he embezzles shogunal money, and ends up being unable to perform the functions on behalf of the shogunate with which he has been entrusted; then, seeing no other way out, he hands his share of membership in the purveyors' association over to others. If he has an heir of his own bloodline, he claims that son is ill and takes him out of the succession, and while outwardly he pretends to seek permission to adopt a son, what he actually does is sell his share.[2] These official purveyors have for generations received great favors from the shogunate and have been able to live in great splendor because of their ancestry; yet they put the house name that they have inherited from their ancestral bloodline up for sale. With the arrangement that they will receive a portion of the house income as a retirement allowance,[3] they sell [their membership share] to persons without any pedigree or to people from distant provinces without even looking into their background and put them in charge of important services on behalf of the shogunate. That is an outrageous way to behave, and it shows utter disdain for received favors. This is what happens when excessive privilege is bestowed on people of low status.

Townspeople who hold membership shares in wholesalers' guilds trading in various goods receive shogunal recognition for their guild in return for paying modest license fees or performing minor services for the shogunate. As a result, they monopolize all transactions in that particular line of trade, and they use the august authority of shogunal recognition to set prices as they wish while taking a set cut that they call "commission." They never suffer a loss and simply rake in a secure profit. If somebody outside the wholesalers' guild begins to sell the same goods, they lose no time in sending a complaint to the shogunal authorities and having him reprimanded. They truly seize [profits] by force. Those closed guilds are of meager benefit to the shogunate, but they do great harm to the world. Seeing the example set by the shogunate, even merchants in the provinces seek to borrow authority for their trade. They have their trade recognized by a daimyo or they borrow the names of imperial princes and imperial cloisters.

The sources of the profit that such merchants gain in all these ways are none other than the warrior houses above and the poor below. Only the townspeople, who stand in the middle, have free access to it. Some of them fill their storehouses with gold and silver and own tens of properties. They do not actually engage in any business but live in comfortable

---

2. *Kabu* (a stake or share) was a hereditary membership in a *nakama*, or "traders' guild," with all the privileges that such membership entailed. *Kabu* shares could be sold only in case of a bankruptcy, and such transactions as well as the adoption of an heir needed the permission of the other guild members.

3. For similar arrangements among bannermen, see chapter 1, pp. 58–60.

retirement. They are businesses in name only, while in fact they collect a set amount of monthly rent from the properties they own. Others lend money against pawned goods. They do not engage in any physical labor, nor do they have a need for large numbers of clerks. Without having to worry about fluctuations in weather and crops, they gain a great amount of profit year after year and gradually stockpile gold and silver coin in their storehouses. In the end, it is completely up to them whether they want to lie in their beds or get up; their situation is truly without compare.

Domainal Purveyors and Storehouse Agents

Merchants also take on the management of the finances of daimyo great and small (they call this "domainal compound purveyance") and lend them money against high interest. More than that, they receive rations or stipends, they are allowed to use family names and carry swords, and they are granted high status comparable to that of chamberlain or domain elder. They lend money when a daimyo is asked to perform services for the shogunate, when his compound has been destroyed in a fire, or when the harvest in his domain has been bad, and therefore they are treated with an intimacy as though they were a relative. When they visit the compound they are welcomed as honorable guests; they may be invited to the lower compound or on pleasure excursions, where high domain officials serve as their hosts.[4]

Lately, large and small daimyo have tended to skimp on their official responsibilities, claiming to lack the funds; but at the same time, they spare no expense in what they call the entertainment of their "money masters." They treat them more lavishly than even intimate members of their own house or the domain elders. They send for geisha and beautiful women to pour the sake, mingle with these money masters at drinking parties, and make sure that there is plenty of lewd singing, music, and other performances. When the party is over, they arrange a palanquin for their townsmen guests and send delicacies to their houses as "presents." At times, those townsmen reciprocate by inviting domain officials to their villas and treating them to a feast, where they show off

---

4. Daimyo maintained multiple compounds in Edo; "lower compounds" (*shimoyashiki*) were often semirural retreats with extensive gardens used by the daimyo for leisure activities.

their wealth and display their beautiful concubines. They are always reaping profits from daimyo requests for goods, and it is their business to be invited to exquisite dinners and be given various products, clothes and textiles, and delicacies from the mountains and the sea. They truly live their lives in paradise.

Domainal purveyors also handle the tax rice collected by the domains every year. They single-handedly take control of the tens of thousands of *koku* of tax rice that hundreds of thousands in the domains shed tears and blood and exhaust all their energy to grow. They manage this tax rice at their leisure, using just one ledger and an abacus. Even when they have already received all the tax rice there is, they prompt for more if it is insufficient [to compensate for the loans they have extended]. Because these purveyors will not provide services to the daimyo unless they stand to gain substantially from it, daimyo large and small are afraid of future problems. They either cut back the stipends of their retainers or impose unreasonable extra levies on the farmers in their domain, just to fulfill their obligations to those townspeople. Thus, these get their hands on rice and gold aplenty and help themselves to profits as they wish. If one were to look for the bold and brave of the state in our age, it would be they.

These townspeople's power makes them conceited, and they look down on daimyo houses' financial situation. They disregard protocol, are unaware both of the obligations of the world and of any other form of refinement, and behave with unwarranted arrogance. They misread the civility of warriors and despise them as inept, stupid, destitute, and fawning. Should a daimyo house happen to fail to pay up as expected, they show no consideration for its troubles and care not at all if the official in charge of the matter ends up in a real pinch. They dupe him by saying that they will immediately make a new loan if only the present loan and interest are both repaid first; in that way, they change the agreement. They do not hesitate to break a long-standing relationship and boast of their toughness. It is their nature to be selfish and willful, and if something does not suit them, they will not even agree to see persons of high status and rank who ask for a meeting. No matter how often one offers them an apology, they will not accept it, but merely take a haughty attitude. If any in the realm deserve to be called callous, inhumane, and immoral, it must be they. Let me give a few examples of their callous, outrageous behavior.

Recently, a rich townsman in Osaka served as the storehouse agent of a certain province-holding daimyo. The official stationed at the domain storehouse office asked this agent for money to send to Edo for the management of the compound there, but the agent dismissed this request out of hand. The New Year drew near, and if this money were not sent, it would disrupt both this daimyo's duties to the shogunate in Edo and the end-of-year expenses of his house. Therefore, the domain representative sent both goods and bribes to the clerks of that agent, imploring him to expedite this money, but still the agent would not listen. Left with no other choice, the representative humbly asked the agent for a meeting, but the agent replied that he was too busy. Since the agent would not receive him, even though he visited his house many times, the representative at last sat down and refused to leave, and so he was granted a meeting. Yet even though he presented his request in various ways, the agent still refused.

Finally, the representative could bear it no longer and said, "This is a regular transaction of our house; it is established practice that you send this money to Edo every year. Yet ever since I have been given this duty and posted to this place, you have never accepted a single one of my requests. This matter in particular is obviously urgent now that the New Year is near. Why do you close your eyes to that fact?" His face clearly showed that he had reached a firm resolution to do whatever was necessary. Pressed in this fashion, the storehouse master replied, "I don't like your manner of asking. That's why I won't send any money." Shocked, the representative apologized: "Then how should I ask? I am from the countryside; I can somehow follow others' example when it comes to military matters, but I have never before conducted such negotiations as this in the big city. Please forgive my discourtesy up to now and teach me the proper formalities."

The master said, "First of all, you must know that I am in charge of all your lord's financial affairs. It is thanks to me that he can perform his duties to the shogunate and manage all his household and public business. I am an important person to your lord. These days, a daimyo can do without the domain elders, but he won't be able to manage without an agent like me. When you make important requests for your lord to such an important person as myself, it is no trivial matter. You ought to put your hands neatly down on the floor and bow your head when you make such a request." The representative flushed. Immediately he pressed his forehead against the tatami mat and expressed his regret: "This was extremely incorrect of me. Please forgive the thoughtlessness of an ignorant country bumpkin." "Now sit there like that for a while," the master said, and he coughed on the representative's head. "It is unthinkable in this world to loan one's important resources to someone who even has to be taught how to make a request. But then again, although you are of no concern to me, I can't abandon your lord. So I will send him this loan." With that, the agent yielded. The representative could not stomach this treatment and considered cutting the man down and then committing seppuku, but his lord's business was more important. Further, he could not bear the thought of ending his life in such a place, so he restrained himself. He saw this business through, and shortly afterward he resigned from his office and retired to his home in the countryside.

There are hundreds of such strongmen in Osaka. They are all as arrogant as that storehouse agent. When one asks them for even a small loan, one must invite their clerks to places of amusement many times, treat them, and ingratiate oneself with them before one can secure the funds. He who offends them will be unable to conduct his lord's business and will run into trouble; therefore, everyone does his utmost to curry favor with them. The wealthy in Kyoto and Osaka are all of this disposition, and they believe that the daimyo large and small all depend on their power. This is the ultimate in impropriety.

Similar things occur also in Edo. Admittedly, this happened a rather long time ago, but once a certain daimyo had promised to return a loan he had received by the end of the year. Because there would be problems with his general year-end bills if he settled this loan, however, the daimyo had no choice but to send one of the officials in charge of the domain's financial affairs to that townsman and explain the situation. The official told the townsman that unexpected problems had occurred due to a poor harvest in the domain and asked him to accept a payment of just the interest for that year, to revise the loan documents, and to extend the loan for another year. However, the townsman would not agree to this. When the official visited him a second and a third time, repeating his request, the man demanded that the domain first repay both the loan and the interest; once those obligations had been fulfilled, he would immediately supply them with a new loan. With this they reached an agreement, and the official brought out all the money allocated for the [domain compound's] year-end bills to cover both the loan and the interest. The townsman took all this money, asked the daimyo's official to wait a little while, and disappeared with the money to the back of the house. Even though he had said he would renew the loan immediately, this did not happen, and the official had to press him. The townsman told him that the law required the money to be kept overnight and asked him to return the next day.

Having no other choice, the official went home and came back the following morning with the contract. This time, the townsman claimed to be ill and unable to see him. Instead, a clerk passed a message to him saying that as unexpected problems had occurred with the cash flow, he was sorry to tell him that he could not be of service. The official was stunned. He protested that if he did not obtain the money now, it would be impossible to manage his lord's affairs. "We have put ourselves on the line by repaying this money," he declared. "Things cannot be left as they are." If the man did not give in, the official would have no way out but to commit seppuku. "I am astounded that you should mention seppuku," came the reply. "That word alone convinces me that I should never renew the loan. One should never lend valuable gold and silver coin to a person so unreasonable as to be ready to commit seppuku at the drop of a hat; after all, such a person may be gone at any time. A debt of that sort is too risky; I cannot accept your request under any circumstances." Even the townsman's clerks would not pay the official any heed, and he could only go home. He tried to solve the matter in various ways, but it was the end of the year. Whatever clever plan he devised, there was no way he could settle all the domain's debts, and this caused great problems for his lord. The official fell into the trap of that broken promise, and I have been told that in the end he was pressed into suicide, ruining his house. He was totally swindled by that townsman.

There are many similar instances. Even if it does not come to suicide and ruination, it often boils down to much the same thing, and in many cases it affects warriors' official duties and status. Those townsmen do not even recognize the favors they are granted—the respect and courtesy with which they are treated, and the extraordinary payments that they receive; they are champions of greed and immorality. If that warrior was driven to suicide, he could have taken some revenge by killing that townsman too, or at least by sitting down to kill himself in that townsman's house; there was little point in dying in his own quarters. However, rear vassals are particularly fearful of the shogunate. If a rear vassal kills someone outside his domain's jurisdiction, the shogunate is sure to take the matter up, and it will affect his lord's name. Quarrels connected to the house's financial affairs and to lack of money are especially shameful to warriors; therefore, the official did not want this matter to come out and decided to put an end to it by taking total responsibility. When samurai put up with the shame of being swindled by townspeople, it is almost always out of fear of the shogunate. This is the underlying cause of the weakening of the samurai spirit.

The Wealth and Arrogance of the Kuramae Rice Agents

Some of the most prominent moneylenders are the rice agents of Kuramae in Asakusa, who earn an immense income and are astonishingly wealthy. They take care of the disbursement of the stipends of bannermen and shogunal housemen and lend them money with those shogunal allocations as collateral. Without any effort, and without any delays, they seize control of these resources. At this time there are ninety-six rice agents. Ninety-six persons take charge of the financial means of tens of thousands of bannermen and shogunal housemen—hundreds for each of them. They give loans based on the size of the stipend, taking a fourth or a third of it as interest—or even half, if the holder is in much debt. As I noted earlier, they are not in the least flexible about the repayment schedule; they simply seize their share as soon as the rice stipend is paid, three times a year. They have a full grasp of the financial affairs of every single bannerman and houseman. They have no qualms about causing a man so much trouble that he can no longer exercise his duties. Even if a man is in such trouble that he hardly has a chance to survive, they close their ears. They break all protocol, rob the warriors to their heart's desire, and lay their hands on huge profits.

Each of these ninety-six houses indulges in great extravagance. Even if we estimate their income at only 1,000 *ryō* per year, that adds up to 96,000 *ryō* for all ninety-six houses taken together. All this is stolen from tens of thousands of bannermen and shogunal housemen. I have been told in confidence that in actual fact, the amount is nothing like 96,000 *ryō* but rather is close to 300,000 *ryō*. Even if we hold to an estimate of 96,000 *ryō*, that corresponds to some 300,000 bales of rice at the current rate. How many hundreds of thousands of people of the soil have exhausted their energies to grow those 300,000 bales? If we adopt the actual number of 300,000 *ryō*, that amount must represent the sweat and flesh of a million farmers. A mere ninety-six men seize all this through the power of money. In the style of those townspeople, they grab hold of the sweat and flesh of a million farmers who work for the realm and the state, and they do so without performing any service, without paying any annual land tax, without making any physical effort whatsoever. Tens of thousands of bannermen and housemen who stake their lives to serve the state are robbed of the larger part of their resources. Unable to receive even their thrice-yearly rice stipends, they fall into destitution. Some among them commit evil acts because of excessive poverty. Some may break the law, and some are forced to sell their house name to others. All this can be attributed to those rice agents.

In the old days, this business was conducted at tea stands made out of rush mats, which served as resting places for samurai who had gone to receive their rice stipends. It is said that those stand holders began to lend small amounts of money and, as this business began to generate a considerable income, gradually became more and more powerful until in the Kyōhō years [1716–1736] they gained shogunal recognition as a guild. From that point on, their influence has increased year by year until matters have reached their current state.

Nowadays, these rice agents treat the bannermen and shogunal housemen—who after all are important customers for them—in an extremely coarse manner, simply because they make such huge profits. They lead their warrior customers to a cramped space on the second floor and make them wait there for a while. They do not put in an appearance themselves but leave it to their clerks to receive them. Whatever notice one may give, they claim to be ill or away and refuse to arrange a face-to-face meeting, while in fact they spend their days and nights indulging in all kinds of amusements. The only task they perform personally is when it is their turn to serve as one of the monthly managers of the guild: then they go to the guild office, known as the "inner gate of the shogunal storehouses," at the fifth hour in the morning, manage the processing of rice bills, and then leave again after the eighth hour.[5] Before, they had their clerks do this, too, but at the time of the Kansei

---

5. The length of hours in the Edo period was not fixed but varied with the season. The fifth hour in the morning would be approximately two hours after dawn by modern count, while the eighth hour in the afternoon would be about four hours before dusk. Office hours, then, were roughly from seven in the morning until three in the afternoon.

reforms they were ordered to perform at least this task themselves.⁶ The association of ninety-six rice agents is divided into six groups, each consisting of about fifteen persons. The rice agents serve as monthly managers of these six groups by rotation, a month at a time.

They say that the association office's monthly expenses used to be enormous because drink and food were so extravagant, but lately they have been reduced and set at 100 *ryō* in "lunch fees" per month. Today, a warrior of five hundred *koku* cannot sustain a lifestyle based on the assumption of having 100 *ryō* for a full year.⁷ Those rice agents spend an amount meant to cover the living expenses of a warrior of five hundred *koku* for one year on a month's lunch fees for one person. It is true that they take their clerks along to the office and put them to work; but the rice agents themselves merely spend their time deliberating whether they will send for food from this place or that today, savoring the delicacies of all the famous establishments throughout Edo, or they discuss various places of amusement they might enjoy. When they get bored they play go or shogi for money, or even worse, they line up gold 1-*ryō* coins and start gambling. This will suffice to show the extent of their extravagance. The rice agents perform only this month-long duty in person; all other business they leave to their clerks, assuming the disposition of a daimyo. It is their everyday practice to have their clerks extort money, which they then squander. The bannermen and shogunal housemen do all their dealings with clerks. These clerks are called receptionists; they are selected for their pigheadedness and behave with extreme discourtesy.

As I have already mentioned, today's lending and borrowing puts the etiquette of high and low on its head. Even persons of high rank and

---

6. As mentioned in "Buyō Inshi and His Times," p. 25, in the Kansei period (1789–1801) the shogunate took various measures to try to limit rice agents' power over the finances of bannermen and shogunal housemen. These included an order issued in 1789 that canceled outstanding debts incurred prior to the twelfth month of 1784 and reduced the interest owed on more recent ones. In return, however, the shogunate also arranged for the rice agents to secure access to alternative sources of capital, and by the time Buyō was writing, the rice agents had regained much of their earlier prosperity.

7. In principle, a warrior could expect to receive as income about 30 percent of the putative yield represented by his stipend. For a warrior of 500 *koku*, this would work out to 150 *koku*, which in the early 1800s would have brought roughly 150 *ryō*. Buyō may be assuming an actual income closer to 20 percent of putative yield.

status behave with great courtesy and politeness in the presence of these rich townsmen and their clerks; they never complain about any discourtesies because they will not be able to conduct their affairs unless they put up with such behavior. Instead, they exhaust themselves in displays of respect and concentrate solely on getting their business done. But even if they put up with discourtesies, stay polite, and offer apologies, rarely are their interests attended to; mostly they return home without having achieved anything. The discourtesy of those rich townspeople in the face of the needs of bannermen and shogunal housemen makes it clear that the etiquette of high and low has been turned upside down. This is most regrettable.

It is true that once or twice a year a quick-tempered man who can no longer put up with rudeness and insults, who is pressed to the brink by his problems, and who cannot accept that no heed is paid to the honor of his house may beat some of those clerks or hit them with the blunt side of his sword. Although people's immediate assumption is that such behavior is totally out of bounds, such a reaction is in fact most reasonable if one knows of the circumstances. Everyone encounters such problems, but people endure them, setting aside the samurai code of behavior out of concern that rumors may get about and the shogunate hear of it.

Only two or three out of tens of thousands of bannermen and shogunal housemen take action of this sort. Yet it appears that those townspeople have made a complaint about it, and recently a shogunal order has been issued stating that if [warriors] raise matters about loans with undue force and the agents cannot cope with them, the agents should send a sealed letter naming the warriors to the town magistrate's office. The rice agents have copied this order in large letters and pasted it on the wall of the room [at the storehouses] where the bannermen, shogunal housemen, and such wait to collect their stipends, just at the level to be right in front of their eyes, so as to intimidate them.[8] When townspeople

---

8. Buyō seems to be referring here to the shogunate's response to a plea made by the rice agents in the late 1760s. As bannermen and shogunal housemen's debts to the rice agents piled up, some warriors adopted the stratagem of trying to cancel their existing arrangement with the rice agents in the name of collecting their rice stipends directly from the shogunal warehouses. In fact, however, for the actual collection of the stipend, they often employed *rōnin* or troublemakers to act on their behalf, and these people, according to the rice agents, caused problems. In 1768, the town magistrate issued a warning against such practices,

threaten warriors with this order—as if to say, "I will make a complaint about you to the shogunate if you do not behave yourself!"—they are humiliating their own long-standing clients. Because samurai cannot make complaints, the discourtesy and immorality of those townspeople know no bounds. The townsmen's troubles amount to mistreatment by a mere two or three bannermen and shogunal housemen out of tens of thousands and is something that occurs only once or twice a year at most; yet they make a complaint about it. Apparently, they have an easy time making their wishes known to those above, and their complaint seems to have gone right through, causing that order to be issued. Thus, we find that in these latter days, matters are turned on their head, and now shogunal laws have been issued by which townspeople control warriors.

Because of this institutional arrangement, a samurai simply cannot win. Among those rice agent clerks, some receive wages of 50, 100, or even 150 or 200 *ryō*; this is more than the income of a warrior with a stipend of 300 to 500 *koku*. Their means exceed that of the bannermen who serve on the shogun's personal guard, and they are so sure of themselves that there is no way a poor samurai can simply cut them down and dispose of them. Their might is such that were a warrior to turn on them, they could easily restrain him. While they were already strong enough as it was, they have now received the shogunal permission I just mentioned and thus added even further to their authority. Many similar matters have occurred, and because only laws that benefit the townspeople are instituted, they have increased their power even more.

Merchants' Extravagance

Merchants are thieves who keep their stealing within "appropriate bounds." Merchants who do not have the disposition of a thief or a beggar cannot make a profit. As the times became more prosperous and extravagance increased among both those above and those below, all lines of trade that were related to luxury, such as clothing and silk, flourished and expanded even into the provinces through branch shops. Merchants selling medicines, women's accessories, and tools; wholesalers dealing in rice, sake, and oil; pawnbrokers and financiers—they all rake

---

including directions to report the names of offenders. See Kitahara, *Edo no fudasashi*, pp. 54–57; Nishiyama, *Edo chōnin no kenkyū*, 1:269–70.

The cotton dealer district in downtown Edo, near Nihonbashi (see map 1). Cotton bales are piled high on the cart and have been unloaded in front of the shop to the left. *Edo meisho zue* (1834). National Diet Library Digital Collection.

in huge profits day and night and gather a fortune. They build residences in the grand style of whitewashed warehouses, using huge timbers of zelkova and oak and putting roofs on them that are like those of temples and shrines or castle turrets. It goes without saying that they furnish their houses and adorn themselves extravagantly. All this extravagance has its source in the favors they have received from warrior houses and in the lifeblood of the farmers.

Warriors and farmers *spend money* depending on the world's fortunes or misfortunes; townspeople *make profits* from the world's fortunes or misfortunes. That is why they have reached such prosperity. What this means is that the circumstances of warriors and farmers on the one hand and townspeople on the other are as far apart as Heaven and Earth. Townspeople have become magnates who look down upon farmers and show nothing but disdain for warrior houses' financial state. It is as in that popular saying: the one to whom one rents a shop ends up the landlord.

Not only in the castle city of Edo but also in Kyoto, Osaka, and all over the country, there are cohorts among those townspeople who live in even greater comfort and indulge in more self-importance than a daimyo. They keep great numbers of men and women in their service, and they even have hereditary retainers. Their managers and clerks are full-fledged house owners and are paid huge salaries. These wealthy merchants pursue the ultimate in personal extravagance and splendor. They go out on pleasure excursions as they wish. They fix up residences that they call their villas and design "scenic spots" for their wives and concubines where they can enjoy views of the sea or the countryside. They gaze from afar at fishermen who work their nets or cast their fishing rods and admire the fires the fishermen light in their boats at night. They rest their eyes and refresh their minds by watching the travails of farmers who, wearing straw hats, transplant rice seedlings, plough the fields with their oxen from morning until night, or carry heavy loads on their backs through the snow. For their own amusement they savor scenes of the poor suffering to survive.

Recently, the clerk of a rich man in the vicinity of Nihonbashi passed on some boasts to me in private. Talking about a daimyo of more than 100,000 *koku*, he said, "Some time ago we were asked to take care of the financial affairs of a certain daimyo, and we went up to his compound to investigate his household and external expenses. The personal budget of that lord is one thousand *ryō* per year, and even hospitality expenses for his guests are included in that sum. Our own master is a townsman, but he has one thousand *ryō* as well, and expenses for hospitality, travel, and the like are paid from a separate budget. Being a daimyo is not a good deal at all!"

[As just one example,] take the case of the wife of a rich townsman in Kanda who went on a tour of the Ise Shrines, Kyoto, Osaka, and Yamato. Before she left, her travel budget had been set at 1,000 *ryō* of gold, but the clerk who served as the tour's overseer was an extremely stingy man, and by the time they had reached Kyoto via Ise, he had managed to use up only 200 *ryō*. She sent an express messenger from Kyoto to inform her husband about this. The overseer was stupid, she wrote; he was too stingy to spend sufficient money on inns, he did not allow her any amusements, and she was most annoyed with him. The husband was livid and said, "It would have shown some sense had he spent 2,000 *ryō* on a budget of 1,000 *ryō*, but he hasn't even managed to get through the original 1,000! What a spineless fellow! We travel to other places and indulge ourselves throughout the year; a woman can do so only very occasionally.

This is a once-in-a-lifetime tour. If she cannot enjoy the sightseeing and the amusements to the full, or if she is forced to put up with any unsightliness, this will affect our reputation and soil our good name. A man must be sent who can take proper care of things." He dispatched another man to Kyoto immediately. One thousand *ryō* in gold corresponds to the annual income of a warrior of 3,000 *koku*. A warrior with holdings of 3,000 *koku* receives that amount to support both himself and his many retainers. He is granted this stipend in return for putting his life on the line, and he uses it to perform his duties. Meanwhile, a woman runs through this same sum without a care in the world. This is truly too shocking for words. The wife of a daimyo would never be allowed such lavishness.

Recently, a daimyo of 20,000 to 30,000 *koku* with a domain in the western provinces of Honshu had financial troubles and was unable to raise travel expenses. If he could not make it in time for his alternate attendance, this would cause problems with the shogunate, and as time pressed, he finally arranged some funds and made it to Osaka. He explained the situation to townspeople there and borrowed 200 *ryō*. Using that money to cover expenses on the road for his large entourage, he set off for Edo. However, on the way his entourage was delayed because of swollen rivers and the like, and soon his limited travel budget was used up. There was no way he could afford to stay at the main or secondary official inns, or even in an inn for common travelers, so he stopped at temples and borrowed both lodgings and food.[9] In that way, I am told, he finally made it to Edo. Rumors about his unseemly troubles passed from one post station to the next, and his humiliation was complete. Other daimyo face similar problems every time they travel to Edo, and few have sufficient travel funds at their disposal. One should compare the situation of that townsman's wife and these daimyo, who are fief holders of districts and domains.

The travel funds not only of daimyo but of lesser samurai as well are extremely inadequate, and this causes problems for all. Therefore, those who run inns along the roads dislike offering lodging to warriors, while they regard rich townspeople as the best kind of customers and do their utmost to please them. What used to be roads for warriors

---

9. In principle, the entourages of daimyo traveling on alternate attendance were expected to supply and prepare their own food when staying at post stations.

have now become townspeople roads.[10] Townspeople take along great numbers of good-for-nothings, spend large amounts of money, visit famous places and historical sites, make poems, drink sake, enjoy any number of delicacies, and stay put for any number of days if it rains. They are pandered to by the inn and offered one treat after the other. A warrior will never obtain any of this. Everything that has become a luxury for warriors is commonplace for today's townspeople.

Townspeople's Ceremonies

The rich pursue the ultimate in luxury when it comes to the clothes and paraphernalia they use for festivities such as weddings, the adoption of a son-in-law, a son's coming of age, the first hair-growing ceremony of a toddler, the ceremony of wearing *hakama* trousers for the first time, the dolls' festival of the third month, and the banner festival of the fifth month. Their wives dress up as if they were the spouses of high-ranking warrior houses, their sons as if they were warrior heirs, and their daughters as if they were princesses or ladies-in-waiting. Before, the daughters of townspeople were so keen to become the wives of warriors that the shogunate went so far as to prohibit such matches, but today they dislike even the semblance of becoming warrior wives. In the old days they envied the apparel of warrior houses and imitated it, but today their attire is so sumptuous that they scorn the warrior style as unfashionable. Instead, the wives, brides, and daughters of warrior houses have become fond of townspeople fashions.

Indeed, it is most reasonable that warrior women should envy and mimic the townspeople, since, as I have already noted, the latter's clothing and hair ornaments and the fashions they adopt for pleasure excursions, summer trips to the riverbank, boating trips, or going to the theater are much more elaborate than those used by warrior houses. These days all warrior houses, and especially the great and small daimyo, are weighed down by the costs of their public duties and driven into poverty. They impose cost-cutting strategies that run five or ten years into the future, and they limit the allowances for their wives and children in order to reduce house costs, with the result that sometimes the whole household—both

---

10. Ordinary travelers such as townspeople paid more for post-station lodgings than did warriors; see chapter 2, note 9.

family members and retainers—has to dress in cotton. Things have steadily become worse than before.

Townspeople have no expenses for public duties; their public duty is to be extravagant. Those who used to be banned from wearing even silk pongee today wear only silk crepe and never touch cotton. Cotton is worn by those who should not be wearing it, while those who should not wear silk crepe use it every day. Townspeople even use foreign textiles such as striped sateen and Dutch imports. They frequently wear felted or worsted wool, velvet, and striped sateen.[11] I am told that the use of felted wool even for spear scabbards was once restricted to province-holding daimyo. Later, it was allowed to lesser daimyo, and subsequently to those holding fiefs of over three thousand *koku*. Today townspeople use it for their haori, for bedding, and even for the thongs of their geta. This shows how radically customs have changed.

When it comes to the betrothal gifts presented at weddings or on the occasion of the adoption of a son-in-law, warrior houses cannot compete with townspeople. Townspeople provide as dowries not only clothes and various paraphernalia but also large amounts of money and property. Likewise, they take beautiful daughters of low-status families as brides, give them large amounts of "preparation money," and provide their parents with living expenses for the rest of their lives. Warriors pay no attention to the personality or the looks of their adopted sons or brides; they prefer those who bring the largest dowries. Townspeople do not care about the amount of money involved; they make their choice on the basis of personality and looks.

Riding on the power of wealth, both the sons and daughters of townspeople naturally become conceited. The children of warrior houses have a lord who supplies their house with its livelihood; therefore, they are aware that they owe gratitude to that lord for their having a place to sleep and food to eat. They exert themselves in the literary and military arts, and, knowing that they, too, like their fathers, are destined to go

---

11. Pongee (*tsumugi*), woven from uneven and coarse silk filaments, was a rough fabric, whereas crepe (*chirimen*) was a high-quality silk. Imported wool of various sorts, particularly felted wool (*rasha*, from the Portuguese *raxa*) and wool dyed a bright scarlet (*shōjōhi*), was a luxury item, and Buyō frequently refers to it as epitomizing extravagance. The term we have translated as "worsted" is a woolen fabric known as *raseita* (from the Portuguese *raxeta*). Striped sateen (*santome*, named after São Tomé near Madras) was a shiny cotton fabric.

into service, maintain an attitude of discreet self-control. In contrast, the children of townspeople do not depend on others at all for support. Throughout their lives, townspeople employ others rather than being employed. Is this not why they do not know loyalty and rectitude? They are never short of anything, and thus there is no need for exercising filial piety. They never suffer any hardship and are used to making selfish demands. When it comes to filial duties, they do not apply themselves to any kind of art. In all this, they are very different from the children of warrior houses. They have no sense whatsoever of self-control or duty; they are strong-willed, and their blind sons and their wives and daughters are similarly wayward and selfish.

When townspeople's children participate in festivals such as those of the Sannō and Kanda shrines, their attire is shocking to behold.[12] The parents dress up their sons and daughters as great generals. The children wear ten or twelve layers of robes of multicolored and gold brocade, crepe, damask, and silk gauze. By way of an entourage they are surrounded by numerous good-looking youngsters, and even their humblest attendants are dressed in felted or scarlet wool, velvet, or Dutch grogram.[13] They are accompanied by their parents and a large number of servants, all of them wearing beautiful outfits and equipped with the most exquisite swords, pouches, and hair ornaments. In short, all are decked out with the very best that is available. In addition, the parents hire whole groups of prostitutes such as geisha and dancing girls, and they pay musicians to play the samisen, *kokyū*, flutes, and drums. All these they supply with hair ornaments and robes of thick and thin silk. Purportedly, the costs of all this amount to more than 500 *ryō*, or even 1,000. For one child's participation in a festival, lasting only one day, they spend the same amount that a warrior of 2,000 or 4,000 *koku* will receive for a whole year.

Of course, these are the doings of the leading townspeople of the area, but also those below them willingly waste sums corresponding to the taxes from 300 or 500 *koku* of land on one day's competition. The

---

12. Together with the festival of Nezu Shrine, the Sannō and Kanda festivals were known as the three "festivals of the realm" (*tenka matsuri*) because their processions were allowed to enter into Edo Castle. These processions were therefore witnessed by the shogun himself.

13. Grogram, known in Japanese as *gorofukurin* (from the Dutch word *grofgrein*) was a highly prized coarse fabric of silk or wool produced in the Netherlands and Britain. In Japan, *gorofukurin* appears to have referred exclusively to wool.

households of a single city block spend hundreds or even thousands of *ryō* on the entertainment of guests and other miscellaneous matters. Their spending matches the annual living expenses of a small daimyo. For such children's festivities as the ceremony of wearing *hakama* for the first time, the first hair-growing ceremony, the dolls' festival, and the banner festival, they invite guests day and night over many days and stage performances of danced drama and comic skits, spending hundreds of *ryō*. It is because so many children grow up in such an excess of luxury and splendor in this city that others in distant provinces and in the countryside are forced to abandon their children to work the land, to send them to other provinces at an early age, to sell them, or even to kill them because they are unable to bring them up. How striking the difference between the city and the countryside, the imbalance between rich and poor!

In recent years, townspeople's funerals have become extravagant as well. The so-called chief mourners all wear "pure attire," and the inner and outer coffins are richly decorated. Food and drink are provided for those who see off the deceased—say 2,000 or 3,000 portions of *manjū* buns, sweets, and rice mixed with azuki beans. Adding the donations payable to the monks, they spend the equivalent of 200 or 300 bales of rice. Therefore, temples depend on the favors of a single great townsman among their parishioners rather than on powerful patrons among the great and small daimyo. They treat such townsmen with great care, give them posthumous names on a par with people who carry official titles,[14] and always do their utmost to please them.

Pricing

The root cause that gives rise to loss and gain, wealth and poverty, is to be found in the pricing of goods. Calculating the market price of goods is a merchant's most important skill. Among all goods, the pricing of rice is most important to the state. The house stipends of warriors consist of rice and grains [which they sell to obtain cash to buy other goods].

---

14. Temples granted (and still grant today) posthumous names to their deceased parishioners, used for mortuary rituals and often inscribed on graves in place of the secular names by which people were known during their lives. Buyō's concern is that townsmen were receiving types of names that were, in principle, reserved for people of warrior status.

Also, rice is vital because the lives of all the people in the state depend on it. Yet as things are today, it is the merchants who settle the price of rice in competition with one another, depending on auspicious and inauspicious events in the world and on harvests in the provinces. The warriors and the farmers are the source of rice and grains, but they are powerless when it comes to pricing. For this they depend on the townspeople, and, as a result, warriors and farmers suffer even when the harvest is good. The townspeople have monopolized the fundamental commodity of the state at the expense of the farmers and the warrior houses. Turning it into merchandise and a rare item, they steal profits. The misfortune of the world becomes their fortune, and the hardship of others has become their main method for making money.

The prime source in all of Japan for the pricing of rice is a place called Dōjima in Osaka.[15] In that place there are powerful people called brokers. Great merchants from many provinces converge here, and any one of them will be selling or buying as much as 100,000, 200,000, 500,000, or even 1,000,000 *koku* of rice and grains. They will not have even a single bale of actual rice at hand; they make all their deals purely on paper, in their ledgers, winning or losing while competing on their wits and luck. This is an enormous gambling party, and their stake is the whole of Japan. They engage in a grand battle by betting whether the weather will be good, wind and rain favorable, and harvests plentiful—or whether there will be natural disasters and bad crops. Betting on the weather and buying and selling the wealth and poverty of the world: the deeds inspired by human greed are frightful indeed!

Human greed likes things to go forward and up, so these brokers do not mind high prices. They call high prices "good trading" and low prices "bad trading." Seven or eight out of ten are buyers. When the harvest is good, prices go down and trading is "bad"; therefore, they prefer bad harvests and rejoice over storms, floods, droughts, and locust plagues in the provinces, because such events add to the competition in bidding and invigorate trading. They wait for disturbances in the world and pray for misfortune in the realm. When the market calms down because of a balance between good and bad harvests, they devise various stratagems to get the bidding going again and move prices up or down. This is called "broker-

---

15. On the workings of this rice exchange and the hands-off policy of the shogunate, see West, "Private Ordering."

induced bidding." If one were to send covert inspectors to the provinces today, one would be able to disclose how those brokers disturb the process of pricing by various evil schemes. To be sure, since those involved are organized in large groups and conduct their scheming in secret, it is not easy to expose their actions. What is clear, though, is that by organizing themselves in large groups these merchants upset the pricing process; they set out to swindle people from the provinces who have come to participate in their great game; and they try to draw amateurs into that game, stripping them of all their financial means and crushing them. They carry such evil schemes through to their final conclusion and flay people to the bone.

Nowadays, there are two thousand rice wholesalers in Dōjima and several thousand middlemen. Moreover, several thousand brokers running so-called cash shops live lives of luxury in Osaka's Edobori.[16] The bidding that arises in Osaka spreads to Kyoto, Edo, and to all corners of the land, and the number of persons who live the good life in this line of business is enormous. Medicines, cotton cloth, cotton wool, oil, coin, and many other goods are all subjected to bidding in Osaka, assessed for value, and priced up or down. All lines of trade have their basis in Osaka. Therefore, it is unavoidable that money accumulates in that place, and that people there grow rich.

People say that this bidding and pricing is a natural process that is beyond the control of the authorities. That is wrong. It *cannot* be so. The fact is that this matter has not yet been subjected to shogunal management. It is unthinkable that the workings of merchants should be beyond the power of the authorities. The authorities have not taken the trouble to manage these matters and have left them to merchants; as a consequence, merchants have acquired such great power that they have ended up measuring Heaven and planning the affairs of the state. Rice and grains are a matter of life and death, have a direct effect on wealth and poverty in the world, and are the prime commodity of the state. How can the pricing of this commodity be entrusted to the workings of townsmen?

To rule the realm, one must consider three matters: the realm, the people, and provisions. The shogunate gives thorough consideration to the first two but has yet to establish a system for controlling provisions.

---

16. Cash shops (*genkin-mise*) operated on a cash-only rather than credit basis.

Even among the first two, much remains to be desired as long as this vital matter is not attended to.

To be sure, it appears that this matter has in principle been regulated, since there is an official limit to the amount of rice that large and small daimyo are allowed to transport to Osaka and Edo.[17] However, there is no limit on the amount of rice that can be transported by merchants. It seems that this was left unregulated because in the old days the merchants were weak and did not engage in excessive transportation of rice and grains. In recent years, however, merchants have grown powerful, and they sell and transport enormous amounts of rice. Is it not wrong to continue to leave this situation unregulated? Today, there is a limitation on the selling of rice by large and small daimyo, while townspeople are totally free to sell rice as they wish. Because townspeople can transport rice to any place in any province, large and small daimyo depend on their services. Daimyo borrow townsmen's names to sell rice in excess of their quota; this they call "barn rice."[18] In this matter, once again things are the wrong way around: townspeople are free to do what daimyo may not. If this is left as it is today, there will always be a shortage of rice and grain in the provinces. Moreover, it will be a source of disaster when there is a famine or a bad harvest.

City Property

When Tokugawa rule was first established, the number of townspeople was kept small. They even say that there were not enough houses to fill the 808 blocks that had been laid out in the city, and that the shogunate resorted to paying ten *ryō* of gold to those who were willing to build a house and start a business in Edo. In the course of more than two hundred years of shogunal rule the city has been filled to the brim, and today

---

17. In fact, the shogunate tried in various ways to regulate the price of rice. One strategy for keeping prices up at times of oversupply, adopted repeatedly from the 1730s on, was to impose limits on the amounts that daimyo could transport to Osaka and Edo for sale.

18. "Barn rice" (*nayamai*) was "private" rice that farmers sold directly to rice dealers. The opposite was *kuramai*, rice that was paid in taxes, sent to the domainal or shogunal warehouses, and converted into cash under official auspices.

there are over thirty-six hundred townsmen's blocks.[19] The same happened in Kyoto, Osaka, and other places. As the number of extravagant townsmen and idlers grew, precious treasures that were once the domain of persons of high rank and status came to fill townspeople's storehouses. Secondary compounds that large and small daimyo have built in Edo on privately purchased land have been taken over by townspeople in exchange for a loan and turned into villas of their own.[20]

Because the townspeople are doing well, their numbers keep increasing. The number of households has doubled year by year, and as a result, property prices in the blocks of the city have shot up. This is very different from the way things were in the past. Today, land near the Nihonbashi and Edobashi bridges in Edo is bought and sold for 1,000 *ryō* gold per *ken* in width. The monthly property rent per *tsubo* is 5 or 10 *monme* of silver, so I am told. The rent for a shop or a house is about the same. The various blocks within the 4 *ri* square area of Edo differ in price depending on the prosperity of the locale, but everywhere the prices go up year by year and have become ridiculously high.[21] I am told that a property in Fukagawa that was worth 180 *ryō* in the Kyōhō years [1716–1736] was recently sold for 3,500 *ryō*. This shows how property prices have shot up as this city has become wealthier. People pay such expensive rents and cover various other expenses besides and still live lives of splendor. So great is the abundance and the profit generated by trade!

Shogunal physicians, attendants, castle servants,[22] purveyors, and artisans were once granted townsman land within the city for their residences. Now that land rents in such areas have become so expensive,

---

19. Buyō's figures seem somewhat exaggerated; "808 blocks" is a common figurative description for the townspeople's quarters. As previously noted, Edo initially had approximately 300 townspeople blocks; by the late eighteenth century, these had expanded to 1,678 blocks.

20. Although the main domainal compounds in Edo were built on lands granted by the shogunate for that purpose, daimyo also purchased land to use for additional compounds (known as *kakae yashiki*) as needed.

21. Four *ri* square corresponded to an area with a radius of about five miles (eight kilometers) around Edo Castle.

22. Buyō refers here to the shogunal servants known as "priests" (*obōzu*) because of their shaved heads and monklike dress. Their tasks in Edo Castle involved serving tea and performing other miscellaneous duties.

they have moved to rented plots in other parts of the city and rent out to townspeople the land granted them by the shogunate. A plot of 100, 200, or 300 *tsubo* not even as big as a rice field of 1 *tan* brings in the equivalent of a warrior fief of 100 or 200 *koku*, and the rent that they raise from such a plot corresponds to the taxes of one or two villages.[23]

In the blocks of this city, a property of 120 *tsubo*, 6 *ken* wide and 20 *ken* deep, has become as valuable as 1 *ri* square of farmers' rice fields. Townspeople who own property collect huge rents without any expense or effort. A property of 6 by 20 *ken* is called one plot. This was the original space for one house in a block, awarded by the shogunate to one person. As time passed, gradually larger properties of 10 by 20 or 30 *ken* appeared; these are worth up to 10,000 *ryō*. There are those who own five, fifty, or even one hundred such properties. It seems that the largest among the magnates of Edo hold some two hundred properties. These bring in an amount equivalent to the resources of a warrior who holds 5,000, 10,000, or even 50,000 or 60,000 *koku*—without the holder having to pay any corvée services or annual land tax or dirty his hands.

This is a sure sign that the city and the countryside are as different as black and white. Because this city is full of wealth, poverty has grown rife in the countryside. Every year, farmers from the provinces gravitate to the cities in great numbers, causing the rural population to dwindle and fields to be abandoned. In the cities, the population increases. Houses are crowded together without a *sun* to spare, land has grown expensive, and people fight over the cost of each and every *sun*.

The above explains how more than two hundred years of great peace have caused the cities to become more and more affluent, giving rise to ever more wealthy townsmen; how these townsmen have risen above the warriors and the farmers, who form the basis of the state; and how they indulge in excessive extravagance and exert great power. This is the state of the richer half of the townspeople. Below I will describe how the poorer half among them behave.

---

23. As previously noted, up to 70 percent of the townspeople of Edo were renters. Further, even many house owners rented the plots of land on which they built their houses (which they might rent out in turn).

Backstreet tenement in Edo. Some dwellers have small stalls selling sandals and other sundries. *Kami kuzu minoue banashi* (1781). National Diet Library Digital Collection.

LOWER TOWNSPEOPLE

As cities have grown increasingly prosperous, many people have moved there from provincial areas year after year. As I have described above, some have succeeded in accumulating wealth and live more luxuriously than nobles or people of high status. And because many want to become wealthy like them, the cities are full of greedy people who resort to nefarious means. It is their wont to seek to be rich without making any particular effort. Taking these wealthy merchants who lead lives of extravagance and luxury as a model, other townspeople similarly concentrate on pursuing greedy and evil means. Those who are not sufficiently greedy can never escape from poverty, while those who become caught up in greed and indulge themselves in drink and delicacies are unable to take proper care of their wives and children.

The Enterprises of the City Poor

Just as there are twenty or thirty poor farmers in the countryside for every well-to-do one, there are many poor people also among townspeople. As

I said above, some have left the provinces because of extreme poverty. Some young men leave because of their dissipation, or because they are drawn by dreams of splendor and wealth. Gathering in ever increasing numbers, they fill the cities and sink into destitution there. Even so, they find life in the cities better than life at home. In rural areas, those who are extremely poor cannot find any means of survival and have nowhere to turn. In prosperous cities, where there are various businesses, even the poorest can at least find some way to live from hand to mouth. Moreover, they find it easier to survive in the cities because, unlike the countryside, life there is not constrained by moral obligation and a sense of shame. People gather in cities because it is easy to do evil or rob others there. Since people have lost their means of survival in the countryside, they crowd into the cities in ever greater numbers, but the more poor people gather in cities, the more difficult it becomes for them to live there, too. Therefore evil deeds grow ever more rampant. Those who fail to make a living in the cities have no means of returning home either, so the only path left for them is to engage in evil crimes.

Let me briefly explain why there are so many poor people in cities and why it is difficult for them to make a living there. First of all, one cannot freely start a new business in a city nowadays. Those in the neighborhood who engage in the same kind of business will protest against any attempt by someone to open a new shop. Should such a person persist, those operating existing shops will appeal to the shogunal government, and the authorities' decision will be in favor of the latter. Wholesalers and brokers have long organized themselves into officially recognized guilds, and since the rules of such guilds prohibit anyone who is not a member from starting the same kind of business, it is natural for such objections to be raised.

Nevertheless, considered from the perspective of the great Way of the realm as a whole, such rules and laws are too narrow-minded and intolerant. Backed by such narrow-minded rules, guilds of wholesalers and brokers monopolize the sale of goods and arbitrarily decide market prices. Should a person buy goods from someone who is not a guild member, the shogunal authorities will take up the matter and levy a punishment. Therefore, no one can secretly buy rice, charcoal, firewood, oil, or any other kind of daily necessity from provincial sources, even if the price of such goods is lower there. Nor can people from the provinces sell such goods. Nowadays, even groups of merchants that are not officially recognized guilds file complaints and make it difficult for a newcomer to start the same kind of business.[24]

Because so many people have gathered in cities and townspeople are crowded all together, it is not easy to find a way to make a living. Even should one manage with great effort to put together the necessary capital, one cannot readily open a new shop for the reasons I have described above. The fact that people cannot freely use their own money to buy cheaply priced goods shows that shogunal law is too narrow and restrictive. Nowadays, whatever the line of business, many people are already engaged in it, and there is no space for someone new. It is thus impossible to start up an ordinary kind of enterprise, and many are at a loss about how to make a living, even if they have considerable capital to invest. In the end, they start up hitherto unknown, unusual enterprises. Much less can those who lack capital engage in a proper enterprise; instead they embark on various aberrant lines of work.

Those who cannot find a proper means of making a living or who lack capital try their hand at various types of jobs. Clever and sharp-witted people scheme to engage in something in tune with the times. Some dupe others. Some cheat others out of their money by taking on lawsuits and turning a lost cause into a victory, or by assisting one of the parties, or by mediating between them. Some contract to undertake a construction project of one sort or another. While knowing that the project will be difficult to carry through, they petition the shogunal authorities to give them the contract; then, with the contract in hand, they entice wealthy investors by making it seem as if the project is about to come to fruition according to plan. Some defraud others by producing and selling worthless things.

There are many people of this kind, all making a living without hard work; they are known as swindlers. Their cleverness and ingenuity are their capital, and they turn everything they see or hear to their own advantage. When they engage in matters under the authority of the town magistrate's office, they tailor their plans to fit the inclinations and habits of the magistrate and the officials in charge, of which they are well informed. They know well how to get along in life. They cheat the gentleman by adopting the ways of gentlemen, the petty person by acting petty,

---

24. For examples of debates over these issues, see Wigmore, *Law and Justice*, 3B:85–91, 141–46.

the wise by acting wise, and the greedy by making use of their greed. They bilk whomever they encounter, even using the Way of the buddhas and gods to bilk buddhas and gods. As a result, they get on in life wearing the clothes of a man of leisure, consuming as much wine and food as they like. This is the fashion of the day, and perhaps we should not despise those who pursue it. As I have explained above, they have become swindlers by drawing on their own cleverness and ingenuity as their capital, because the constricted circumstances of the world leave them little room to pursue some other means of living.

Money Lending

Nowadays, those who have a small amount of capital or have acquired money by swindling others often start lending money at high interest. In principle, as I have said earlier, the lending of money should be a form of circulation to the mutual benefit of all parties, based on mutual sympathy and sincerity. In today's world, however, borrowing and lending is not in the least based on sincerity. Moneylenders will not lend money even to their childhood friends if the latter lack substantial property, but they will lend readily to a complete stranger as long as that person has ample possessions. Money lending is simply a means to squeeze out a profit, and it has nothing to do with sincerity. Were money lending to be conducted on the basis of mutual sincerity, lenders would not take interest from borrowers. To set interest at such and such a rate is contrary to moral principle. When did the concept of interest appear in the world? It seems that it was the doing of those engaged in the marketing of goods. How contemptible!

Recently, however, even the noble houses who serve as imperial regents, imperial cloisters, and other high-ranking houses have begun to make their living by engaging in money lending. [Other lenders] borrow the title [of a noble house or cloister] to add authority to their own money and use that as an excuse to seize exorbitant interest. Imperial regent houses, being of the highest status, should take pity on the indigent, but nowadays, quite to the contrary, they exploit the poor. Imperial cloisters, which stand at the head of the Buddhist world, are supposed to come to the aid of all sentient beings, but instead they act in a totally unconscionable manner. Avaricious swindlers borrow this villainous authority to collect usurious interest to their heart's content.

Let me explain how such usury works. When a moneylender lends a sum to a borrower, he first sets the due date—say in three months—and deducts the interest, 10 or 20 percent, for that period from the sum lent. In addition, he extracts a service charge, which comes to another 10 or 20 percent of the principal. Therefore, when the borrower contracts for a loan of 10 *ryō*, the lender in fact hands over only 6 or 7 *ryō*. At the end of three months, when the term comes due, the borrower has to "return" the principal first and then borrow it once more. At that time the lender again extracts interest and service charges in the same fashion. In this way, if a moneylender lends a sum for a year, its value doubles; he gets a return of 20 *ryō* on 10, 200 *ryō* on 100. No other business would produce such a large profit. This shows how moneylenders utilize all manner of nefarious means.

In the name of encouraging the circulation of funds throughout the world, the shogunal government, too, engages in lending money.[25] Since the government loans money at lower interest than private moneylenders, it may serve in a sense to encourage circulation. Yet such governmental loans seem to have appeared only after the Kyōhō years [1716–1736]. There was no official arrangement of this kind in earlier periods. Those who receive such loans must put up some sort of security in return. If they have no security to offer, the government will not yield, even if they starve to death. This is far from benevolent government. Should a warrior undertake this kind of activity, it would be regarded as a culpable offense. How is it that the shogunate engages in activities that it holds to be a culpable offense?

Quite a few temple and shrine priests do not bother going through swindlers but lend money at high interest themselves, under the pretext of raising funds for repairing a temple hall or paying for its preservation.[26] Such conduct is not appropriate to one who is a priest. As I mentioned earlier, the buddhas and gods are supposed to save people. How could it please them to know that priests are causing hardship to the poor and snatching money from them? Nowadays, those in financial difficulty are often forced by necessity to borrow money at usurious rates. What with double the amount they borrowed being sucked out of them, they ultimately come to ruin. Bitterly, they come to rue that what they received in

---

25. See chapter 1, note 5.
26. See chapter 1, note 6, and chapter 3, pp. 112–13.

the name of a benefice was in fact a poisoned cup. How grievously wrong it is that the shogun's government should profit from the ill-gotten gains that are the source of this bitterness and that temples and shrines should make a business of dealing in such matters.

In today's world, even the shogunate, people in important positions, and people who lead the worship of the buddhas and gods—persons who are revered and looked up to throughout the world—are eager to gain the profits of usury. How much more is this true of townspeople and farmers of even the slightest means. They do not hesitate in the least to pursue this path as far as they can. They accept as security the houses in which people live, their land, their tools, their business rights, or guild membership, and they build their own fortunes on pressing poor people mercilessly. Moneylenders do not complain if someone else starts up the same business. There is no problem even if someone opens a new money-lending shop next door to an existing one. Yet another convenience compared with other forms of business is that a moneylender need not employ many clerks and apprentices. And since the profits are large, it is a popular business. But only those of a cruel and harsh disposition can make a success out of this path. The popularity of money lending fosters the rise of evil means throughout the world and is the source of the people's impoverishment.

There are various special forms of lending money: monthly installment loans, daily installment loans, chattel-lease loans, and crow loans. These are exceptionally usurious loans made to poor people of very limited means. With crow loans, money lent in the early morning when the crows begin crying has to be returned by evening when the crows go home. From a single day's circulation of funds, the lender gains as much interest as an ordinary loan would bring in a month. In the case of chattel-lease loans, the lender leases clothes, nightclothes, bedding, mosquito nets, and the like for a set daily fee. The destitute borrower then pawns the leased goods; he thus has to pay double interest, on both the leased goods and the pawn.[27] In tune with the times, evildoers can thus turn a small amount of cash into a large fortune in no time at all by lending money.

---

27. In the case of chattel-lease loans (*sonryō-gashi*), the borrower in effect borrowed the collateral for the loan, which made it possible for the lender to collect more than the usual interest rate. See Wigmore, *Law and Justice*, 3A:240–43, 248–51.

The good-natured, who tend to lag behind the times, borrow money, pay interest on top of interest, and soon become destitute. Seeing how the fates of the good-natured and evildoers run contrary to the principle of Heaven, we can gauge the right and wrong of today's world.

Quite a few people earn their living by collecting a service charge for mediating between lenders and borrowers. Some, falsely claiming that they will arrange a loan, extract money from potential borrowers by charging them for so-called miscellaneous costs. Others defraud poor people by demanding that they pay a service charge in advance. They are nothing more than smart-looking muggers, and the turmoil presently caused by borrowing and lending is immense. Out of ten lawsuits, eight or nine concern loans. As I have repeatedly pointed out, loans are the medium that has brought about the imbalance between rich and poor. Evil people become lenders, and many succeed in becoming well-off without working hard. With the disposition of a demon, they act as if they were offering solace to the needy when in fact what they offer is the poison with which they wring profit from their victims.

Good people borrow money with the expectation that it will take them through a time of need, only to find, like those who have fallen into the realm of hungry ghosts, that the solace they sought has turned into the flames of usurious interest. Should the borrower be late in paying back what has been borrowed, the lender will with demonic force take possession of his house and storehouse, seize his furniture, tools, clothes, and cooking pots, or force him to sell his wife or daughter to raise the necessary funds. Should these measures fall short, the lender will bring suit with the shogunal government. The borrower will undergo interrogation at the magistrate's office, and whatever he owns will be confiscated. He may be handcuffed or jailed.[28] Not only the borrower but also his relatives and guarantors may find themselves in trouble. The staff of the magistrate's office responsible for investigating the case will act as mercilessly as demons so as to force the borrower to repay. In today's world, evil people exhaust their own means to strip their victims to the bone. When their own efforts are insufficient, they rely on the power of the magistrate's office. Using the staff of the magistrate's office as the agents of their own greed and wickedness, they press the borrower to pay. How

---

28. Putting handcuffs on the accused for a set or unspecified number of days was a standard form of punishment.

much more audacious can one get than to use even the shogunal government as the agents of one's greed and villainy?

City Crime

The destitute in distant provinces and remote regions never engage in illegal acts, even when they [face difficulty] in settling their accounts on the specified days.[29] Should a famine last for two or three years, and they have to eat tree bark and grass roots because they cannot get even coarse grain, they do not resort to the kinds of evil deeds that destitute townspeople often commit. In the rare instance that they do steal something, the crime is easily uncovered since they are not at all shrewd. Those living in towns are familiar with a luxurious mode of life. They have to maintain associations with their equals and keep up a style of life appropriate to their family rank. Consequently, they cannot eat barley instead of rice but have to consume delicacies. If they do not maintain the same standard of living as their neighbors, they cannot stay in their current residence. Their expenses for rent and daily necessities are thus high, and should they be unable to keep up with the cost, they will be forced to move out. Confronting that likelihood, they can do nothing but resort to evil deeds.

There is another reason [why many crimes are committed in cities]. Since the people who have gathered in cities come from various villages and provinces, they do not share any bonds of mutual sympathy, even if they exchange pleasantries on the surface. Although neighbors are separated from each other by only a thin shared wall, either may move away unannounced to unknown parts the very next day. They share no sense of moral obligation or mutual encouragement. The young people I mentioned above may cannily avoid being arrested by keeping themselves hidden, but those who are honest and obstinate cannot manage such clever ploys and are caught and punished right away.

These days, true criminals never meet with punishment. They cause turmoil and rob others while sitting comfortably at home without dirtying their own hands. In today's world, the definition of who is good and who is evil has been reversed. The laws of retribution for good and evil,

---

29. Buyō refers to "the matter of the thirtieth [the last day] and five and ten days (*misoka gotōbi*)." The last day of the month and days with a five or ten were often designated as days for settling accounts for debts or things bought on credit.

pernicious and correct do not apply at all. In this world, those who are honest and kind to others will sooner or later find themselves stripped of their belongings by evildoers. Evildoers cheat them and snatch their possessions by counting exactly on that honest and kind nature. Many criminals who have been sentenced to banishment continue to live stealthily in this castle city of the shogun. They become the leaders of gangs of troublemakers, who admire them as gallants. Some of them manage gambling parlors or act as the banker there. Others extort money from people in a weak position, such as women living on their own, kept women, tea-stand operators, or entertainers. Keeping an eye out for those who have done something wrong, they intimidate such people into lending them money. Acting as if they were the ringleader of a band of thieves, they take kickbacks from them; they also swagger about and menace even those with no particular weak point.

Those who were admired as gallants in the past, such as Banzuiin Chōbei, Tōken Gonbei, and Ukiyodo Hyōe, sacrificed themselves to shoulder others' burdens.[30] I have heard that they let people with no place to live stay for free in houses they controlled. They challenged the strong and helped the weak. When others requested them to do something, they willingly took on the task if only it accorded with the Way of loyalty and filial piety, and they did whatever was required to accomplish it, regardless of the cost. Those known as gallants today are totally different.

First of all, those called gallants today are troublemakers. They devote themselves to illegal matters such as gambling. In addition many become what are known as undercover agents or informants.[31] In the past,

---

30. The operator of an employment agency for supplying servants and low-level retainers in early to mid-seventeenth-century Edo, Banzuiin Chōbei came to be known as an archetypical gallant (*otokodate*), a Robin Hood–like protector of the weak and challenger of the powerful and overbearing. He was immortalized in the Kabuki play *Banzuiin Chōbei*. Tōken Gonbei, an Edo townsman who was arrested and executed by the shogunal authorities in the late seventeenth century, also figured in the same play. Mid-nineteenth-century woodblock prints of a Kabuki actor playing the role of Ukiyodo Hyōe suggest that this was a similar character.

31. As Buyō's subsequent description indicates, undercover agents (*okappiki*) and informants (*meakashi*) occupied a semiofficial place in the Edo law-enforcement system. In many cases, they were by origin criminals who agreed to provide evidence on others in return for a reduced sentence. The lower-level staff officers in the town magistrate's office came to hire them privately as a conduit of information about the Edo underworld, in which, as Buyō notes, the agents often

the function of such people was to ferret out troublemakers such as arsonists or thieves and privately inform the officials responsible for investigating these matters. Now, however, they no longer stay behind the scenes to secretly pass information to the officials in charge; rather, they openly throw around their weight as if they were the officials' agents. People are intimidated and dare not raise objection to what they do, so the agents become even haughtier. Since the officials depend on these agents to help them carry out their tasks, they tend to connive at the latter's unlawful acts, and as a consequence, the agents engage in wrongdoing all the more freely. Should investigation of one of their own crimes become unavoidable, they turn in their underlings as culprits in their place. Or should they harbor a grudge against someone, they trump up charges against him and have him imprisoned. When they find a fool with a little money, they encourage him to engage in illegal activities.[32] Having cheated him out of his money, they then turn him in as a criminal. They steal others' wives and concubines and use these women as bait to get their hands on yet others' property. Such lowly deeds hardly befit the name of "gallant."

Among both the upper and lower classes, it is those who are good at cheating others and taking advantage of people's feelings who are regarded as skillful in getting through the world. Those who are not skillful at such things end up being cheated and taken advantage of. Therefore, people want to be good at cheating others. For one who seeks to become good at cheating others, honesty and conscientiousness are obstacles. People who are concerned about moral obligation and shame cannot be good at cheating. Those who feel sympathy for others cannot either. Nor can those who [adhere to] the Way of sages and worthies or who are afraid of the divine punishment of the buddhas and gods. Least of all can persons who observe the government's laws be good at cheating others. Those who are skilled at cheating others regard such scruples as nothing more than tools to keep up appearances and are possessed solely by the desire to rob others.

This is the normal state of mind among today's townspeople, and such customs have spread widely throughout the world. Confucian

---

continued to be involved. By the end of the Edo period, the staff officers in the town magistrate's office were said to employ some four hundred such agents.

32. By "illegal activities," Buyō probably means gambling.

scholars, doctors, warriors, temple priests, and farmers all deviate from their own Way and have come to regard trustworthiness as nothing more than a signboard to keep up appearances and conceal that, inwardly, their only concern is to rob others. This is a serious problem. This bad custom is spreading more and more widely. Where will it stop? Will it continue to spread endlessly until the world falls into chaos? At this time, when the world is on the verge of decline, the customary cruelty and villainy of the people can explode at any moment.

Arson, Firefighters, and Robbery

Nowadays, should a fire break out, low-ranking townspeople all turn into thieves and feel free to steal the clothes and goods people keep stored away. They are always on the lookout for a fire, and on days when there are strong winds, they even set fires. In addition, the number of carpenters, plasterers, roofers, and steeplejacks has steadily increased.[33] They find it hard to make a living if townspeople do not lose their residences to fire, but when a large-scale fire breaks out, they are elated and in high spirits, for at such a time the wages and costs they can charge almost double. Steeplejacks and their followers are organized into some forty firefighting groups, each of which is named for a letter of the syllabary. But instead of paying proper attention to their responsibility to put out fires, they regard it as an opportunity to loot. Recently, they have begun to engage in a devious practice called "diverting the fire." Pretending as if they are trying to prevent a fire from spreading, they lead the flames to a place where the fire would not likely reach by itself. They do so in hopes that after the fire, they will be employed to rebuild the houses. Quick-witted and rich townspeople manage to save their own houses by secretly bribing the head of the firefighters not to burn them—an unconscionable deed at a time of emergency.

33. Steeplejacks (*tobi no mono*, literally, "kite people") took their name from the tool associated with them, a pole with an iron hook at the end that was seen as looking like a kite's bill. They used the hooked pole in their normal occupation of erecting the scaffolding for construction projects, but because firefighting in the Edo period consisted primarily of quickly pulling down buildings to create a firebreak, *tobi no mono* also came to play a central role in the firefighting apparatus. See also Takeuchi, "Festivals and Fights," which confirms many of the points Buyō makes about steeplejacks.

Steeplejacks are known in the town as "the lads," and they receive "felicitous gifts"—large sums of money for drink—when townspeople build new houses and storehouses, open shops, or have a wedding or funeral. If the sum is smaller than they expected, they are resentful and take revenge later. Should a townsman employ steeplejacks from another block, the ones in his own block will complain and create trouble by starting an argument or a fight. In the end, they will get money from that townsman under the pretext that they need wine for a drink of reconciliation. In this way, steeplejacks treat the blocks they live in as their own designated territory.

Since they expect the block residents to employ them unquestioningly, they are lazy. With an eye to shaking down larger wages, they spend two or three days to complete a task that they could do in one. Because too many people have crowded into the cities these days, they struggle to make a living, and thus some long for fires. Townspeople have to pay a lot to hire opportunistic workers [from their own block] and cannot easily employ those of their own choice. They cannot manage their own affairs to their own liking. It does not stand to reason, a prime example of how tangled things have become.

In the transition from autumn to winter, some poor people cannot change their clothes from thin summer ones to warm winter garments. Naked as trees in winter, year by year they cause ever greater disturbances by committing arson, robbery, mugging, and murder. Many engage in petty theft, such as stealing people's clothes and belongings in the public bath. In this season, the shogunal authorities therefore appoint additional staff to the office that deals with incendiaries and robberies. To be sure, in other seasons as well, night robberies, muggings, and murders have doubled in number in recent years. Thieves known as purse cutters rob passersby of their purses, pouches, and other belongings; they also snatch hair ornaments from women. Particularly after dark, many troublemakers prowl about with an eye to snatching women's hair ornaments and other possessions. This shows that towns are always full of robbers.

In this way, it is not at all uncommon nowadays to suffer theft or robbery. If a warrior or a townsman loses his possessions in the confusion of a fire or if he suffers an ordinary theft, he tends to keep this hidden. To submit a formal appeal to the authorities would cost him a considerable sum, and being summoned [for an official hearing] would be time-consuming and cause him to incur various expenses. In addition, a government investigation rarely turns up stolen goods. Seven or eight out of ten stolen items will be lost forever, and should a stolen article be found, it has often cost the owner more in the end than its worth. It is thus pointless to report a theft to the government. Further, since people tend to speak ill of the victims of thefts and robberies, wealthy people try to keep their losses from being known out of concern for their reputation. As a result, thefts and robberies go without being investigated, which means that they increase steadily.

The more numerous thieves and robbers become, the less effective the governmental system for controlling them. At present, thefts and robberies are so numerous that they have become a part of everyday life. I have heard that in Korea there are so many thieves and robbers that the government cannot punish all of them. If a thief whose crime comes to light returns what was stolen and negotiates with the owner, the owner may withdraw the charge. As a result, stealing has become a daily matter and is regarded as if it were something to be proud of. In recommending a woman as a wife, a matchmaker will often say, "She is good at stealing as well." Will this not happen in Japan, too, before long? Since Korea is a small country, it may not be such a problem there, but Japan is a large country, and should things decay to the same degree here, gangs of scoundrels are sure to cause large-scale disturbances.

At present in Japan, the decay has not yet come to the surface, but it cannot remain hidden for much longer. Theft and fraud have become everyday matters. Things may look fine on the surface, but such appearances are not reliable. As I have described above, the world is full of troublemakers, many of whom are waiting for an opportune moment of disorder. Among the lowly there appear to be many bold men who think that if the world shifts further out of kilter, they will be able to take advantage of the situation to perpetrate villainous deeds. We must keep on guard.

Derelicts and Beggars

Apart from such problems, people without any family to rely upon for support are increasing in number in the city outskirts. There are large numbers of beggars such as lay devotees, nuns, the blind, the deaf, and the crippled. Although they may not commit serious crimes, they have

Indigent paper scrap collector in backstreet tenement area. *Ukiyodoko* (1814). Waseda University Library.

been left behind and have exhausted ordinary means of making a living. Some have vainly used up their energy in trying to keep their daughters or sons from being lost to dissipation. Others fell ill. In the end, they have become derelicts. Obviously, there must be many people of this kind in both the provinces and this shogunal city.

Some of these people have resigned themselves to their fate; they turn to Buddhist teachings and see their current situation as a result of bad karma. Others bear a grudge against the world. Some rely on handouts from others and become a burden on the world as they leave the provinces for the cities. In other cases, they have left the flourishing cities for the provinces. Kneeling at people's gates and doors, they beg for mercy, or else they grovel at the feet of passersby. Since few willingly offer them a copper coin, they sink into a morass of cold and hunger. In the end, old and too weak to walk, they can no longer even beg. They do not even have a place to lay their dying body, nor a drop of water to moisten their lips. Lost on a roadside far from home, they collapse in misery and die.

One might argue, of course, that such people are the scum of the earth and do not deserve serious consideration. Flourishing and decay, rise and fall are the way of the world, it may be said, and if there are those who are noble, there are also sure to be those who are lowly. Or it may be said that outcasts and beggars have certain roles to play in the country or that they do not deserve pity because their present state is the consequence of their own deeds. Should we take such a stance and pay them no heed, there is no argument to raise in opposition. Even so, we should bewail a situation where, because the Way of swindling runs rampant, people have been brought to ruin because they are old-fashioned, stubbornly honest, or slow-witted. If good people are brought to ruin because they are unable to trick others, this is indeed to be regretted for the state's sake.

In an age of calm and order, all people, down to inconsequential commoners of the lowest rank, should be able to live in peace and security. People without any family to rely on should be few in number, nor should there be large numbers of human scum such as outcasts and beggars. It is said that if a country has many outcasts and beggars, this casts shame on the ruler. I heard that the Divine Lord declared that people should show pity for those without any family to support them, and that this is the foundation of benevolent governance. Is this not to say that benevolent government means to keep the numbers of people without anyone to rely on, outcasts, and beggars to a minimum? In fact, however, at this present time customs have degenerated and the ways of luxury and ease, greed and robbery run rampant, causing people to easily go astray, become ill, and fall into destitution. As a result, many such derelicts have appeared. Is it not essential to correct this absurd situation? Should it be left as it is, circumstances will arise that are beyond the capacity of the state's institutions to control.

At the present time, to be sure, there are the Edo Town Office and the granaries founded during the Kansei era [1789–1801] at the direction of the shogunal government as relief measures for the destitute.

The shogunate carried out an investigation of the expenses of the city blocks of Edo, which had yearly been growing larger and larger, ordered the blocks to reduce their costs, took 70 percent of what was saved, and used it to buy and store unhulled rice. I have heard that the shogunate plans to distribute this rice in times of famine. In the town this arrangement is called the "70 percent."[34] Not only in times of famine but also in ordinary years, the shogunate distributes rice and money saved in this way for the support of destitute people who suffer from chronic illnesses, infants without parents, and those who are too poor to bury their deceased family members. In truth, this policy helps the weak at the expense of the strong and should be termed as an instance of benevolent governance. However, the fact that things cannot be managed without such a policy is a sign that the world is coming closer to the end.

It seems that the shogunal authorities enacted these measures after seeing the situation of the destitute during the Tenmei famine [1782–1788]. Before that time, the shogunate was able to administer Edo without depending on such a policy. Henceforth, should a famine continue for two or three years, the government should be able to provide adequate relief by using the unhulled rice stored in granaries. But such measures will not suffice if people continue to move into the city from the countryside, if it is flooded with the destitute and derelicts, and if, on top of that, disasters such as storms, floods, earthquakes, and fires occur for five or six years in a row. Even under ordinary circumstances such acts of benevolent government are not sufficient, for as I mentioned earlier, destitution leads some to desert their parents or children, while others engage in various evil acts or become derelicts, and not a few die unnatural deaths.

---

34. In 1791, the government ordered the Edo town elders to carry out the policy that Buyō describes here and to set up the Edo Town Office (Machi Kaisho) to manage the funds collected, which the shogunate expanded through additional grants from its coffers. Apart from relief measures, the Edo Town Office was also charged with lending out a portion of the funds at low interest so as to stabilize the finances of the house-owner stratum of townspeople and low-ranking shogunal retainers. The specially designated shogunal purveyors (*kanjōsho goyōtashi*) whom Buyō describes disparagingly earlier in this chapter played a central role in the management of Edo Town Office funds.

The Danger of Serious Riots

Generally speaking, those living in towns are of no use to the realm and the state. These useless people fill both the three major cities and the provinces. Some of them proudly lead luxurious and indolent lives. Some fall into poverty and destitution. Others become heinous rogues. All of them use up huge amounts of rice, grains, and other products. Warriors and farmers have to cover what these people waste. Indeed they are great thieves of the realm and troublesome burdens on its lord, the shogun. Farmers, who exhaust themselves toiling in poverty, eat miscellaneous grains instead of rice. Therefore, they are able to survive by licking sake lees and fermented rice-bran paste or by chewing grass and vines if there is a famine that continues for two or three years. They do not engage in wrongdoing or long for an upheaval to change things. By contrast, when townspeople and idlers encounter impediments to their livelihood for just twenty or thirty days, they begin to perpetrate outrageous acts. Should they not be able to earn a living for one hundred or two hundred days, they are sure to cause serious disturbances. Since they are accustomed to eating only rice, they will be a terrible nuisance for the shogunal government if bad harvests continue for two or three years, causing a shortage of rice. If the government should fail [to supply them with sufficient rice], they are sure to cause a major disturbance, and who can say where the matter will end.

At the time of the Tenmei famine, violent outbursts and riots occurred in Edo, and people broke into the stores of rich merchants and smashed them.[35] Compared with that time, the overall city population has increased, as has the number of the destitute. Further, people have become twice as evil-minded. Those of low status have become strong and bold, while warriors, who are expected to control them, have become weak-kneed. Will it thus not be difficult to [put down a riot, as the government] managed to do in the Tenmei era [1781–1789]? To be sure, since the degree of evil-mindedness has increased, all parties plot against one another, so a riot may not easily occur. But if it does occur, it will be difficult to put it down. The lowly today are so cunning that they are certain to set

---

35. In the fifth month of 1787, attacks on the stores of rice merchants believed to be hoarding grain broke out almost simultaneously in several Edo blocks and continued throughout the city for the next three days.

fires, and they may even use swords and spears. At a time when things are still calm, people should be aware of this likelihood and prepare themselves for it.

The population of the cities is sure to continue to increase further. People's taste for luxury will grow stronger, and destitution will become more severe. Competition among the greedy will be fiercer. People will prey upon one another without a moment's pause. The desire to seize others' property will well up, and heinous ways will flourish. Those who long for disorder and are willing to disturb the world will gain in strength, and the warriors will be exploited by them and fall deeper into poverty. As the warriors become weak-kneed, the military Way will decline. The people's cooking stoves, which should be the felicitous symbols of everlasting peace and order, will continue to decay.[36]

Townspeople and idlers are all worms. During two hundred years of peace, myriad worms have appeared, and ceaselessly they continue to consume the state's wealth. Because of them, high and low in provinces far and near are brought to violate governmental laws, and perverse evil flourishes all the more. They should be swiftly subjugated. If we cannot reduce them in number, will not the state decline and its continuity be endangered? Is there no possibility of restoring the entire realm to a solid and proper condition? There is indeed a way for the government to reform the situation; I will describe it elsewhere.

---

36. The phrase about the populace's cooking stoves alludes to a poem in the *Shin kokinshū* (no. 707), which is in turn based on a story about Emperor Nintoku in the *Kojiki* and *Nihon shoki*:

Viewing country folk, who have been exempted from taxes and are enjoying prosperity, Emperor Nintoku made the following poem:

Having climbed to the top of a tall building, I look out.
How vigorously the smoke rises from the people's cooking stoves!

Chapter 6

PLEASURE DISTRICTS AND PROSTITUTES

It is difficult to depict in words the large buildings in the pleasure quarters, the grand multistoried bordellos, and the splendor of the bedchambers that go with the world's affluence. Nothing today or in the past can compare with such opulence. This is indeed to be expected, given that in these places the wealthy and the debauched throw gold and silver about with abandon. This business is based on luxury.

Today is no different from the past in that the prostitutes have no fixed abode and suffer from being swept along by the current, living lives of shame. On the other hand, their hardships have increased far beyond ancient times, because ours is a world in which people are insincere by disposition. It is an easy enough business, but one without kindness, and the prostitutes' expenses are great. In today's world, the high-ranking courtesans of Yoshiwara known as *tayū* and *chūsan* cannot cover all their expenses unless they take in 500 to 600 *ryō* or as much as 700 to 800 *ryō* a year. The customer, to be sure, must pay the so-called summoning fee for a courtesan, both during the day and at night, but the standard practice is for the brothel owner to take this for himself; this money is not something that the courtesan keeps.[1] Thus, all she thinks about is how she can trick and coax her customers, because she will be unable to survive in the cruel world of prostitution if she cannot acquire the large sums of money needed for her expenses.

---

1. The term *tayū* was used until the middle of the eighteenth century; thereafter the most expensive prostitutes were known as *chūsan*. The "summoning fee" (*agedai*) for a prostitute of this rank was 1 *ryō* 1 *bu*; other expenses involved in being entertained by her (for food, drink, and so on) were in addition to this.

The main street of the Yoshiwara pleasure quarter. High-ranking courtesans can be identified by their elaborate hairdos with many ornaments and the padded trailing skirts that they hold up in front of them. *Edo meisho zue* (1834). National Diet Library Digital Collection.

Right now, bedding and nightclothes cost from 50 to 100 *ryō*, and the hair has to be decorated with over ten tortoiseshell hairpins, which cost 100 to 200 *ryō*. Clothing for each of the four seasons and everything else has to be in the same range. Today 600 or 700 *ryō* is the price of 2,000 bales of rice. A hundred *ryō* for bedding equals 300 bales. Compared with a warrior's means or a farmer's livelihood, this is a huge sum. Even the prostitutes lower in rank cannot afford the things suitable to their position unless they take in a large amount of money. Because the entire world has become accustomed to luxury, and splendid surroundings are indispensable for their line of business, expenses have increased enormously in comparison with the past, and it is difficult to keep up with them. This basically means that the prostitute's mind, which is her only resource, becomes totally absorbed with tactics for gaining more and more. She exerts herself day and night to acquire huge sums of money, knowing that her life depends on it. Selling her natural true feelings places severe hardships on a woman's limited spirit.

In today's world, the customers on whom a prostitute depends truly lack all human feeling. Since prostitutes have to take irresponsible play-boys as their partners in order to appropriate these large amounts of money, they have no other choice but to make up lies and get money by deception. Such lies become their habitual practice, so that everything today's prostitutes say is a falsehood from beginning to end. Since even children know this, deceptions become more and more difficult. All the customers have become skilled at deceiving and tricking courtesans and prostitutes. Because conditions have gotten to the point that prostitutes always lose in matching trickery with trickery, it becomes difficult for them to endure [their lot], and from that we can know the depth of their hardships. Is it not a hard profession that violates a woman's chastity, the core of her femininity that she received from her parents and with which she was endowed by Heaven? One that turns the roots of her feelings into objects for sale and teaches her the technique of ceaselessly competing in trickery with all manner of men day and night, morning and evening? She is the most pitiful of people, to have been born a human being but with nothing to rely on as she struggles futilely only to fall into a profession devoid of humanity.

Brothel Keepers and the Women Who Run Their Brothels

We should not hate prostitutes. Rather, we should hate the brothel keepers who engage in the business of selling women. Theirs is a business that goes against the Way of Heaven and the Way of man. They are not human beings; their behavior is like that of beasts, and it is more than hateful.

In this business, first they buy up someone's beloved child for a small sum of money, then they cage her like a domestic bird inside their house, and finally they force her to deplete her true feelings down to their very roots. They lead hot-blooded youths into debauchery without a care for whether those youths might cause hardships for their parents, be formally expelled from their household, or be separated from their wives and children. They show no restraint in snatching other people's goods; they do not mind doing business with robbers, swindlers, Buddhist priests who have left the world, pariahs, or outcasts; they easily treat muggers and murderers as honored guests; and they turn on all their charm to plunder people of everything they own. When those whom they have plundered fall into destitution, they spare them not the slightest glance, and should one of their victims come to pay a visit, they will not even offer him a cup of tea, in glaring contrast with before. If among those honored guests there is one who breaks the law and becomes the subject of an official investigation, they make a secret report and have him arrested. Sometimes it happens that the brothel keeper himself drives someone to break the law by squeezing him too much, but even at such an extremity, the brothel keeper cares not a fig for the obligations he owes that person and, having stripped him of all he has, lets him become a criminal. This is not the deed of a human being.

The brothel keeper always wears silk crepe with a haori of imported felted, worsted, or grogram wool. Sometimes he wears sateen, batik, or stripes, all in the latest Chinese or Dutch fashion. His wallet, short sword, pipe, tobacco pouch, and accoutrements are delicately inlaid with gold, silver, and coral. He leaves the running of his business to his wife and concubines, while he goes to see plays and sumo. When he goes on sightseeing trips or even pilgrimages, he rides in a palanquin with attendants in tow. At shrines and temples he spends great sums of money in making offerings of canopies, draperies, lanterns, washbasins, votive pictures, and so forth, spreading his reputation as far as possible. Free to do as he pleases, he gathers with his cronies to make a regular practice of drinking parties, wagers on games such as go or shogi, or gambles, treating money lightly. He sets up a second house or retirement cottage where he installs a prostitute he has selected and indulges in carnality to his heart's content. Whether at home or abroad, he satiates himself on tasty food, drink, and sweets. Unlike other people making their way in this world, his business is such that his face is soft, glistening, and plump, and he decorates everything about his person. He throws gold and silver coins lavishly about as though they were pebbles, and no matter where he goes, he is recognizable to anyone with eyes to see as the master of a brothel.

With several tens of prostitutes under his employ, he drives them to deplete the roots of their human feelings in exchange for gold and silver and brings hundreds of customers to financial ruin—or else he makes them into disloyal, unfilial types who indulge in robbery, mugging, and murder while he alone devotes himself to pleasure. The term for brothel keeper, "lost eight," was originally written as "forgotten eight," meaning that such men had forgotten the eight human qualities listed in the *Gozasso*: etiquette, duty, uprightness, shame, filial piety, deference, loyalty, and trustworthiness.² To abandon these eight human feelings means you are not a human being, that is, you have the face of a person and the heart of a beast. If you have even one of these eight qualities, you cannot run a business like this.

Only a woman can accomplish the task of breaking in a prostitute. It is said that old women are particularly good at this. For that reason the brothel keeper employs his wife or concubine, or else the brothel handler or manager—any mature woman of bad disposition—and leaves the matter up to them.³ A woman selfish to the marrow of her bones, greedy, with a bad basic character, and, in particular, a strong disposition, is good at breaking in the women under her care. The more mature such a woman becomes and the further she travels down the road of greed and ill temper, the less she minds the lack of sleep at night or the lack of time to eat, but concentrates on her work. For that reason the brothel keeper builds up his business by making use of his wife or concubine or a woman treated as his daughter, or else he brings a woman over to his side through adultery and such, or ropes in a disreputable old woman. This is his secret. In all the ways of erotic desire, beginning with greeting and seeing off a customer, the entire management cannot be done well except by women. Because a man who tries to get involved will only be in the way, the brothel keeper is merely a façade for the house. Without any work to be done, he indulges in pleasure noon and night.

Because the business will get done even without such a master, a woman can also openly act as the proprietor while her husband stays in the shadows. In some cases he wants to keep his face hidden because he is a criminal. In other cases the wife assumes the role of official proprietor, while the husband acts as her adviser. Sometimes the husband will set up a separate establishment at a different place, and when he makes deals with the shogunal authorities and other people, he receives them at that other place, which he calls his official business office or reception office. You can get away with a lot in this business.

---

2. The pun was based on the characters 亡八 ("lost eight") and 忘八 ("forgotten eight"). Both were read as *bōhachi*, a term that also came to be used of brothel keepers. *Gozasso* (Ch. *Wuzazu*) is a late-Ming encyclopedia, compiled in 1619.

3. Handlers (*yarite*) took care of various aspects of the management of the brothel, particularly supervising the prostitutes; often they were former prostitutes. Managers (*mawashi onna*) typically oversaw matters such as equipment.

The Life of a Prostitute

Now, when these sorts of women break in a prostitute, they ordinarily do not give her much to eat, they check on her occasionally to make sure she curries favor with her customer without nodding off, and at times when she looks sleepy or not very appealing, they scold her severely, all to ensure that she does not become lazy in spirit. Fearful of such scolding, the prostitute treats her customer very well. She ingratiates herself with him by tolerating him even if he gets drunk to the point of making unreasonable demands. Should he become so drunk and overflowing with food and drink that he vomits, she nurses him. She gets some young nobody who knows nothing of obligations even to his parents and brothers to fall in love with her, she plays up to a country bumpkin, and she manages to curry favor with a white-haired old man over twice the age of her father by rubbing, stroking, holding, and helping him along. In this way she has relations with all sorts of customers, sometimes three or five from morning to night, sometimes six or seven. To each she turns a smiling face while hiding her grief in her heart, and she depletes the roots of her feelings in allowing each to do as he pleases.

If she is unable to ingratiate herself with a customer and he becomes unruly, or she is indisposed and does not provide good service, or she is left at loose ends when no customers come, she will surely receive a beating. In all this the old woman is the one who metes out the punishment, with the wife, concubine, or so-called daughter giving the command, and the prostitute is beaten with the force of a demon. When that punishment is not enough to bring her around, she might be denied food for several days, or put to work cleaning the toilets or some other dirty place, or stripped naked, bound with hemp rope, and doused with water. When moistened with water the rope shrinks, causing her to shriek in pain. Sometimes a woman will be tortured to death. Such severe reprimands did not exist in the past.

According to the proverb, a courtesan is a wife for a night or a spouse for a day, which shows that a woman used to have no more than one or two customers a day. With no more than one or two customers, a prostitute could not fail to ingratiate herself with them. Laws against trade in people were issued at the beginning of Tokugawa rule, and it is said that strict regulations stipulated that a prostitute could have only one customer during the day and one at night.⁴ Recently such laws have broken down, and now we have what is known as "revolving," whereby a prostitute has to move from one man to the next so long as there are customers, whether she goes through five or ten. Not only does this force her to work at an occupation unsuited to her natural human feelings, it is too much for her to have so many customers, especially because nobody cares whether she is an adult or still a child. Because she is made to work unreasonably, forced to deal with strong and lusty adults, and tormented regardless whether she is sick or well, she unintentionally stops providing good service and earns a reprimand. This is truly unreasonable and unjust.

Should it appear that she has contracted a disease such as syphilis or exhaustion, she is sold to some other lower-class house of prostitution. This is known as "changing the horse's saddle." The amount of money she has earned up to that point is treated as profit, and she is sold for the full value of the original contract. She might as well be a horse or cow. Even if a prostitute tries to get through life avoiding that sort of misfortune [she will not be able to because] everything has to be splendid, from fashionable ornaments for her hair to the style of her clothing, and she has enormous expenses for fete days.⁵ Seeing that she is a woman, everyone around her tries to take advantage of her, interferes with her, and steals from her. Since she has lots of expenses, which have doubled since times in the past, she can never earn that much money on her own. In today's world, customers think it clever to deceive a prostitute. Because she needs to make a fortune while dealing with such insincere men, it is not easy indeed for her to pull off such a trick.

Regardless of right or wrong, she deceives a youth into spending so much on her that his parents formally expel him from the household, or she gets a man to divorce his wife, or she makes a promise to any num-

---

4. Tokugawa law did prohibit the outright sale of human beings (*jinshin baibai*), as distinguished from long-term indenture; since Buyō does not specify to which level of prostitute he is referring, and regulations governing brothels differed depending on region, it is difficult to know whether his other points have any basis in fact.

5. On fete days (*monbi*), prostitutes were expected to get their patrons to pay for the cost of the extravagant clothes and ornaments they wore on such occasions. On such days a prostitute's fees doubled, but she had to secure her customers in advance. See Seigle, *Yoshiwara*, p. 275.

ber of men to marry them by pledging her troth—presenting them with a written deed, cutting off her finger, or cutting her hair—and she ruins them financially. Monks who have left the world steal alms and utensils from their temple, bringing it to ruin. Warriors are tricked into absconding or even committing suicide, employees embezzle from their masters or run away. Even when her customers do even worse and commit the crimes of robbery, mugging, arson, or murder, she still shows no qualms at all, for it will not do unless they are stripped of everything. Words cannot possibly describe behavior that strips people so completely. From this we can know how the prostitute's hardships have doubled since ancient times, and how they have been led to an entirely evil, perverted Way. Today, there is not a single courtesan of a graceful and modest spirit as in the past; they are all like foxes and tanuki, at heart muggers and murderers who make their way through this cruel world by deceiving people as long as they have life.

Should a woman prove unable to endure this life, go crazy, and try to escape, seeking the help of an accomplice, breaking a window and climbing up to the roof or crawling under the floor, going over the embankment and trying to cross the moat [that demarcate the boundaries of the Yoshiwara], she will be punished when she is discovered. If she succeeds in running away but her hiding place is found and she is reported to the authorities, no censure will attach to her master, whose misconduct was the cause. Rather, the authorities will regard it as a matter between master and servant in which the servant has absconded and will put the blame solely on the runaway, who will be censured and scolded and then returned to her employer with no excuses allowed. Punishment on such occasions is particularly severe. She may be beaten with a bamboo stick until she faints, or be stripped naked, gagged with a hand towel stuffed in her mouth, her four limbs tied together behind her back, and suspended from a crossbeam to be beaten. This is called "stringing up." As I said before, the wife, concubine, or the old woman administers ordinary punishments, but the brothel keeper himself does the beating with the bamboo stick or the stringing up. For the brothel keeper to terrorize by occasionally displaying his authority in this manner is the basis of his business. This is another of his secrets. Throughout the year this is his only duty.

In addition to being punished like this, the prostitute may be sold to some other place. This extends the length of her contract and piles up expenses for legal procedures and other things. Twice the money of her original contract is collected from her, and despite having already endured hardships to no avail, she embarks on new ones. If she becomes ill from exhaustion of mind and body, or if her body is destroyed by syphilis so that she cannot be sold off to become a lower-ranking prostitute, let alone recover, she receives no treatment for her illness and is as much as left to starve to death. Some women die an unnatural death by hanging themselves, throwing themselves into a well, piercing their throat, or chewing off their tongue. In some cases these unnatural deaths are investigated according to the law, but most are covered up. The dead are buried in a temple's collective grave or simply dumped. In some rare cases, they revive when they are being washed prior to burial or at the grave. I have received definite information that this has happened in two or three places. Tormented to an unnatural death before having lived out her natural span of life, left to starve to death, and thought to have already died while she was still alive, once in a great while she started breathing again.

As I said before, the laws instituted at the beginning of Tokugawa rule have become disordered, and benevolent government that shows mercy to the people cannot penetrate this far. This is truly something to be lamented. Because a woman who dies this kind of unnatural death holds a grudge against the house that employed her and curses it, the corpse is bound hand and foot, rolled up in a straw mat, and buried that way as a charm against the curse. This is the secret method employed in this business. It is the way cats and dogs are treated, signifying that she has been turned into a beast. It is said that these extreme measures mean that she cannot curse human beings. It is truly a brutal deed.

Some women are punished by the authorities because they commit arson out of resentment against their severe treatment. Arson occurs fairly frequently, but in most cases [the brothel keepers] see that it is hushed up. [When it does come to light], the authorities punish the arsonist strictly in accordance with the regulations, but they do not take action against the brothel keeper, who, breaking the laws of former times, treated the woman so cruelly that she was unable to endure her suffering and was driven to set the fire. This is a truly heinous situation. Further, since it is the authorities who punish the woman for the clear crime of committing arson, the brothel keeper need not fear retribution [from her resentful spirit]. Instead, as in the expression "to fatten after a fire," the affair ends with its becoming the basis for subsequent prosperity.[6]

Even though a prostitute may be driven to extremity by her misfortune, no one will come to console her. When a kind soul shows her some sympathy, truly her long-cherished only desire, how could she regret to give up her life? Those rare double suicides occur when a couple has mutual sympathy for each other's misfortunes. Indeed, someone who has even the slightest resources will never become a partner in suicide. A man who becomes a partner in a double suicide has no standing of his own. Neither he nor his lover has a reason for living on; they simply are completely overwhelmed. It is not at all the case that they choose death because they are drowning in love. Having talked together about their bad luck, they die because sympathizing with hardships that are impossible to bear has left the man confused. People say that this was decreed by karma, or that it is the sort of thing done by beasts, and no one really takes the matter to heart. There are also women who falsely pretend to be ready to commit double suicide. They claim to endure terrible hardships, and having exhausted all other means of trickery and deceit, they appear ready to die. Nowadays, such devices as cutting one's hair or cutting off a finger have become old-fashioned, and these will not convince a playboy of a woman's seriousness. She has to show herself willing to wager her life. That people go through such contortions shows how much more complicated the cruel world of prostitution has become compared with former times.

The Transformation of an Ordinary Woman into a Prostitute

Even when a prostitute has endured these various hardships, evaded death, and completed her contracted term of service without a hitch, it is still impossible for someone who has fallen into prostitution to return to being an ordinary woman. Because she is ruined for life, it is said that making a woman a prostitute is to send her to hell. There is good reason for this.

When an ordinary woman first becomes a prostitute, her entire body becomes wracked with pain within two to three or five to six months, or

---

6. The phrase refers to someone's business prospering more after a fire than before, whether from receiving condolence money or otherwise.

else it swells with pus, and she truly suffers. In her profession this is called "getting accustomed to the chicken coop." While she is thus afflicted, she is shut up in a separate room and nursed. It is called a coop because it is like the conditions under which a chicken lays an egg. While she goes through these afflictions, her body loses its fat, and she becomes pale, thin, and frail. Thereafter, she is truly a woman of the floating world. Since at the outset she was an ordinary woman, her true feelings were engaged to the utmost every time she had sexual intercourse with men. These feelings penetrated to her bones and produced the afflictions seen above. Once she has gone through such afflictions, she is called an expert in her profession. Thereafter she has been stripped of ordinary human feelings, and no matter how many men she meets, she never loses her heart, nor does she get pregnant.

This transformation from an ordinary woman into a woman of the floating world is an affliction that washes away her natural chastity. There is the saying that "a loyal retainer does not serve two masters, nor does a chaste woman serve two husbands."[7] Not serving two masters has its source in the feeling that arises from a sense of righteousness, and not serving two husbands is the commitment that arises from natural chastity. This natural feeling of commitment leads a woman to cleave to the husband to whom she has entrusted herself and not to allow her heart to be swayed even at the cost of her life, or even if it means putting her parents aside. Prostitution is a profession that makes a woman take countless men as her partners and thereby crushes the natural chastity that ties a woman's body to one man for life. As such it is an atrocious practice impossible for an ordinary human being to perform. If a woman does not go through the transformation described above, she cannot do it. This perverted Way truly contradicts the Way of Heaven. You should know that in our world, this sort of perverted Way is flourishing.

Once she has become a prostitute by going through this transformation, a woman will not bear children, she will not perform manual labor, and she will not do weaving or sewing, laundry, or cooking. In short, she is no good for any kind of normal work in this world. Instead, she becomes a wastrel for her entire life. The only things she knows are how to fix her hair and makeup and to dress herself up every day, to spend her

---

7. This widespread saying can be traced back to Sima Qian's *Historical Records*. See Watson, *Records of the Historian*, p. 34.

time singing and playing the samisen, to ingratiate herself with men, and to melt the hearts of honest men. As a consequence, it is said that whenever a man of means makes a prostitute the woman of his house, all his relatives bewail it as betokening the house's ruin.

For that reason, the only ones who will marry prostitutes are men of low status who do not even have a fixed dwelling place, and [the prostitutes who become their wives] know no security their whole life long and end up as derelicts and drifters. A prostitute who fails even to become the wife of such a lowlife will change her abode from one place to another without ever being able to leave the world of prostitution. As she becomes older she will gradually fall into ever lower categories of prostitute. Even when she has aged she will not be able to do any other work, so she may become what is called a "night hawk," or "everyone's bride,"[8] or end up an outcast or a beggar. Truly, becoming a prostitute is nothing other than falling into hell. As the proverb says, "Seen from the outside it is paradise; once inside it is hell."

The Causes of Prostitution

Various reasons lie behind women's becoming prostitutes. Women from Edo or other similar places are sometimes sold into prostitution because they have fallen into an adulterous relationship. Or they may have been seduced by a young man or abducted by troublemakers and thrown into prostitution after that. Needless to say, there may be cases in which women become prostitutes because of their parents' faithlessness or dissipation. However, it is contrary to the principle of the Way to sell a daughter, to abduct a woman for sale, or to sell a wife or sister. It is particularly inappropriate for a parent to sell a child. If such a thing should happen out of filial piety, as a result of extreme poverty, it is somewhat understandable, but that is rarely the case in today's world. Women are sold owing to the seller's dissipation or lust. It is contrary to the laws of Heaven. If this were times past, such things would have become subject to government sanction.

---

8. "Night hawks" (*yotaka*) and "everyone's brides" (*sōka*) were the lowest class of unlicensed prostitute, streetwalkers who in popular imagery carried with them a rush mat to ply their trade by the side of the road.

However, the prostitutes who come [to Edo] from faraway provinces and remote regions do not do so for the reasons given above. They all come because of their parents' hardships. Out of all the provinces, most come from Etchū, Echigo, and Dewa [in the north]. It is said that when parents are pressed for as little as three or five *ryō*, the sale is done. Sometimes it is at the approach of winter at the time of accounting for taxes. Or perhaps the destitute have somehow managed to get through the end of the year but are unable to hold on until summer through the lean months of spring. Anticipating that the destitute will be unable to survive, brokers called *zegen* go into these regions to buy girls.

Even for people with a city disposition it is not easy to sell a child, and it is a fearful thing to send her to hell for life. In distant provinces and remote regions, where people grow up with constant shortages and live together in hardship, what must it be like to sell off a beloved child raised at your bosom to a faraway place you have never seen, and for parents and child never to see one another again? Even to send a child off for legitimate employment causes a parent anxiety and worry. Think then how it must feel to send a daughter off to work as a prostitute. Indeed she goes bravely off, wholeheartedly determined, knowing that she can save her parents from their suffering. These are the true feelings between parents and child. And that is as it should be. Of course, it is said that in the past, everyone used to point their fingers at a person who had sold a child and shun him as inhumane, even in Etchū and Echigo. The seller too would be ashamed and reluctant to show his face among his fellows. That is not the case anymore, and it is said that the number of people who sell their children has gradually swelled.

Another point is that places where children are sold have little circulation of money. You may think that money is so precious in those places that people will exchange a child for just a meager amount, but the matter is not so simple. In those areas there are extremely wealthy people. As I have said before, the wealthy suck up the soil's abundance, and therefore an excess of destitute people appear; some strangle or drown themselves, and others sell their children. This accords with the principle that peasant uprisings break out in places where there are extremely rich people. Generally speaking, the old customs remain in remote areas: each is strict in his obligations to others, all money accounts are kept honestly, and borrowers try to repay both principal and interest without fail. Therefore, the prosperous gradually become even more prosperous, the destitute even more destitute, and poverty and wealth become sharply divided.

Townspeople are not taxed to the extent that they have to sell their children. They never sell their children out of a sense of obligation to others. Whenever a townsman sells a child, it is for selfish reasons. Even if by some chance a person is driven by destitution to make a sale, destitution in the provinces is different in kind from destitution in urban areas. If a farmer sells his daughter in the fashion described above, the parents do not thereafter live a secure life. They will not even be able to survive at ease for one or two years. Rather, they use the money to compensate for immediate hardships into which they have been cornered. But the daughter who has been sold becomes permanently derelict, and neither parent nor daughter benefits from that sacrifice.

Parents carefully raise their children in hopes that they will grow up to become respectable people and take care of them when they grow old, but they lose this all in trying to gain a moment's respite. By expending the filial piety that she owes her parents in order to overcome a moment's hardship, the daughter ends up separated from them for life, and she too becomes an object abandoned for a lifetime. Generally speaking, it is standard practice for a person who exercises filial piety to receive a reward from the government,[9] and if it is a form of filial piety to vainly abandon one's life for the sake of one's parents, no one should be less overlooked than a woman who has ended up a prostitute for this reason.

Let me say this as an aside. In the three cities and other towns, people often receive rewards for filial piety. In the provinces and the countryside, such rewards are rare. However, the sort of filial people who receive rewards in the cities are so numerous in the provinces and countryside that they cannot be counted. Whether one is close or distant to the authorities makes a big difference in benefit and loss. In general, people of the soil are the ones who perform corvée for public works levied by the shogunate, and for that reason it would be appropriate that the filial among them be the ones to receive prizes. Townspeople and idlers do not pay annual land taxes or perform corvée labor, and thus it is a waste for them to be granted a prize for what they consider to be filial piety. Besides, it is

---

9. The shogunate adopted a policy in the Kansei period (1789–1801) of rewarding and publicizing instances of filial piety. See Sugano, *Kankoku kōgiroku* and *Edo jidai no kōkōmono*.

deplorable to distribute to townspeople and idlers the tribute in taxes that the people of the soil have produced through severe austerities. Yet in the everyday way of things, it is all like this. We ought not to remain indifferent to the fact that farmers sell their children out of an excess of poverty, which results from their devotion to the duty of paying taxes and performing corvée for public works levied by the shogunate.

Kidnappings

In various provinces, kidnappers abduct children at play who have wandered off at places where crowds gather, or at dusk. They take them along to distant provinces and sell them there. Because the eight Kantō provinces are close to the seat of power, kidnappings are few, but they occur frequently beyond the barriers. Such practices are not thoroughly investigated in faraway provinces but are just overlooked.

In the provinces around Kyoto, where children go in groups to make pilgrimages to Ise or travel around a pilgrimage circuit,[10] the kidnappers press their way into the group. They select a good-looking child, trick her into separating from the others, and take her. In these cases, people back home do not know that she has been kidnapped and think that she was hidden by the gods. Some are delighted, some are grieved, others may mark the day of her disappearance as her death day or hold a funeral. I have heard that in Hyūga province, people buy old and young men to make them into servants for farmers. For that reason, there are kidnappers for boys in the provinces around Kyoto. In Hyūga such boys are treated like dogs or cats. They are not even given clothes, straw sandals, or geta to wear and are left to sleep on the ground. What I have heard is so inhumane that words cannot do it justice. Since my subject here is young girls, I will not pursue it further.

Let me describe the situation for a young girl of this sort bought and brought here from the provinces at a young age, particularly one abducted by kidnappers. Dragged to a place where she is totally at a loss, she is handed over to deplorable people, taken to those brothel keepers, and called a trainee from the age of seven or eight. As such she meets

---

10. Leaving home without formal permission to go on pilgrimage (*nukemairi*) became a widespread popular custom in the eighteenth century. In some areas it served as a rite of passage. See Nenzi, "To Ise at All Costs."

with strict discipline, sometimes being punished with large doses of moxa burned on her skin.[11] Always bullied by fellow workers, she wakes up early in the morning, is chilled by the night cold, and is not allowed to sleep during summer nights. Not conscious of night or day, she aimlessly passes the years not knowing whether her parents in the provinces are alive or dead, unable to remember even their names or their province, forgetting how many siblings she has. The only thing she knows is fear of her master's strength and the importance of doing as she is told. Penetrating to her bones, all this becomes her ceaseless torment.

Not having anyone to rely on, she has nowhere else to go, no matter how severely she is punished. Knowing nothing of the ways of the world, she relies on an inhuman house as her sole support and believes she must consider the brutal brothel keeper as important to her as a master or a parent. Her enjoyment consists of seeing a plenitude of exotic and tasty food and admiring the hair ornaments, makeup, and clothes of the elder prostitutes, so she, in her young heart, is encouraged to grow up as quickly as possible and become a good prostitute so as not to be scolded by the master, to have free access to hair and cosmetics, to wear beautiful clothes, and to eat delicious food. Finally she falls into the cruel world of prostitution, and she ends up a being that is no longer human.

Under such circumstances, the parents who struggled to raise her are set aside, she is bound to a man who should have no place in her life, and the fullness of years that should have been devoted to the benefit of her all-important parents end up being plunged into inhuman suffering because of the doings of evil people. The most unfortunate will fall ill, and as I said before, not a few of them die because they have not received treatment. During the previous measles epidemic, it is said that over 120 women died among the prostitutes and trainees employed at Ogiya in the Yoshiwara. From this you should know the lack of care provided for the sick that leads to unnatural deaths.

---

11. Use of moxa involved placing a small wad of dried and powdered mugwort (*mogusa*) on different parts of the body and igniting it. Apart from being widely employed as a therapeutic treatment, moxa was also used to "cure" misbehavior.

Brothel Keepers' Profits and the Spread of Prostitution

Despicable above all is the brothel keeper. For just a small sum, he plunders people's jewels, he has no qualms about employing a man's wife or daughter or kidnapped children, he unjustly uses up the full bloom of their maturity, he turns a person into something no longer human in order to secure an immense profit for himself, and he takes in at least a hundred times more than he has invested. If during her term of service a woman has a good customer who redeems her contract, the brothel keeper collects a huge sum. For a child whom he has bought and raised for 3 to 5 *ryō* cash, or a woman whom he has bought for 30 to 50 *ryō*, he collects all the profit she would have made for him in the future. No other business can compete with his. When a woman who has no special customer to redeem her contract but who has worked for the length of time specified has received advances or goods against her earnings, not even a tiny portion will be forgiven. She will be charged high interest on those advances and goods, which adds months and years to her contract and ends up requiring extra years of service. Should she manage to finish working without problem and without such debts, she will be driven away without the slightest concern for what will become of her. This too leads to lifelong destitution. In any case, every woman who falls into the hands of these brothel keepers loses her life.

Long ago, in the Tenshō years [1573–1592] during Lord Hideyoshi's reign, a survey of the number of courtesans in and around Kyoto showed that there were over 230. It is said that this was seen as insufficient, and thus permission was granted for a total of up to 1,000. At present, there are twenty-seven locations in Kyoto with prostitutes, and they must number at least 20,000. In Osaka, previously there was just Hyōtanmachi, but now there are also Kita no Shinchi, Shimanouchi, Naniwa Shinchi, Horie, and other places, which between them have tens of thousands of prostitutes. Following unification [under Tokugawa rule], prostitutes appeared here and there in the shogun's capital. I have heard that in 1617 a man named Shōji Jin'emon appealed to the authorities and received a grant of land measuring two *chō* square below Fukiya-chō, where for the first time he put up a fence and gathered in one place all the brothels previously scattered here and there. The number of prostitutes at that time was around 300 to 400.

Today, however, the number of prostitutes in Yoshiwara has reached 3,000 to 4,000. In addition, there are said to be 300 to 400 women called geisha.[12] Other places where prostitutes are found are called "restricted areas." They can be found in the six sections of Fukagawa as well as Shinagawa, Senju, Itabashi, Naitō Shinjuku, Kozukappara, Nezu, Yanaka, Ichigaya, Akasaka, Honjo Matsui-chō, [Honjo] Irie-chō, and other places. As the term implies, these are places where prostitution is "restricted," so they all operate under the guise of restaurants, taverns, and tea stands while secretly engaging in prostitution. I do not know how many thousands of women they employ. In the past, the authorities ordered the land seized or confiscated and cleaned the place out whenever secret prostitution was exposed. Such things are rare nowadays. Whenever the secret trade in women is exposed, the facts are twisted this way and that with promises for the future, and a lid is put on the matter so that the houses of prostitution can make a living. For these reasons, "restricted areas" and "secret prostitution" have become only empty words, and houses of prostitution operate openly.

In places like these, men referred to as bosses undertake to solve any problems that may arise in connection with this line of business. They are in constant contact with the lower officials in charge of city administration, whom they are forever sending presents. Whenever something happens that might hinder business, such as a quarrel, murder, arson, robbery, or a prostitute's unnatural death, those bosses immediately send a bribe to get the matter smoothed over. Since the lower officials have been well primed, they readily show favoritism in disposing of the problem. Generally speaking, the bosses distribute gifts more lavishly than do great and small daimyo when seeking some favor, and so the lower officials go out of their way to bend the outcome in a manner beneficial to the bosses. To cover their expenses, the bosses collect money on a monthly basis from the masters of the prostitution houses.

It is said that in Nezu, the amount of money regularly collected by the bosses in this fashion is over one thousand *ryō* a year. The same is true in Yanaka. I am told that in Honjo Irie-chō and other places, it is

---

12. Although geisha had to prostitute themselves in order to survive, that was subsidiary to their main business of entertaining customers with music, dance, and song.

Prostitutes in the Naitō Shinjuku "restricted area" (see map 1) with *zatō* blindmen as customers. *Suichō kōkei* (1779). Waseda University Library.

also over one thousand *ryō*. This is just the basic charge, and when there are emergency expenses, additional funds are collected to cover them. The other places follow suit. By using such large sums of money to manage affairs, the bosses keep all flanks covered, they enjoy fame as gallants, and they indulge in arrogant extravagance. This is what the business of secret prostitution is like today. Flourishing without the slightest hindrance, the business of hidden prostitution is said to employ several hundred women inside the capital, but in the near future such women are more likely to be counted in the tens of thousands. And what must be added to this number are the so-called geisha. They have increased a hundredfold since former times.

What are called entertainers in the townsmen's blocks began to appear around the Hōreki era [1751–1764], and I have heard that according to an Edo census, by An'ei [1772–1781] there were at least 106. Now it is said that there are over 3,800 geisha. These so-called entertainers engage in the same kind of business as prostitutes. With this sort of trend in the three cities, the number of prostitutes all over the country—in places such as Nara, Sakai, Fushimi, Shimonoseki, and Nagasaki, as well as in the post stations throughout the provinces—must be several tens of thousands. Totaling up all the places in Japan, the number must exceed 100,000 women.

At the beginning of Tokugawa rule, prostitution districts were allowed in the three cities and in two or three other places as well. It was strictly forbidden in all other provinces. Two hundred years later, these regulations have collapsed one by one, and now prostitution is everywhere. In truth, good ways are easily abandoned and bad ways readily arise. It does not do to be negligent in running the state. The Way of prostitution goes against the Way of Heaven, it is against principles of the Other World, and it is the prime cause of disaster for the state. The practices of the Honganji sect of Buddhism and prostitution are the two great perversions of our world. They must be reduced. However, since these two great perversions have become ever more popular with the passage of time and have risen up everywhere, will it not be difficult to find a means to eradicate them at the root? This is something that should be considered. There are indeed means to reduce them. I will say more about this later.

KABUKI

The basis for entertainment in today's world is Kabuki. No one now regards Noh, uncostumed Noh dance, Noh music, poetry, linked verse, tea ceremony, and so forth as entertainment. To people, entertainment means koto, samisen, *nagauta* long songs, *jōruri* story chants, danced drama, and so forth. Kabuki is at the root of these entertainments.

Kabuki first originated in *nenbutsu* dances;[13] [it was picked up by outcasts who performed on riverbanks and who] added risqué mingling between men and women; thereafter, praiseworthy elements such as *nenbutsu* dancing were lost, and Kabuki took on the character of being only about relations between men and women. This became the basis for fostering debauchery in our world, and, perhaps around the Kan'ei era

---

13. *Nenbutsu* dances, in which the participants chanted the name of Amida as they danced, accompanied by bells and drums, originated in the Heian period. By the Muromachi period they were widely performed at the Bon festival to welcome the spirits of the dead, to bring the dead to the Buddha, to drive away pestilence, and to pray for rain.

[1624–1644], it was prohibited twice. Nevertheless, as the world under the shogun's rule became more splendid, there was no stopping the spread of entertainments. Kabuki repeatedly made a comeback, so the shogunate forbade men and women to dance together while allowing dances performed by children called "youths." The youths' dances became more and more elaborate until their appearance was like nothing seen before.[14] Today's Kabuki actors are not youths, nor are they outcasts, and even though the name "people of the riverbank" remains, they do not live on riverbanks but in houses just like ordinary people. What distinguishes them is their attitude of superiority to ordinary people and the great amount of money they make.

The Extravagance of Actors and the Theater World

Actors are ranked according to their artistic skill. The less skillful get a salary of about 200 *ryō* a year; the more skilled make over 1,000 *ryō* a year. In addition, they receive vast amounts of money, clothing, curtains, banners, and piles of decorated items known as "heaped presents" from leagues of fan clubs and people referred to as patrons. Nowadays, an actor making 1,000 *ryō* has the income of an official of the 3,000-*koku* stipend level and boasts that he earns the same amount as the magistrate who administers all the townspeople's blocks in Edo.[15] The stage props are splendid, and although it is said that the theaters' facade, railings, gates, and tower are built to resemble the battle camps of old, those battle camps could not possibly have been built as solidly as today's theaters. The decorations for the stages and the boxes for the spectators are splendid and can hardly be compared with the dances performed on turf in former times or with the way people sat on the ground to view them.

The beauty of the costumes is beyond description. When performing the roles of emperor, shogun, or princess, the actors wear clothing of

---

14. In 1629, the shogunate prohibited women from appearing in Kabuki on grounds that it incited licentiousness. This was followed in 1652 by a prohibition of performances by "youths" (*wakashū*) with unshaved forelocks. Subsequently Kabuki actors were supposed to be adult males. See Shively, "Bakufu Versus Kabuki."

15. The town magistrate was expected to be a bannerman holding a stipend of 3,000 *koku*, either by virtue of his original status or through the provision of a *tashidaka* stipend supplement.

brocade embossed with gold, brocade, silk twill, or velvet, sometimes thickly stitched with gold and silver. It is said that the clothing for a man playing a woman's role in a dance play costs as much as 100 *ryō*. Even a real princess would not be able to wear such expensive goods. I have heard that around the Genroku era [1688–1704], the government prohibited even humble cotton costumes on which thin gold and silver foil had been pasted to look like gold-embossed or patterned brocade.

Ever since the Kansei reforms [of 1787–1793], there have been so-called clothing inspections, with officials occasionally coming to make an examination. On that single day, the actors deliberately wear old and plain clothing to pass the inspection. Because the actors have to wear ugly rags when the officials come to inspect their clothing and the officials get in the way of the performance, the latter just peer in for a little while and leave almost immediately. When they come to see the spectacle for their private enjoyment, they bring along their wives and concubines or entertainers and see it through to the end. What was supposed to be an inspection by the public authorities ends up being nothing of the kind, and the actors are left free to indulge in their usual splendor. Things have really gone too far.

The actors' residences too are magnificent; their wives, concubines, and even their children have male and female servants; they live in exceptional splendor, toy with rare Japanese and Chinese objects, and satiate themselves on exotic foods from mountain and sea; their extravagance in everything is beyond compare. Once I went on an excursion to the villa near Fukagawa of a chief actor making five hundred *ryō* a year. First of all, the rock on which I stepped to remove my shoes was granite of the highest quality, five *shaku* in width and over three *ken* long. The main sitting room looked like the study in a daimyo's palace with its double sliding cedar doors and paper sliding doors covered with gold leaf, all decorated with famous paintings and pictures of popular places done by renowned artists. The garden contained countless species of trees and flowers. Here and there were unusual rocks, stone lanterns, hand-washing basins, silver tubs, and silver pitchers. From the accoutrements of the sitting room to the enclosure for exotic foreign birds, nothing was commonplace. Whether from past or present, everything was a rarity.

When I praised the house as marvelous, a wonder to behold, I was told that it was supposed to have been the private residence of a certain daimyo but that it did not suit his taste. It had been unused until this actor inquired about it and fixed it up, even though it was out of keeping with his status. Although he spoke with fake modesty, saying that he had not deliberately sought such splendor, in his heart he was proud to have a dwelling equal to a daimyo's. Detestable words! There is a rumor that a villa belonging to one of his colleagues is of the same style and even more splendid.

Had anyone put on such an appearance in the past, he would have been censured. Nothing like that happens today. Even if the government tries to take measures, people find some way or other to get around them. When in fact there is an inspection, someone stealthily brings a warning beforehand. On that occasion, the stones will be buried in sand or wrapped in rough straw mats; as a temporary expedient paper will be hung in the sitting room to cover the wood; and the officials will do nothing. In contrast, a poor, honest, and long-suffering person is immediately arrested, tied up, and ends his life in jail for having committed some slight wrong. The gap between those who are in tune with the times and receive favorable treatment and those who do not is as great as that between Heaven and Earth.

Owing to this sort of treatment, actors have become exceedingly arrogant in disposition. On the surface they have not yet been able to lose the label "people of the riverbank," so when out and about they fawn and flatter, but in their hearts they feel like daimyo. Even though they receive money for displaying their art, they are just as arrogant as a daimyo, and they are not in the least bit thankful. They take what they receive as no more than their due. They do not make the slightest gesture of gratitude, nor do they feel in the least bit thankful. Worse, they take on an air of despising money while receiving so much of it that they throw it around heedlessly.

A few years ago, an actor playing female roles named Segawa Kikunojō Rokō was invited by a province-holding daimyo to dance the piece called "Dōjōji."[16] As a reward he was sent a bundle containing 100 *ryō* in gold. The official in charge of this transaction was a samurai from that distant province who had come to Edo on alternate attendance, and he

---

16. Buyō presumably refers here to Segawa Kikunojō III (1751–1810), one of whose most famous roles was in the dance play *Dōjōji*. Kikunojō III was such an accomplished and popular performer that he served as troupe chief, something unusual for an actor specializing in female roles.

was extremely surprised when told to hand over such a large sum to such a person. Yet Kikunojō did not show much appreciation at all. The official expected that perhaps he did not know it was 100 *ryō* and had mistaken it for just a small sum, and so he said to Kikunojō, "You have received as much as 100 *ryō* for work that did not take even an hour, so how happy you must be." "I am indeed delighted," Kikunojō replied, "but I myself have given more to others." The country samurai's face turned red with embarrassment, and he was humbled by the temperament of a chief performer who could really be called a 1,000 *ryō* actor.

After that, Kikunojō took the bundle back to his house and gathered together the musicians who had accompanied him, his regular staff, and others who had assisted. "Because all of you worked so diligently today I could perform even better than usual, and I am all the more delighted and satisfied. I am giving you this as a token of my appreciation." He took out the 100 *ryō*, added another 100 *ryō* to it, and divided the total of 200 *ryō* among them. He did this because he could not be satisfied with simply having humiliated that country samurai and felt that he had to match words with deeds. From this one can understand the arrogant disposition of the "people of the riverbank" and the derisive way they treat money. Having become ever more prideful and arrogant, actors visit the three cities and other urban centers. Wherever they go, they attract fans and idolizers; they receive mountains of money; they suffer not the slightest setbacks, but wander around floating on splendor.

The Theater's Influence on Women

Generally speaking, townspeople and idlers really like these Kabuki actors, though this is less true of warrior households. In particular, their wives and daughters are deeply infatuated and besotted, and they all try to ingratiate themselves with the actors. Pulled along by their wives' and daughters' infatuation, men too become fans. Women of the floating world who are entertainers and dancers see Kabuki as the basis of their art, and they attach themselves to the actors, respecting them as masters and teachers. The actors then make these women their underlings and lose themselves in sexual pursuits to their heart's delight. Sometimes they select a beautiful woman to become their wife or concubine. They have wives and concubines as it suits them in the three cities and everywhere else, and with debauchery as their usual state, they indulge in extravagance beyond all compare. Pleasure for women and girls in today's cities begins and ends with Kabuki; Kabuki actors are the only people who appeal to them, and they think about nothing else. Consequently, it is no longer the case today that plays imitate life; rather, plays come first and life imitates plays.

In popular parlance, encountering something really splendid, like a prostitute all decked out in her finery, is said to be comparable to "watching a play." The way to praise the figure of a man of high rank and status is to say it is like seeing such and such actor. Even the shogun's awesome authority or the imposing dignity of a magistrate's office or other offices and government officials are likened to what is seen in dramas; such has become a common mode of speech. The way things are dyed for the stage and stage styles of clothing become popular fashions. Likewise, actors' argot becomes common speech. Women and girls relish all this. It is often said that there are no men who hate girls and no women who hate plays, and indeed a woman who has once seen a play becomes so besotted that she would exchange eating three meals a day for seeing it again. When young women go to the theater, they are completely swept away. They forget their parents and husbands, they imitate the actors in their hairstyles and the way they present themselves in face and form, and [the theater] becomes their standard point of reference.

Actors use every possible mode of lascivious pleasure to capture women's hearts and sweep them away. Many plays involve amorous encounters or people going mad with longing in their relations with the other sex; in others, men and women break the bonds of loyalty, abandon filial piety, drown in pleasure, and throw away their lives in crimes of sexual passion; or else there is jealousy between wives and concubines, two sisters competing for the love of one man, or a fierce contest over one beautiful woman, and so forth, all artfully designed to melt women's hearts. Among the actors, father and son, older and younger brothers perform their risqué arts together. In some cases, the father becomes the husband and the son his wife or concubine. Sometimes they are divided by playing the roles of enemies, or they perform roles in which parent and child or elder and younger brother strike or even kill each other. From this we can know how different such performances are from the earlier dances in which people chanted the name of Amida and preached Buddhist doctrine!

Actors and audience at a Kabuki play. Candles illuminate the night performance. *Satemo baketari kitsune tsūjin* (1780). National Diet Library Digital Collection.

Women are of shallow understanding and fickle, so they in particular are easily swayed by self-indulgence and cruelty. When women see a play depicting someone falling in love with a man, they imitate it. Even though they should be directing their love to the master or husband on whom they depend, instead they adore the actor before their eyes who plays the male role, and they hate the actor who plays the female role. For that reason, actors playing female roles have few fans among women and girls. One way or another, women are easily moved by what they see. Even when they say they believe in the Buddha, they do not practice the Buddhist precepts but are simply infatuated with the Buddha. Worse, at some point their adoration of the Buddha is such that they deviate from the essence of Buddhism and wander into side paths. It is said that even Śākyamuni experienced difficulty in leading women to enlightenment. Since women who say they are praying to the Buddha in fact tend to become infatuated with the preacher, how much more likely are they to have their heart snatched when they fall in love with an actor in a theatrical performance.

When her love becomes intense, a woman will summon the actor to a theater teahouse, a restaurant, or some other place and busy herself entertaining him at a banquet. She may bring him along on an excursion or even summon him for a visit to her residence and give him huge amounts of presents. She might even run away to the actor's lodging and give herself over to becoming his wife or concubine. Recently, this fashion has spread even to women in warrior houses, and, as is suggested by the saying "Women's quarters fill with chatter about the stage as soon as everyone gets up in the morning," they are fixated on gossip about the theater. They put their favorite actor's crest on their clothing, combs, hairpins, and other accessories; they are obsessed about him as though he were their master or husband; and they secretly send him gifts. A wife may know nothing about the name of her husband's superiors or the pedigree of his house, but she is well versed in the Kabuki actors' dwelling places, house names, whose children they are, and how old they are.

It is, of course, true that among men, too, there are decadent sorts who indulge themselves with courtesans and geisha. Men who enjoy taking pleasure with women tend to like plays as well. They take their favorite women along to see the spectacle; share delicious food such as sake, savory tidbits, sweets, and rice cakes with them; squeeze five or six men and women into a small theater box measuring just six *shaku* square, in intimate proximity; and spend an extravagant amount worth five, ten, or even twenty bales of rice inside that tiny space in just one day. It is said that in former times people who went to see spectacles carried about a hundred to two hundred coppers worth of money, or about two to three *shō* of rice.[17] Today, even if you are so stingy and behave in such an unsightly manner that people point fingers behind your back, you cannot watch the spectacle from a box for anything less than one and a half *ryō*. This is equivalent to more than three bales of rice. In anything to do with women, [men] do not stint on money or bargain about the price but throw money around, so the circumstances are such that prices simply go up at will.

Seeing sumo is cheap because no women are involved, food and drink are not so extravagant, and expenses are few. Furthermore, tournaments are held only twice a year in spring and fall on ten days of fine weather, and with only a total of twenty days in the course of a year, spectators are few. This too is something that flourished in the past, but business has slackened off over the years. Sumo itself has gradually

17. One *shō* would be roughly 0.03 bales.

declined, and there are no wrestlers like those of former times. Plays, in contrast, are performed throughout the year at a number of places, and every day spectators flock to see them. Above all, sumo is a sport in which victory and defeat are immediately apparent, making the sight exhilarating. Plays are decadent and cruel, so that they contaminate those who see them. Right now, no one likes clarity; in one way or another people prefer something sexy.

From this you can tell that people's dispositions have changed from what they were in the past. This invites Heaven's displeasure. Already heavenly disasters have occasionally befallen places that flourish by catering to self-indulgence and cruelty. Blocks with theaters and teahouses or with prostitution suffer fires two or three times within each decade. But because they are popular places, they soon return to business as usual and suffer no lasting ill effects. Each time they are burned out, they are immediately rebuilt even better than before. One should be very careful of places that prosper by catering to the evil ways of the times. It does not do to be negligent.

Since the theater holds sway in this way, plays based on those of the three cities are popular in provincial castle towns and cities as well. It is said that theaters are permitted only in the three cities and strictly forbidden everywhere else. These laws have broken down, and nowadays the youth groups in villages and rural towns imitate plays under the name of "festival dramas." Even youths so poor that their parents have had to seek work in other provinces are lured into participating, and the sons of the wealthy too are swept along and squander an immense amount. The festivals that in former times took place at sites for *kagura* dances have disappeared, and the classical rural ways of the people of the soil, such as the Bon dance and the harvest dance, are no longer performed.[18] Everything follows the trend of theatrical performances, luxury, and debauchery just like in urban areas. Everything the gods hate goes into festivals.

---

18. Sacred dances performed to invoke the gods and then entertain them, *kagura* have deep roots in Japanese history and folk religion. Bon dances are performed in midsummer at the time of the annual rites to deceased family members. On the influence of the theater on *kagura* and festivals, see Breen and ᴼuwen, *New History of Shinto*, pp. 158–64, and on the increasingly "festive" ¯ter of shrine festivals in the decades around 1800, see pp. 98–106.

Entertainments Driven by Lust

Prostitution has become popular in the three cities and also in the provinces, and it captures men's hearts. Likewise, theatrical performances have become popular in the provinces and outlying areas and capture women's hearts. With the appearance of these tools to lure men's and women's hearts and lead them astray, disorder has arisen. All the songs that at present are sung with samisen originated in these theatrical performances, and they take lust as their essence. They lure men and women into debauchery.

Popular dramas today are such that parents and children cannot sit side by side to watch them. Up to seventy or eighty years ago, plays might show dalliances between men and women, but according to what I hear, the characters would do no more than nestle their cheeks together, and if the man took the woman's hand, she would just hide her face in her sleeve. Even with that, I have heard that the old people of that age would get angry and call such behavior outrageous. Women too were circumspect and would blush when watching the scene from *Treasury of Loyal Retainers* when Yuranosuke holds Okaru to lift her down off the ladder.[19] Nowadays, men and women are shown in outright copulation. Women in the audience take it in their stride without the slightest blush. Things have really fallen into disarray.

This style has become fashionable today, and if things do not resemble theatrical performances in one way or another, they will not find favor with people. Consequently, there are many people who get through the world by imitating the deportment of Kabuki actors and mimicking their voices. They lead dissolute lives as the favorites of pleasure-seekers and receive lots of presents, or they deceive a woman who loves the stage. Here and there in the blocks of the city are so-called vaudeville stages where interpreters of military tales, imitators of Kabuki, shadow plays, impersonators, magicians, tellers of comic stories, and so forth incorporate the style of the theater and mimic actors' voices. Female artists as well as singers of story chants collect an audience and take their coppers. If the destitute or the poor living in the back alleys have a daughter, they hope she will work as a concubine or a kept woman, or as an entertainer

---

19. In this scene, Yuranosuke asserts that he can see up Okaru's skirt to her private parts; see Takeda, Miyoshi, and Namiki, *Chūshingura*, p. 117.

or dancer, and they encourage her to learn the entertainment arts seen in theatrical performances.

Consequently, actors are worshipped as though they were the main object of veneration at a temple. Parents look to them as teachers of the arts who will enable their daughter to rise in the world, and if the daughter does succeed, this will enable the parents to get through life in comfort. Since they depend on the actors as their source of strength, they believe theatrical performances to be the best thing in the world, and they are truly grateful to the actors. Out of an excess of affection, wealthy townspeople have their daughters learn dance dramas, decorate their daughters' clothing with the same sort of gold-embossed and other brocade as theater actors, put on plays at home, and sometimes invite actors and lavish food and drink on them. They employ a troupe of musicians for their daughters and take them all along for flower viewing or sightseeing or to a villa to put on dance dramas for others to watch. The daughter performs in dances that show risqué behavior between men and women; that set aside loyalty, filial piety, and social obligations; and that depict lovers drowning in lust or men and women copulating and throwing their lives away out of sexual desire. When a daughter becomes skilled at performing such dances, her parents, grandparents, and other relatives all gather in delight to watch her and praise her to the skies.

Restraint in sexual desire is absolutely the most important thing in the relations between parents and children and between siblings, and desire should not show on one's face at all. Restraint is the norm for human beings; sexual desire should be kept secret from the world. For family members to see a girl perform in these dances and to take delight in this and praise her for it is therefore another example of the truly deplorable disposition characteristic of today's world. This type of behavior has become more and more prevalent among warriors as well, and there are many who have their daughters learn Kabuki dance. They even perform the dances themselves. They have their wives and concubines take up the samisen, hand drum, or big drum to accompany the singing, they make special friends with people of lowly origins, and they lead a dissipated life.

It is said that long ago the daimyo Imagawa Ujizane loved dance, and the young samurai in his household gave their all to have beautiful dance costumes. Poor warriors sold their military equipment to procure the necessary robes. It pained the people of the [Tokugawa] house to hear of this, and they took it as a sign that in the Imagawa house, the military Way was in decline.[20] What was known as dance at that time was the Bon dance, performed to the accompaniment of a large drum with no other instruments. Costumes were not fancy, and there was no risqué behavior between men and women. Even so, for a military establishment this was enough to make the Tokugawa give up on them.

Today, daimyo large and small employ scores of young and beautiful girls as dancers, musicians, and the like to put on their own theatrical performances as a debauched diversion. These warriors are clumsy at drawing their large sword, but they are highly skilled and knowledgeable regarding gestures in dance and modes of performance in artistic circles, and they are particularly well versed in the ways to pluck a samisen and sing. The samurai below them let their daughters dance while father, mother, and sisters sing and play music. Such aspirations have filled even the military houses; the townspeople and idlers carry on all the more shamelessly. These practices have spread through the provinces out to the countryside and have fostered extravagance and debauchery.

There is no limit to the sorts of spectacles that imitate the theater, such as puppet theater, acrobatics, mechanical dolls, and peep shows, and they have all come to use splendid costumes. In particular, various spectacles have appeared in recent years that are lavish operations with huge costs, as much as one thousand to two thousand *ryō*. They take in money by startling the eye and seizing one's attention. All of these are designed to intoxicate people, and they are tools for destroying the Way of loyalty and filial piety. It is the complete opposite of the artistic forms of the past, which offered encouragement to promote good and chastise evil. Beginning with theatrical performances, entertainment arts and spectacles have gradually increased, and today who knows how many tens of thousands of people make their living in this fashion. They all become the idlers of the realm, not paying taxes and not working at corvée labor. Instead, they indulge in luxury and pride to their heart's

---

20. The Imagawa were major feudal lords in the medieval period. Ieyasu spent some years of his childhood as a hostage of the Imagawa and broke with them after they were defeated by Oda Nobunaga in 1560. Imagawa Ujizane (1538–1614) was subsequently driven from one domain to another. He spent much time in Kyoto honing his skills at poetry and football (*kemari*) and leading what Buyō would call a dissipated life.

content and waste resources. What is more, they disrupt the customs of high and low, and at their worst they promote lust. Above all, they become a tremendous hindrance to the state in years of famine or upheaval. This is likely to become more prevalent by the day. They must be stopped.

Recently, a great many writers of light fiction have appeared,[21] and they too lead people's hearts astray. They twist and bend the true accounts and correct explanations of the past, mix in all sorts of false reports, and change the story to suit the taste of today's people. Their chief device is to put relations between men and women at the center. They mix in what is popular in the theater districts and pleasure quarters, patch in ghosts and other apparitions, and turn old-time customs and plots that once promoted the principles of loyalty and filial piety into a joke. This is a device that misleads people and promotes debauchery. These books of light fiction have become widely popular, and few people buy the true Confucian classics that have come down from ancient times or other regular books, even if these are available at a discount. Even though the volumes of light fiction are more expensive than the Confucian classics, many people buy them; new printings appear every year, and they circulate throughout the provinces. They are all intended to please women.

And then there are the erotic prints and amusing illustrations that depict men and women copulating, which appear in various editions with new printings every year. These too are elaborately colored with gold and silver leaf. Sometimes they are displayed at the front of townspeople's shops. They even become playthings enjoyed together by parents, children, and siblings with no sign of distaste. When women collect these pictures, they say they are magical devices that make clothes multiply; they place them between their clothes in trunks and sets of drawers and hand them down from mother to daughter. The popularity of such prints promotes lasciviousness throughout this world. Occasionally, the government issues directives banning them, but this does not put a stop to them; instead, they spread further. Of course, the authorities do nothing about theatrical performances that depict actual copulation when portraying risqué relations between men and women, and even though the number of prostitutes has grown ever larger, the au-

---

21. Buyō speaks here of *gesaku*, a term subsuming various forms of fiction that became popular from the late eighteenth century onward.

thorities show no concern. Compared with these, pictures and the like are trifles. The main evil in all of this is ignored by the authorities, so one can hardly expect them to take action against this lesser evil.

Restaurants

Today's fashions and customs have led to debauched people and entertainers growing ever more numerous and sinking ever deeper into debauchery. As a consequence, places of entertainment and restaurants have appeared everywhere, and they all flourish. Because the government previously did not allow extravagance at restaurants, these establishments outwardly call themselves by plain names such as tavern or sake shop, whereas inside one may find an extraordinary appearance, totally out of line with such appellations.[22] The construction, furnishings, carvings, sliding doors with decorative paper designs, tea pavilions, bathhouses, large stone lanterns, planted trees, and other curious objects are all of the most lavish style, no different from the residence of someone of high rank and status. Sometimes a concubine's dwelling, called a villa or retirement house, is set up in an attractive setting to which customers are invited. There high-quality objects are used, and the rare and delicious dishes served are all superior to a banquet put on by persons of high rank.

Now, the prosperity of these restaurants is such that should ten or twenty friends go to one of them in a group without advance warning and want expensive dishes costing five to ten *ryō*, they have no problem at all preparing them at once. Ten *ryō* today is the price of over thirty bales of rice. The restaurants lay in stock every day and make preparations sufficient to deal with large groups of customers without the least hitch, no matter how many may come. Places like this can be found throughout Edo. Restaurants also run catering services that will provide servings to order anywhere, for no matter how many hundreds of people, as soon as someone comes with the order. From this one can gauge the prosperity of these businesses, and the great number of people who live in luxury. When they have created such a splendid establishment

---

22. Taverns (*niuriya*) and sake shops (*sakaya*) were in principle places where food was presented casually or was sold to be taken out rather than proper restaurants with private dining rooms.

preparing food day after day, restaurants then employ attractive women. They keep any number of beautiful girls, whom they call "adopted daughters," and have them serve at banquets, making them into playthings freely available for selfish desire. No one among the general populace seems to find this distasteful!

People who go to such places are of course the wealthy, but even people whose pocketbooks are light put on a big show and pretend they have more than enough money. People who are usually stingy and pay not the slightest attention even to their relatives' hardships throw their money away as soon as they become caught up in the current, and they never ask if the price is high or low but pay as much as it takes. For this reason, profits in the entertainment business are enormous. By not selling on credit, this business never suffers losses, and it succeeds by pleasing people.

Because restaurants and entertainers succeed by pleasing the world at large and enjoy good fortune, they suffer no constraints on their livelihood or other worries. From dawn to dusk they entertain cheerfully both the highborn and the base. Showing no deference to those of high status, they consider samurai customers with light pocketbooks to be a particular nuisance and treat them roughly, while they respect even a baseborn man as an important guest if he has lots of money. Far removed from a normal disposition and free from any sense of duty, they get through the world by cajoling and softening people up. To be sure, just as customers are divided into three grades of top, middle, and low, restaurants too are of high, middle, or low quality. They have appeared everywhere in the city blocks, and even low-quality restaurants flourish thanks to today's taste for luxury in food. Large numbers of eel shops, dessert shops, sweets shops, taverns, and others have appeared, and countless food businesses prosper at every corner. Delicious tastes from land and sea are collected at such decadent and outrageous places, and more than enough idlers eat as much as they please. This should be seen as a most untoward development.

There are also places called pleasure-boat inns on the riverbanks; these operate large, small, or two-person roofed pleasure boats that transport extravagant people to enjoy entertainment spots on the cool of the river. They employ numbers of boat captains. These captains are not the ones who do the work of rowing the boat; rather, they wear the clothes of a man of leisure and keep the guests company. When they reach the place of entertainment, the captain bargains for everything just like a jester and receives payment in return. Sometimes, the master of the pleasure-boat inn builds a two-story building just like a restaurant, a structure that does not conform to what the lodging for a boat master should look like, with an alcove and elaborate shelves hung with hanging scrolls painted by Chinese-style poets and artists popular in today's world. When courtesans and entertainers come along to accompany customers to their destination or welcome them back, the boathouse master provides a banquet; for a fee, he will even arrange rooms for secret assignations.

Just as nowadays many people have come to ride in palanquins, so too has it become quite ordinary for baseborn people and even lowly employees such as clerks from merchant houses to ride in boats. They too bring courtesans and entertainers along with them and hold banquets or enjoy other amusements on the boats. Tea stands have also appeared throughout the city, and they have taken on a splendid appearance. Customers who sit down just to enjoy a cup of tea are deemed the lowest-class customers, so tea stands prefer to employ girls and beautiful women as waitresses and to provide space for banquets. In this fashion, the restaurants, boathouses, and tea stands have come to resemble brothels. Some of them engage in secret prostitution, and places where men and women can meet are nothing out of the ordinary.

Kept Women

Kept women have become widely popular in recent years, and they have appeared in great numbers throughout the city's blocks and back alleys. From wealthy townsmen to farmers, priests, and other idlers, and even down to clerks and samurai servants, somehow they all keep a woman. A lot of warriors do so as well, but because samurai have limited assets, they cannot keep a woman for long. For the most part, this is something done by townsmen, idlers, and priests. I know an extremely wealthy townsman who has nine kept women. All of them are of a beauty rarely seen in this world. I have heard that there are many men who keep two or three.

Consequently, the lowest-ranking townsmen train their daughters, if they have any, in the performing arts; if they do not have a daughter, they adopt one, hoping to make her into an attractive young woman. Even a poverty-stricken man will have his daughter take lessons in singing story chants, samisen, Kabuki-style dance, hand drum, large drum, or *kokyū*. Unable to wait all the years it takes for her to grow up, he rushes to make her an entertainer or else a kept woman while she is still immature. The daughter, too, has long been prepared for this and prays that she will catch someone's favor and live in ease and comfort. She chooses a good man to whom to entrust herself, and calls it taking a master. What she means by a "good man" is not someone of high status or good looks. It makes no difference to her whether he is baseborn, ugly, or old, and she does not look into the man's background to see if he is a monk, temple priest, pariah, or outcast; she reveres any man with lots of money as a good man. In some cases, kept women get pregnant and collect huge sums for the birth, but at other times, if they receive only a small allocation, they will act like inhuman monsters and abort the fetus.

In former times, people even regarded it as shameful to send a daughter as a concubine to a daimyo or other warrior house. People criticized them, and their relatives thought it to be abhorrent, sometimes to the extent of cutting off relations with them. Even today, these old ways remain in a few warrior houses, and when it becomes known that the daughter of a retainer has gone to work as a concubine, the family will be dispossessed of retainer status or receive some other form of censure. In most cases, however, no action of this sort is taken. Consequently, the daughters of retainers may put on a front of going out on regular service, but secretly they are going as a concubine. When worse comes to worst, retainers rely on a friendly townsman and send their daughters out to become unauthorized prostitutes, entertainers, or a townsman's kept woman.

Previously, everyone down to the lowest of the baseborn despised living on love, but now it has become a usual thing. Now that it has gotten to the point that even samurai secretly get by thanks to a daughter, and thanks to the townspeople—how much more is it so for the hordes of baseborn. All regard it as a great accomplishment to get such work. Daughters, too, consider it something of which to boast, outsiders are envious, and parents brag about their attractive daughters, proud of the good impression it makes on others. It even happens that people willingly lend clothing and money to parents with such a daughter. For that reason, everyone hates boys and likes girls, and a daughter with a pleasing face becomes the treasure of the entire family, relatives and all.

People today envy parents with girls because they would like to have a daughter whom they can turn into a diversion for baseborn townsmen, farmers, and men of even lower standing. In today's world, concubines of daimyo large and small do not get a good allowance. Therefore, such concubines often reckon that it would be better for their parents' sake if they became an entertainer or a kept woman. Even when they are so lucky as to be favored by the lord himself, they take their leave without good reason and choose to enter into that kind of business. From this one can tell how much this world has declined, and how debased people's dispositions have become. For a girl to become someone's plaything, right before her mother's and father's eyes—is this not behavior far removed from proper human relations?

Among kept women there are gradations, from superior to inferior. There are pretty girls, beautiful women, and mature women. There are also couples who collude to hide the husband so the woman can appear to be a widow and draw in a man, and women who have two or three men. Indeed, payment is based on the woman's grade. Even though monthly allotments and the like vary depending on the individual, all these women get sufficient income to live a life of pleasure day and night. Right now, nothing can compare to such comfort. For the baseborn nothing could be better than this.

Let me describe the circumstances for a superior kept woman. First, she is installed in a splendid dwelling with male and female servants. In the morning she gets up as late as she pleases and takes a bath, scrubbing herself from her face to her toenails. A hairdresser comes to fix her hair, and she makes herself up with red and white powder. She always eats delicious food three times a day, as well as snacking on various dishes in between. Waiting for her master constitutes her entire day's work; she has no other. When the man comes, they sit face-to-face while she plays the samisen and sings songs. She satiates herself on banquets and amusements. Her mother, father, and sisters are at her side, preparing sake and food, changing her clothes, and assisting in the bedchamber. Whenever she goes to plays or spectacles, makes a pilgrimage, goes sightseeing, or takes a boat to enjoy the river's coolness, her hair ornaments and clothing are gorgeous. Sometimes she will bring along a performer who has struck her fancy, at other times she has her mother come along as though her mother were her attendant, and she makes her way through the world by trading in the risqué games played by men and women.

Through her own capacity the daughter takes care of mother, father, and siblings, and because she has unlimited access to delicious food and clothing for them, as a matter of course she becomes proud and willful. Because her parents no longer have to live through endless hardships but enjoy a life of comfort thanks to their daughter's fortune, over time they come to see her as their master, and in the end the distinction between parent and child disappears. The loss of proper circumspection for each other is worse than in the case of prostitutes, for a prostitute does not ply her trade with her parents next to her. By contrast, these parents do not just look on from the side as the kept woman, their daughter, goes mad for a man, and tightly wraps herself around him as a vine twines itself around a tree so as to melt his heart and wheedle him into giving her clothing, hair accessories, and money. No, they even assist in the bedroom by placing the pillows next to each other. When the man comes or goes, they deferentially arrange his sandals for him, and they do everything to humor him. Since long ago, prostitutes have been said to be animals. Today, some engage in an enterprise even more despicable than that of those beasts called prostitutes.

In today's world, both men and women have acquired the disposition of such beasts. They are not ashamed of their greed and lust. Even old men with white hair keep women and toy with girls the same age as their grandchildren, while women care nothing for character or age but fawn only on men with money. Both in Edo and in other areas where numerous people live in close proximity to one another and struggle to earn a livelihood, there are inequalities between poverty and wealth. Some people pursue greed and become rich, indulge in luxury and lust to their heart's content, and commit inhuman acts. Others who are poor but who have a single daughter not only can live comfortably, by depending on their daughter they can obtain plenty of hair accessories, clothing, and the like; therefore, everyone follows their suit and ends up committing acts beyond the boundaries of proper human behavior. This arises from being unable to bear poverty and withstand the temptations of wealth; what is to be resented is this trend of the times.

The usual yearly wage for a servant woman is between two and three *ryō* a year. Thus, even if she works for a lifetime and saves several decades' worth of wages, it would be difficult for her to get even one expensive object [such as a tortoiseshell hairpin]. To be sure, today's servant women are adorned with luxurious items. When the wife of a small-scale warrior goes out, the servant women who accompany her have exactly the same appearance [as she has]. The tortoiseshell pins on their heads, the silk crepe of their clothing, the sandals with thongs in velvet or felted wool are all the same, to the extent that mistress and servant are indistinguishable. Since none of this can be accomplished on a servant's measly wage, it has to be supplemented by her parents. In former times, girls sent their parents part of their wages to help them get through life, but now the parents send their daughter a portion of what they can scrabble together through toil and hardship so that she can outfit herself properly.[23] When a woman works as an ordinary maid in this fashion, her parents undergo hardships and the daughter does so too, but to no avail. Even though wages for servant women have doubled from what they used to be, they still do not suffice, and few women work as servants. Only girls whose parents are extraordinarily honest, rigid, and old-fashioned or who are so ungainly that they are useless for love do this kind of work. If a girl's nose is even a little bit shapely, her parents polish her up and send her out to be a performer or a kept woman or to work in a restaurant or tea stand.

If she should meet with this good fortune, she does not have to work at weaving, sewing, or cooking, and she can ride in a palanquin or on a boat to see spectacles or go sightseeing. In recent years, many hairdressers for women have appeared, and she can have them do her hair; she can lie at ease and have a massage, and it is truly as though she were living in a dream. Furthermore, many men want to marry women who have experience in this kind of love work. Since these women can marry easily, many get their husbands to put out money to support their parents, to provide their trousseau, or even to supply a lifelong allowance for their parents. In any case, such women get along the best from beginning to end. For baseborn people to sell their love so as to live at ease, or for them to get caught up in the greed that is part of the practice of love, is an evil custom that was rare until recently. Such customs have arisen because all things have come to be based on prostitution and the theater.

---

23. Not a few wealthy Edo townsmen and farmers from nearby areas sent their daughters to work for a period of time as maids in the women's quarters of upper-level bannermen, daimyo compounds, or Edo Castle with the expectation that they would acquire training in good manners. Such families often paid a substantial amount to provide their daughters with appropriate clothes and such. See Ōguchi, *Josei no iru kinsei*, pp. 169–72; Masuda, "Yoshino Michi no shōgai," pp. 121–26; Walthall, "Fille de paysan."

Kept women have become popular in the past fourteen or fifteen years. To be sure, a few did exist before then, but both parties cared about what others thought and concealed their relationship. I hear that keeping women began in Kyoto and Osaka in the Tenmei era [1781–1789]. Up to fifteen years ago, people in Edo said contemptuously that there are such frivolous customs in Kyoto and Osaka. The custom that they then criticized has now appeared in Edo and probably involves tens of thousands of people. Moreover, such people are not ashamed of what others think, nor do they conceal their relationship. Quite the contrary, they see it as a great deed and make it out to be the height of fortune.

This should show you how in just fifteen years customs have changed for the worse, and the world has gone downhill. These evil customs will surely spread gradually throughout the provinces and even to rural market towns. The expansion of luxury in dress and hair ornamentation that goes along with them is also a recent phenomenon. Extravagance in all things is enormous compared with fifty years ago, and it is enough to startle an old man. No wonder! The amount of goods from the provinces that in today's world has been spent on and by these prostitutes, performers, and kept women is beyond calculation. Is this not an outrageous waste?

Lust as a Threat to the State

The Way of men and women is in accordance with the harmony between Heaven and Earth; it is pivotal for governing the state, the house, and the individual; and the married couple is the foundation for proper human relations. It is not at all a private matter. Consequently, the Way of proper human relations and the proper practice of the realm is to use a go-between to arrange a contract, and then perform the engagement and marriage ceremony in accordance with etiquette. But now these procedures are not followed. The daughters of the baseborn have absolutely no sense of discretion, and it is not unusual for them to engage in illicit relations. They have no scruples with regard to their parents, and they pay no heed to what others may see or hear. Some of them sneak out and run away from their parents, or they refuse the marriage connection urged by their parents. There are many couples who live together without benefit of a go-between, and it has become normal to take a husband [of one's own choice] and break ties with one's parents. It has also become a regular practice for wives and concubines to commit adultery. Both partners betray and rob each other.

Swept away by passion, men are tricked, women are tricked, or couples collude together to extort money. A man may force another man to give up his wife or abduct her, just to show what a man he is. A woman sometimes takes her husband's property, sends it to her paramour, and runs off with him, ruining her husband. Even when the husband and wife get along well together and have a child, the wife may sometimes be tricked into having a relationship with another man, who then takes her off, leaving her husband no choice but to divorce her. The daughter that parents look to depend on is snatched away from them, and the husband loses the wife who ought to protect his house. Children lose their parents, and they too are led astray.

Since this sort of illicit sex is a villainous crime that leads the state into lawlessness, it would not do for it not to be severely punished. It is most appropriate that in former days, wise and good generals set up strict laws against this. Today, there are types who sell their wives and concubines into prostitution, or push them to have illicit relations with another man. For a husband to disrupt the Way of wives and concubines by handing his wife over to someone else is abominable. Adultery is such a serious crime that wives or concubines who commit it are sentenced to death. Even the baseborn are allowed to slay a man who has cuckolded them, and the wife as well. Since the punishment for adultery is as severe as execution, and since it is even allowed for a wronged husband to kill the adulterous pair himself, surely the government should punish a man who contravenes the great Way of the proper relations between men and women by putting his wife into prostitution for his own benefit, or who makes her engage in adulterous relations.

Women usually entrust themselves to men, and even if a woman tries to sneak past the barriers [erected to control travel], only the man who guides her is punished, whereas the woman is not. For other evil deeds as well, whenever a man is involved, the punishment falls entirely on him and the woman escapes. Even when a husband and wife jointly commit evil deeds such as theft, the husband alone is punished and the wife is not. All this happens because it is a woman's Way to follow her husband, whether for good or bad. Since a woman is forgiven even such grave crimes because it is her Way to follow her husband, the husband should not be forgiven in the least when he violates the Way. What a woman must guard is just this one thing: chastity. One who causes her to violate chastity is the greatest criminal in the entire realm. Even if he is not punished for that crime itself, some severe punishment should be inflicted on him.

As we have seen above, prostitutes, courtesans, kept women, and illicit sex have proliferated, and the Way of women has become greatly disordered. It has become the usual custom for women to make light of and deceive their parents, or else neglect their husbands and act selfishly and willfully. If we look at today's lowly people who live in rented rooms on back alleys or who perform day labor, we see that while the parents barely get through life, the daughters adorn their hair and make up their faces, wear good clothes, practice the performing arts, or chase after men. While husbands get up before dawn and go out to pursue their household occupation as a peddler or the like, wearing straw sandals and shouldering their goods, wives delight in their husbands' absence. They get together with the other wives in the neighborhood or on the same row to talk about how useless their husbands are and discuss fleeting pastimes. Or they may gamble at different sorts of card games, or invite young men to go drinking with them or accompany them to the theater or spectacles, or go sightseeing or on a pilgrimage. They go to scenic places on the edge of the city, and because lots of restaurants and tea stands have recently appeared along the approaches to these sites, they stop there, sometimes even going up to the second floor and wasting money while taking their ease. When evening falls and the husbands return home, these wives pay no attention to the labors their men have performed all day but instead send them off to draw the water and cook the food. Thinking it a great deed to use their husbands by deceiving and cajoling them, wives act like masters, and husbands become like servants. In the unexpected eventuality that a wife does not take a lover, she keeps reminding her husband of his indebtedness to her for her chastity and lords it over him. This too can only be seen as willfulness and selfishness.

Beginning with the consorts of daimyo great and small, women have reached the epitome of willfulness and selfishness, while among the baseborn, the lower one gets, the more disordered is the Way of husband and wife and the Way of women. Today's people are distracted by desire for what is in front of their eyes; they destroy their bodies, shorten their lives, and bring disorder to the realm and the state. If reforms are put off, will not heavenly disasters befall us and tumult occur on earth?

Chapter 7

PARIAHS AND OUTCASTS

Pariahs, outcasts, and others of their ilk, such as those known as hut dwellers and watchmen,[1] are on the increase not only in the three cities but throughout the provinces too. Their numbers are now vast, and they are invariably more ostentatious and arrogant than regular people.

Take, for example, the Edo-resident chief of the pariah community, Danzaemon. His lifestyle is that of a holder of 3,000 *koku*. The chiefs of the outcast community, Matsuemon and Zenshichi, are not far behind.[2] Those beneath them occupy different rankings, but all live the good life. The pariahs of Kyoto and Osaka have become ever more overweening, and the man known by the name of Taikoya Matabei of the pariah village of Watanabe in Osaka is worth an estimated 700,000 *ryō*. His storehouse overflows with treasures from Japan and China, and his extravagance is second to none. He is said to have seven or eight beautiful concubines. He, too, has followers beneath him, several score of whom are exceptionally wealthy. When Nishi Honganji monks head down to Osaka to solicit funds, members of the pariah community line up *masu* measuring boxes and fill them brimful with gold coins. They display bag after bag overflowing with silver coins. All of this is by way of offering to Nishi Honganji monks. Such people as these are removed

---

1. Hut dwellers (*koyamono*) and watchmen (*banta*) were terms used in some areas for outcasts. Although many villages and town wards hired outcasts as watchmen, in Edo watchmen were recruited from among ordinary townspeople as well; the latter were also known as *banta*.

2. On Danzaemon, Matsuemon, and Zenshichi, see "Buyō Inshi and His Times," p. 18.

from communication with the rest of the world. They accumulate vast sums over the years, but their only expenditure is in the form of gifts to Nishi Honganji. How great the Way of the Buddha!

Again, there is a pariah village called Norata in the domain of Hikone in Ōmi province. There they purchase for a pittance aging cattle and horses, which people bring them from far and wide; they feed them poison and, having killed them, skin them. They remove the hair from the hides, render the fat from the flesh,[3] and manufacture glue. The pariah community there is headed by two men known as Saiji and Saibei. Each is said to be worth between 300,000 and 400,000 *ryō*. Cattle and horses are of benefit to the people who sustain the state, and it is immoral to dispose of them when they grow old on the grounds that they are now valueless. In due course, we should give thought as to how this manner of business might be stopped. Norata used to be unique, but now similar places have sprung up elsewhere, too. The good tends to wane while the bad waxes. Everywhere, pariahs and their like are in ascendance.

Outcasts in Kyoto and Osaka all do nicely, too. Their residences all have gates and entrance halls. On display is their arsenal of weapons for making arrests: staffs, poles, sticks, ropes, and other weapons for capturing and restraining criminals. The authorities employ these people as agents to go after arsonists, robbers, and troublemakers and take them captive. As a result, they comport themselves as if they were shogunal officials. They are forever flaunting their authority and, on the pretense of pursuing troublemakers, intrude into town houses without a by-your-leave. In their interrogations, they point the finger where there is no suggestion of guilt, so much so that regular people live in abject fear of them. It is all the wrong way round. Indeed, these people make as if they are hunting down troublemakers, but the truth is they are out to line their own pockets. They always take the down payments in gambling and insist on their own cut from kidnappings and night robberies. Outcasts in the provinces everywhere are of this type. In some places, they are allowed to wear swords, but everywhere they enjoy the good life.

In former times, these people were entrusted with the disposal of anything polluted; they would make their way through life loitering on street corners or by houses, begging for food, and taking anything offered them, even a single penny. They have now declared a halt to small

---

3. The rendered fat was used as a salve for burns and wounds.

donations of coins or food and take a year's allotment in one fell swoop.[4] Thus, without expending any effort, they obtain a standard income. They also make plenty of money on those occasions when either celebration or commiseration is called for;[5] again without personal effort. They no longer appear as beggars; they simply act as if they are taking their due, as though it were a fixed stipend. They are known by such names as "outcasts" or "hut dwellers," but they actually live in fine houses and wear silks and silk crepe. They are well able to afford the various festivities for sons and daughters. When one of their daughters weds, they go so far as to arrange a ceremonial procession to send her off to her new house. They prepare fine food and gifts for the main guests. When they set off on pleasure trips to visit famous sites or temples and shrines where large numbers of people gather, they dress quite as regular people, without reserve. Because these people obtain money easily, entirely without physical labor, and do not need to use it for anything other than personal indulgence, they can spend more on food and wine than can regular people, and they do so without a second thought. Money in any case flows down to the lowest, and it likes to attach itself to those who are without any human qualities. This does not conform to Heaven's Way; this is topsy-turvy.

Again, these outcasts take up positions in temple and shrine precincts and at street intersections, and they put on performances of danced drama, mime, and story chants put to music. They draw crowds and make money. They get ever more ambitious, and their performances have come to resemble theater. They dress in fine costumes; their womenfolk call themselves "female ballad singers," and, wearing deep straw hats, [they walk around] playing the samisen and singing story chants.[6] There was a time when these performances would earn them a copper or two a time. Now, though, they bring in fifty or a hundred coppers a

---

4. Outcasts established ongoing relationships with particular neighborhoods, which paid them donations on a lump-sum basis rather than have them go begging house to house.

5. Like the blind, some groups of outcasts had sanction to collect alms on the occasion of weddings and funerals. See chapter 4, pp. 129–30.

6. Although Buyō did not have a high opinion of the various performers who called themselves *tayū* and accompanied themselves on the samisen, his point here is that the even more lowly female outcast street performers were putting on airs by referring to themselves as "female ballad singers" (*onna-dayū*).

performance. Such women dress well, wearing sateen; they decorate their hair with pins and combs made of tortoiseshell and use ivory plectrums to strum their sandalwood-necked samisen. These items are not Japanese; they are all foreign imports. These women's faces and hair are made up beautifully, and there is no hint that they were ever outcasts or beggars. Their appearance is one with which a regular town dweller could not compete.

In the early days of the Tokugawa reign, not even the wives of daimyo adorned themselves with something so luxurious as items made of tortoiseshell. Now, though, the womenfolk of the outcast communities all wear it freely. One might say that this is a consequence of the splendid age in which we live, but this is not so. This defies Heaven's principles. It is a sign that the decline of the age is upon us and that [splendor and wealth] are flowing to those below the people who sustain the state. This is no good thing at all. The expenditure for it comes from nowhere other than the warriors and the farmers, who are the very foundation of the realm. This is why warriors and farmers are all impoverished. Nowadays, a small-scale warrior cannot afford the wedding ceremonies and bridal processions of old. Under the pretext that she is making only a temporary stay in her new household, for the most part the bride will have already moved, going secretly at night [so as not to attract notice]. Her clothes and trousseau will be altogether pitiful; the feasting will be minimal. Many poor farmers spend their entire lives without a bride or groom. Yet these parts beyond the pale of ordinary human existence have grown ever more extravagant, and people who never had things like marriage celebrations now perform them with a flourish. [As a result] warrior and farmer have lost their original meaning.

The rice-producing farmers cannot eat rice except on a small number of occasions in the course of the year, but throughout the year pariahs and outcasts have ample white rice of fine quality. Nowadays townspeople eat better rice than warriors; the same applies to clothing, wine, and sweets. But more than the townspeople, it is the pariahs and the outcasts who indulge inappropriately. The fine things of this world make their way steadily down to the lower extremities. The pleasures of viewing the moon and flowers, the rare and fine treasures of Japan and China old and new, the finest flavors from the seas and the mountains, the most beautiful daughters and wives: these prove to be all for the pleasure of the lowliest. Fine clothes, hair ornaments of tortoiseshell and coral, even sandals and geta are all for the use of the lowliest of women. Luxuries and a life of ease belong to the lowly. Warriors and farmers suffer out of their sight. The profligacy of these sorts of lowly people, the competition driven by greed, the evil goings-on, the flourishing of pariahs and outcasts—all this has been gathering momentum over the years. They are now the norm. Such things may not appear unacceptable to the average person, but to look upon the world through the eyes of Heaven is to understand that this state of affairs cannot be allowed to continue for a moment longer.

ON JAPAN BEING CALLED A DIVINE LAND

I have heard it said that Japan is a Divine Land and that in ancient times the feelings of its people were clear and bright, without duplicity and never obscured by a single cloud or wisp of mist. Those times are thus called the Age of the Gods, and its people the people of antiquity. Today, the ways and feelings of the people of antiquity survive in distant mountains and hidden valleys where the people are illiterate and untouched by money. Among them there are neither "good" people nor "evil" people; none are poor and none are rich.

The Negative Effect of Confucianism, Buddhism, and the Way of Yin and Yang

Some say that with the coming of Confucianism to this Divine Land, the notion arose that for all things there is a particular moral obligation, and that such obligations led to quarrels about priority and status. In addition, the arrival of Buddhism infused all things with duplicity. Buddhism ignores the reality of things as they appear in front of our own eyes, and it makes up arguments about things that cannot be seen, such as a previous life and that to come. It regards the present world as a temporary matter, and it presents evidence for this by claiming that people's intelligence or stupidity, poverty or wealth is due to karma from their previous lives. It leads people by making threats about the future and by sowing in their minds the desire to become buddhas in their coming lives. Because of these teachings, people became obsessed with matters of the previous life and that to come, and naturally, duplicity arose. Gripped by the desire to be the one alone to attain the status of a buddha, people began to differentiate between self and other, and thus they constrained and hampered the pure and straight Way of the Gods.

As the moral obligations of Confucianism mingled with the selfish desire of Buddhism, it contaminated people's disposition. Confucianism duly became a precious treasure of the state, but it was still too early [for the authorities] to begin using Buddhism. There is no place for Buddhism when people are secure in their Heaven-endowed true nature, are without desire, and keep righteousness between ruler and minister and trust between father and son. That land where Śākyamuni presented the dharma was in an age of decline. It was a land where evil desires abounded and where humans behaved like beasts. That was why Śākyamuni, on the one hand, scared the people with strange occurrences and, on the other, out of compassion taught them about ultimate reality, thereby seeking to lead them toward a state of no self and no desire. When this teaching was brought into our country of Japan, which as yet had no notion of desire, it had the converse effect of fostering desire and inspiring clever deceit.

Of course, in our age, with its abundance of outrages and evil, it would be hard to do without Buddhism. Without the reverence taught by Buddhism, how much more would such outrages and evil spread. Yet one wonders whether all this moral corruption may not also have its cause in the proliferation of the Buddhist Way. After all, this Way puts the principles of the true Way to one side. It teaches that the bond to one's own actual parents is a mere transient phenomenon, and it claims that the misfortune of one's lord or of one's parents is due to bad karma from a previous life. When someone receives a favor from another person and gains some benefit, the Buddhist Way does not teach him to be grateful to that person but rather claims that this benefit is a karmic result he himself sowed in an earlier lifetime, or that it is due to the protection of a buddha or bodhisattva to which he has secretly offered prayers. People come to behave in a duplicitous manner and do not see things as they really are. Should people thereby ignore their natural duties of this world and think of the benefits they have received as coming from elsewhere, it is truly the extreme of selfish desire. If one cheats and tricks others with greedy cleverness, as is the custom of our times, should then the wealth one acquires in such a manner be understood as a reward resulting from the positive karma of one's previous life? Then again, were a person to abide by the true meaning of the Buddhist Way and abandon all desires, he would instantly fall into destitution or become a derelict and a burden to the world. Should this then be held to be owing to bad karma from a former life? This is in truth a teaching that will drift wherever the current may take it.

The Buddhist Way is acceptable as long as it is taught only to the lowly classes as a way for them to control their bodies and minds. For those of middle rank and above, it becomes a great obstacle that prevents them from handling their worldly duties and from leading others. Especially for one who is a warrior retainer, to have faith in the Buddhist Way and pray for his afterlife is to act like a woman who has intercourse with a secret lover: it is the extreme in disloyalty toward his lord. As his heart is taken in by Buddhism, he fears for his next rebirth and, looking upon this life as something transient that may not last another day, seeks to avoid getting trapped in the affairs of this floating existence. He thus leaves aside his moral obligations, loses courage, and becomes unable to stand up and put his life on the line for the Way of loyalty and filial piety. Those Honganji followers who rebelled in Mikawa are an example of this.[7]

An Age of War

Human beings are the ultimate spiritual entity among the myriad things. Noble and lowly, strong and weak, all have received the nature of Heaven and Earth, the sun and the moon, and are alike endowed with a nature that is good. When one preserves the goodness of this nature and one's heart is unsoiled, one is identical with both gods and buddhas. There is no need to rely on the gods and buddhas as something separate from oneself. To be sure, there are degrees in the richness of this endowment of the good nature, with some being wise and others stupid, some quick and others slow. Regardless of their endowment, however, people today end up falling into a state of perverse cunning and greedy lust.

As the years have progressed, people have fallen ever more quickly into this state of cunning and greed, and now it has come to the point that people already acquire an evil heart while still in their mother's womb. Those born fifty years ago would be totally shocked to see how quick young people today are at calculating profit and in using their wits

7. See chapter 3, note 25.

at bargaining. The customs of an age of upheaval permeate the being of those living in it from the time they are in the womb. Fierce from the moment of birth, they take killing others for granted. On the other hand, those born in an age of order know peace from the time they are in the womb; by nature they are upright and calm and thoughtful in manner. In this way, the people who lived in the period from the beginning of Tokugawa rule until around the Genroku-Kyōhō era [1688–1736] were calm and thoughtful. People of the present day, by contrast, learn an attitude of deceitful cunning and greedy lust as soon as they are born. Just as you will not have good seedlings if you plant bad seeds, human progeny, too, have steadily worsened until now there are only bad people. In the present age, those who have strong passions and are clever, quick, and sharp are victorious, while those who lack strong passions and are dim, slow, and dull lose out, living their lives in vain.

With the raging of this war, the Way of Heaven is lost, the Way of the buddhas and gods falls into the realm of demons and heresy, and the Way of man collapses entirely. One sees not a trace of good nature, only people with human faces but the hearts of beasts. At present, people are practiced in pursuing their greed for riches, freely abandon themselves to their lascivious impulses, and compete with one another in extravagance. In their pursuit of all that is nonrighteous and part of the inverted Way, their disposition is like that of an age of war. In an actual age of war, those who win and those who lose, those who kill and those who are killed alike know what the stakes are. Bandits, pirates, and troublemakers openly display their strength and force, putting their lives on the line. By contrast, people at present put on a show of sincerity but are masters at fawning obsequiously on others, from whom they snatch their prey when the moment is ripe. When it comes to deceitful cunning and cruelty, even those of an age of upheaval would be no match for them; they represent an extreme of evil perversity.

An age of good government is said to be one when people do not encroach on or steal from others either by strength or cleverness. At present, people prey on others as in an age of war, but with a degree of deceitful cunning and greed that goes beyond anything seen in an age of war. Will not this war grow ever more fierce until eventually, people will engage in evil without any fear of death? And will not that then lead to an actual clash of weapons and a renewed age of upheaval? One should not let down one's guard.

Competing Interests in a World of Fixed Limits

The source of these evils can be traced to the fact that for more than two hundred years people of the soil have suffered from mistreatment while merchants have been the recipients of largess; people who sustain the state have declined while idlers have increased; people who sustain the state have been despised while townspeople and idlers have been cherished. As a result, people who sustain the state have grown weaker and weaker, and the Ways of townspeople and idlers alone flourish, until townspeople and idlers have come to make up over half the population.

The strength of the people of the world has fixed limits, and because at present the townspeople and idlers of Edo, Osaka, and Kyoto, as well as of the provinces, consume enormous quantities of grain and other products, the people who sustain the state and constitute the other half of the populace have become exhausted in the effort to produce this grain and other products and know no peace of mind. Townspeople and idlers having become far too numerous, the country's products are not enough to feed them, and thus they go to extremes in cunning and greed. The cunning and greed rampant in today's world have led to the devastation of forests; the exhaustion of gold, silver, copper, and iron mines; and the devastation and abandonment of wet and dry fields.

But even though townspeople and idlers have grown numerous and available resources do not suffice to feed them, cities offer many opportunities to give free rein to cunning and greed, and the possibilities for evil pursuits are infinite. Compared with remaining one of those who sustains the state, it is easier to pursue a living in a city. In a city, even should one end up an unregistered wastrel, troublemaker, pariah, or outcast, one will be much better off as far as clothes, food, and lodgings are concerned than those who, remaining in the provinces, sustain the state. As a consequence, day by day, month by month, the number of people sustaining the state decreases, and townspeople and idlers grow more numerous. Because townspeople and idlers grow numerous, the burden of costs to the state increases, and warrior houses and farmers sink deeper into poverty.

Since the millions of townspeople and idlers use up the various goods produced throughout the country, prices go up, causing difficulty for warriors and farmers. On the other hand, warriors and farmers sell rice and other grains, but townspeople and idlers manage to buy these from them at a low price, leaving warriors and farmers doubly hard-pressed. Being ever more hard-pressed, farmers grow weaker and weaker and decline in number, but for warriors the only recourse is to force more from the already exhausted people who sustain the state. Daimyo and fief holders raise the annual land tax, but even this is not enough. Daimyo impose extra levies, extract extraordinary forced loans, establish monopolies on local products for their own profit, and devise ways of collecting various license fees. Or they lend out money at high interest or force people to exchange their gold and silver for paper money called "rice bills," "silver bills," or "copper bills," collecting a premium in the process, only to halt the circulation of such bills and turn them into wastepaper, causing a loss to all. They press the populace mercilessly in all sorts of other ways, too, bringing about the destruction of those who sustain the state. At present, benevolent rule by daimyo and fief holders has ceased altogether, leaving those who sustain the state no place to stand.

Loss of Control

In today's world, the various merchants, artisans, and transporters by ship, palanquin, and ox and horse all form guilds and associations of people in the same line of business, setting up a variety of internal regulations and arrangements. It is not easy to take action against these guilds. If their activities were suddenly halted, it would cause all sorts of inconveniences. Even unregistered persons, troublemakers, fake dispensers of medicine pretending to have circuit licenses, gangs of gamblers, prostitutes, brothel brokers, abductors, thieves, shoplifters, confidence men, pickpockets, pariahs, and outcasts join together. Not only in the cities but also in the provinces, such gangs act arrogantly, and as they tie up with one another throughout the countryside, they cannot easily be brought under control. Gangs and associations of people who engage in such disreputable activities grow more numerous by the day; they are a great impediment to the state and cause harm to the people of the world.

Every once in a while attempts are made to bring gamblers and thieves under control, but their activities are so extensive and they are found so widely throughout the world that a force of fifty or one hundred men cannot possibly stop them. If one tries to put a stop to them in Edo, they go to Kyoto and Osaka, and if one pursues them in Kyoto and Osaka, they disperse into the provinces. If one pursues them in a daimyo domain or bannerman fief, they move into shogunal holdings, and if one tries to put a stop to them in shogunal holdings, they hide out in temple or shrine lands. It is thus extremely difficult to search them out and eliminate them. Particularly when they lie low in the provinces and countryside, one cannot easily find them, and a policy of control cannot be implemented in both distant and nearby places at the same time. It is just like chasing flies off a bowl of rice; the authorities pretend to exert full control while in fact they merely repress those among the troublemakers who stand there triumphantly in broad daylight. As a consequence, gamblers and thieves flourish everywhere in the provinces and in the countryside. Words cannot express how terrible the situation is.

When it comes to the shogunate's laws, too, as the saying goes, "The regulations proclaimed throughout the realm last for a mere three days." No one fears them; no one obeys them. Regulations have long existed that townspeople and farmers should not wear clothes made of anything finer than rough, sturdy pongee, that they should not use gold and silver implements, and that they should neither purchase nor sell tortoiseshell items costing more than one hundred *monme* of silver. The government has issued regulations about all sorts of other things as well, but all of them are ignored, and today it is impossible to enforce a single one. As the world has gotten more and more out of kilter, the government has put out ever more laws, but they all are abandoned almost immediately. Because the number of laws has become so vast, even officials, from the magistrates on down, cannot remember them all. When the need comes up in the investigation of a case, the officials find out about a law's existence only upon checking the records. Naturally, the lowly classes neither know these laws nor obey them. And of course, under the present conditions, in which it is impossible to enforce laws even temporarily, people will not obey a law even if they know and understand it. Since it is pointless to issue repeatedly laws that cannot be implemented, the Way [of proper government] should be opened up so that legislation can both be applied and kept standing.

Of course it will need more than ordinary measures to open up the Way of governing for the people's benefit. The essential thing is first to reduce the numbers of townspeople and idlers and return them to their original status as people of the soil. People of the soil obey laws. Townspeople and idlers break them. Now it may be considered harsh to reduce the numbers of townspeople, idlers, and other bad sorts who at present stand their ground so confidently. Unless one uses the force of the military Way, it will be difficult to carry out such an attack. Quite likely, implementing such an attack may lead to riots. It is like applying moxa to a child.[8] Although the moxa serves to make him behave correctly, at the time he writhes and screams. Since it is a matter of applying moxa to the troublemakers and such who at present roam freely throughout the entire country of Japan, they may well cause an uproar. It is indeed a radical, fearsome approach.

If things are left the way they are, extravagance, lust, and greed will gain further strength; the military Way will become weak and soft; poverty will spread; those who sustain the state will become exhausted and decrease in number; townspeople and idlers and other bad sorts alone will increase and eventually will bring chaos to the state. To do nothing about this, saying it is the inevitable course of events, is like failing to give a sick person medicine.

Acting in Heaven's Place, Before Heaven Does

The Way of man cannot simply be left up to the Way of Heaven or the Way of the buddhas. Everything depends on keeping control. The Way of Heaven shines on eras of turmoil as well as those of order. People commit the enormous crimes of assassinating their lords or murdering their parents and brothers in full view of the sun and moon, and yet these do not cloud over. Since these entities just let things go as is, they are hardly dependable. Buddhas and gods are the same. It is said that what happens to people is up to the buddhas and gods, but also that the gods and buddhas will not go against people. Whatever sorts of things someone does, they just let it pass. They are indeed trusting. Even if it is a matter of desire and greed that will result in harming others and taking what is theirs, the gods and buddhas will grant worldly benefits and will also listen to curses and incantations against others, if only one prays to them. They lend support to evil intentions, connive with evil people, and encourage evil deeds. If the Way of Heaven and the Way of the buddhas are allowed a free rein, who knows what degree of havoc they will wreak in the world. The temple and shrine priests of the present turn the buddhas and gods into salable objects and hold to a Way that is evil and

---

8. For moxa, see chapter 6, note 11.

inverted. Yet they do not incur retribution; on the contrary, they obtain bountiful rewards. They thus increase their evil deeds and become ever more proud and arrogant. How could one count the slightest iota on gods and buddhas that are used in this manner as the tools for deeds of evil and arrogance? When leaders in the past have destroyed the state, it was with the assistance of the gods and buddhas.

The Confucian Way, too, holds that what flourishes will weaken and that "when a series of changes has run all its course, another change ensues."[9] This resembles the Buddhist notion of karma. And although Confucians always speak about the Way of benevolence, this is something that, like faith in the buddhas and gods, cannot be counted on. It is true that those who do evil may soon be defeated and those who indulge in excessive extravagance meet with disaster or fall ill and see their lives shortened. This may appear to be Heaven's punishment or punishment meted out by the gods and buddhas, just as the teachings of Shinto, Confucianism, and Buddhism say. But because it comes after the evil has been done, such punishment is useless; it is as much as making people into evildoers first and then punishing them. Is not the true Way of Heaven and of the buddhas and gods to lead people to the ultimate good *before* they become evildoers? If those Ways cannot do that, they are of no use whatsoever. Clearly, neither the sun and the moon nor the gods can overcome selfish human desire. Since it is said that the buddhas and gods cannot control human action and people cannot follow the intentions of the buddhas and gods, it is all the more certain that only man can govern man.

This is something that needs to be incorporated in the state's Way of government. Benevolent governance means to ensure that people do not first do something wrong and *then* be punished for it by Heaven or the gods and buddhas. This is how things were done for about one hundred years after the establishment of rule by the Tokugawa house. Whether the age is good or bad, whether things accord with Heaven's Way or not, whether karmic responses are good or bad, whether Heaven or the buddhas and gods take punitive action or do not—all this depends on the fundamentals of the Way of government. Since all blessings and all miseries alike have their source in what people do, the ruler of the state

---

9. A quote from the "Great Appendix" to the *Book of Changes*; Legge, *I Ching*, p. 383.

should himself establish a strict system for rewarding good and punishing evil, acting in place of Heaven and before Heaven does, in place of the gods and buddhas and before the gods and buddhas do, thereby ensuring that the people of the world do good and receive all blessings.

To let wrongdoing go, saying that it is the inevitable course of events for people to tend toward badness, or that to mount an attack against wrongdoing is making a mountain out of a molehill, is what I described above as leaving things up to the Way of Heaven or to the gods and buddhas. It may be presumptuous of me to condemn the current state of affairs, but the situation at present looks indeed like leaving things up to the Way of Heaven and the doings of the gods and buddhas. People are just left to go bad, the world is just left to go bad, and then, when people do something bad, punishment is levied out. In the *Analects* it says, "To put the people to death without having instructed them—this is called cruelty."[10] Thus, should not the present mode of government be called "cruel"? It is a very shortsighted approach. The ruler should act in place of Heaven and establish institutions that will force the buddhas and gods to submit; he likewise should adopt methods of governance and instruction that will make it difficult for people to commit evil deeds and thereby keep them from becoming evildoers.

To be sure, it is not an easy thing to act before Heaven does and in place of Heaven. If the ruler adopts methods of governance and instruction that are truly in accord with the Way of Heaven and that realize heavenly virtue, the buddhas and gods will rely on him. If instead he prays for their assistance, he will not obtain protection and may even be punished. Unless he shows a heavenly virtue great enough to pull the buddhas and gods in his wake, he cannot act in place of Heaven. That is to say, he must carry out government using the military Way that is fundamental to the Japanese spirit. Whether one stirs up unrest or succeeds in establishing order, all depends on one's use of the military Way.

Since the flourishing or decline of the world and the prevalence of good or bad customs depend entirely on governance and instruction, we should reform the manner of governance now, attack those evildoers and miscreants who disobey the edicts and laws issued by the successive generations of shogun, and establish laws that will restore the populace to their former state of goodness. In carrying out this attack, one should

---

10. *Analects* 20:2; Legge, *Chinese Classics*, 1:353.

not use either the Confucian Way or the Buddhist Way. Instead, to restore the world to order, one should rely on the military Way that served originally to secure order.

THE LAND, PEOPLE, AND RULER

At present, the people's dispositions are disordered, the mountains and rivers are disordered, laws are disordered, and people's households are disordered. The foundations of the state's land have become weak and attenuated. With the decline of the state's foundation, warriors have ceased to be righteous and brave; weak and spineless, they indulge in luxury. Vassals have appeared who extort from the populace and steal from their lord; they freely commit crimes against their lord and mercilessly extract what they want from the lowly. As for the people of the soil, they have become trapped by the Way of greed and have wearied of producing goods of use to the state. They have lost their original disposition as common people and have become impoverished; only the Way of the peripheral townspeople and idlers flourishes. The millions of townspeople and idlers in the world today are no more than noxious worms who eat away at the warriors and farmers. In the past two-hundred-some years, such worms have steadily proliferated; they have become particularly dominant in the course of the past century.

In this way, millions of worms eat away at the foundations of the state. It is impossible to count how much of the products of use to the state are wasted day and night in this way. Some such worms have fed so voraciously that they have become fat and languid; others are caught up in a frantic quest to become fatter; and then there are those who, unable to find enough to feed on, are so emaciated that they turn to preying on their fellows. Both those who are fat and those who are emaciated are alike noxious pests that sap the state's strength. They turn against the realm, break the ruler's laws, block up the Way of benevolence and righteousness, and violate the teachings of the gods and buddhas. These pests are the root of the present illness of the realm and state. The disasters they bring are ultimately extravagance, lust, and greed. The numbers of these noxious townspeople and idlers must be reduced and the roots eradicated of the illnesses of extravagance, lust, and greed that eat away at people's hearts.

If the Way of Heaven exists at all, things cannot continue long as they are. Will not disasters soon arise throughout the realm? To bring things under control before heavenly disasters, earthly upheavals, famines, crop failures, and the like all occur at once—this is what may be called benevolent government. If there is a delay in establishing effective methods of control and what is broken becomes yet worse, will not Heaven be angered and the spirits [of mountains and rivers] rampage? And then will not the populace all turn into rebels and bandits, while storms, floods, earthquakes, fires, swarms of locusts, famines, and pestilence come one on top of the other, leading in the end to violence and chaos? In such circumstances, there is a tried-and-true method: before such disasters arise one should act in place of and in advance of Heaven and, leading the spirits under one's command, establish proper means of control. Without getting bogged down in age-old precedents and standards, one should formulate new laws, put the people on a fresh footing, and transform a bad age into one that is good.

When disorder reaches its ultimate, order will be achieved, and when order reaches its ultimate, things will fall into disorder—this is the norm of the Way of Heaven. At such a time, there is a way to bring about the ultimate shift whereby disorder is transformed and order restored: the ruler must carry out benevolent government correctly; his ministers and officials must be loyal and stalwart and not twist the laws; rewards and punishments must be administered fairly; the ruler and his officials, acting as one, must ensure that the blessings of good rule are distributed widely throughout the realm and thereby save the world.

To reform customs and practices and renew the people, the first priority is to eradicate the extravagance and lust running rampant through the world, put a stop to the Way of greed and avarice, get rid of the wealthy, and save the impoverished. Further, more than half the townspeople and idlers who fill the bustling cities and those who, throughout the country, feed off others should be returned to their original status of people of the soil. This is the method by which the greedy robbers who prey on the state can be reduced, the abandoned fields throughout the provinces be restored, the proper pursuits of the people, now attenuated and faltering, be expanded, and, above all, the foundations of the country be made firm and strong.

Warriors will then be provided with the economic means befitting their status and will reform their conduct. Even the weak and decadent will be frugal and revert to a sturdy uprightness. Committing themselves to behaving in a trustworthy and righteous manner, they will polish away the rust that has accumulated on the military Way and devote themselves to military preparations. Farmers will give up extravagant elegant pursuits that are inappropriate to their status, root out the inclination to greed, and return to a simple and spare manner of life. The impoverished will thereby regain their footing, and families will no longer be dispersed as a result of poverty. Things will be evened out so there are no extremes of poverty and wealth, suffering and pleasure. Temple and shrine priests, too, will abandon impure desires and reform defiling behavior. They will hold to the precepts, strive to carry out the principles of the Way, and, basing themselves on the Way of great compassion, protect the state. Practitioners of the Confucian Way, as well, will keep a distance from flamboyant extravagance and a life of idle ease. Instead they will implement the methods of benevolence and save people's lives.

The number of townspeople will be halved; in particular, the wealthy who take pride in extravagance will be reduced in number and the might they flaunt before the world suppressed or broken up. Popular writers, artists, entertainers, unregistered persons, and troublemakers will find it difficult to continue in their dissipated, reprehensible behavior and will no longer be able to make their way through the world as they choose. Unconstrained pursuit of evil enterprises will cease to be possible, and many of these sorts can be brought back to their original status as people of the soil. The differentiation between honorable and lowly and the distinctions among the four classes will be firmly established, and people will become modest and straightforward. Since the people of the soil will become more numerous, two hundred people will do the work that up to now has been done by one hundred, while those who eat off them will become fewer. Expenditures will be smaller and additional levies reduced, and thus the people will prosper.

Overall, in governing the realm and state it is crucial to ensure that those above and below have sufficient food and dress. If food, dress, and housing are inadequate, people may fall ill, their lives may be shortened, or they may turn to wrongdoing. On the other hand, if they have an excess of food, dress, and housing, people may become lazy, extravagant, or greedy, and again, they will turn to wrongdoing. For people to have too much and not enough are both bad. At present, things have become unbalanced, and thus there are many who do not have enough and many who have too much, and both turn to wrongdoing. When things are leveled so there is not an imbalance between poor and rich, suffering and pleasure, the people can be readily governed and live in security.

Current officials do not grasp that it is possible to establish such a benevolent government at the present time because, having grown up in an age of peace and taking security for granted, they have become indolent. They have decided that the current state of affairs is something natural and do not put any effort into thinking about what should be done. Occasionally, someone may appear who does have aspirations to rectify things. But then what happens is that, being of high rank and stipend, he becomes concerned about the negative consequences for himself if he acts. Or else, being of low rank and stipend, he fears the reaction of his superiors and, not having direct access to the lord, is unable to achieve his aim.

What I fervently hope is that a loyal vassal, endowed with both ability and virtue, will appear in the world and that, without thinking about what may happen to his own person, he will act upon his heavenly virtue and take as his own responsibility the difficulties of the realm, the security of the state, the preservation of the ruling line, and the world's moral corruption. Memorializing the ruler about these matters, may he mediate between the ruler and the people, carrying out the ruler's commands and establishing new, rigorous laws. May he thereby dispose of those lost in extravagance, indolence, and living off others, eradicate the heinous actions of the plunderers of the state, and save the people from impoverishment and untoward death. Ensuring that the ruler's benevolence extends to the entire populace, may he relieve the people's laments, seeing to it that the people do not hold a grudge against the ruler and that the ruler does not hate the people. May the blessings of virtuous rule then extend throughout the realm and state, and may the great task of securing the prosperity of the ruler, his ministers, and the people be achieved. I pray for the appearance of an outstanding figure who can bring about such a world, whose praises both high and low will sing, calling for it to last unto eternity.

At such a time, I pray that I may assist this virtuous and able figure and that, without giving a thought to the survival of my house or name or the fortunes of my descendants, I may strive body and soul to correct the deleterious customs that I have repeatedly described throughout this book. May the ruler thereby completely restore the ancient style [of the Divine Lord] and establish a regime of good rule, peace, and order that will last for another two hundred years. This is the great task whereby "a thousand autumns bring the folk ease, ten thousand years make for the blessings of lasting peace."[11] The key method for accomplishing this great task is something I know well from my observation of the workings of Heaven and Earth. But because it is a matter that bears on the great secrets of the realm and state, I will not speak of it here and will rest my brush.

Longing to recompense ruler and people
I pray fervently, with all my might,
Before Heaven's successor![12]

Bunka 13 [1816]

---

11. Buyō alludes here to a passage from the Noh play *Takasago*, often recited on auspicious occasions. The translation, slightly modified, is from Tyler, *Pining Wind*, p. 40.

12. Although Buyō adopts Kokugaku-like terms in this poem, he does not seem fully familiar with their implications. In particular, he seems to use the term *amatsuhitsugi*, usually applied to the imperial line, to refer to the shogun as the ruler recognized by Heaven.

EDITIONS AND REFERENCES

EDITIONS OF *SEJI KENBUNROKU*

Harada Tomohiko, Takeuchi Toshimi, and Hirayama Toshijirō, eds. *Nihon shomin seikatsu shiryō shūsei*, vol. 8. Tokyo: San'ichi Shobō, 1969.
Honjō Eijirō, ed. *Kinsei shakai keizai sōsho*, vol. 1. Tokyo: Kaizōsha, 1926. Reprint, Tokyo: Kuresu Shuppan, 1989.
Honjō Eijirō, ed. *Seji kenbunroku*. Kaizō Bunko 1–42. Tokyo: Kaizōsha, 1930.
Honjō Eijirō, ed. *Seji kenbunroku*. With an introduction by Takigawa Masajirō. Tokyo: Seiabō, 1966. Reissued, Seiabō, 2001.
Honjō Eijirō and Naramoto Tatsuya, eds. *Seji kenbunroku*. Iwanami Bunko 33-048-1. Tokyo: Iwanami Shoten, 1994.

INCOMPLETE EDITIONS

Takimoto Seiichi, ed. *Nihon keizai sōsho*, vol. 34. Tokyo: Nihon Keizai Sōsho Kankōkai, 1917.
Takimoto Seiichi, ed. *Nihon keizai taiten*, vol. 52. Tokyo: Keimeisha, 1930. Reprints, Tokyo: Meiji Bunken, 1971; Tokyo: Hō Bunshokan, 1992.
A digital facsimile of an undated (1850s?) woodblock print version of chapter 1 can be found in the Kotenseki Sōgō Database of Waseda University; see www.waseda.ac.jp/kotenseki.

REFERENCES

Aoki Michio. "Seji kenbunroku no sekai." *Rekishi to chiri* 519 (1998): 33–37.

Botsman, Daniel V. *Punishment and Power in the Making of Modern Japan*. Princeton, NJ: Princeton University Press, 2005.

Breen, John, and Mark Teeuwen. *A New History of Shinto*. Chichester, UK: Wiley-Blackwell, 2010.

de Bary, Wm. Theodore, Carol Gluck, and Arthur E. Tiedemann, eds. *Sources of Japanese Tradition, Volume Two: 1600 to 2000*. New York: Columbia University Press, 2005.

Drixler, Fabian. *Mabiki: Infanticide and Population Growth in Eastern Japan, 1660–1950*. Berkeley: University of California Press, 2013.

Fritsch, Ingrid. *Japans blinde Sänger: Im Schutz der Gottheit Myōon Benzaiten*. Munich: Iudicium, 1996.

Groemer, Gerald. "The Creation of the Edo Outcaste Order." *Journal of Japanese Studies* 27, no. 2 (2001): 263–93.

———. "The Guild of the Blind in Tokugawa Japan." *Monumenta Nipponica* 56, no. 3 (2001): 349–80.

Honsaroku. In *Fujiwara Seika, Hayashi Razan*, edited by Ishida Ichirō and Kanaya Osamu, pp. 269–302. Nihon shisō taikei, vol. 28. Tokyo: Iwanami Shoten, 1975.

Howell, David L. *Geographies of Identity in Nineteenth-Century Japan*. Berkeley: University of California Press, 2005.

———. "Hard Times in the Kantō: Economic Change and Village Life in Late Tokugawa Japan." *Modern Asian Studies* 23, no. 2 (1989): 349–71.

Hur, Nam-lin. *Death and Social Order in Tokugawa Japan: Buddhism, Anti-Christianity, and the Danka System*. Cambridge, MA: Harvard University Asia Center, 2007.

Katō Takashi. "Governing Edo." In *Edo and Paris: Urban Life and the State in the Early Modern Era*, edited by James L. McClain et al., pp. 41–67. Ithaca, NY: Cornell University Press, 1994.

Katsu Kokichi. *Musui's Story: The Autobiography of a Tokugawa Samurai*. Translated by Teruko Craig. Tucson: University of Arizona Press, 1988.

Kitahara Susumu. *Edo no fudasashi*. Tokyo: Yoshikawa Kōbunkan, 1985.

Kitō Hiroshi. *Bunmei to shite no Edo shisutemu*. Tokyo: Kōdansha, 2002.

Lau, D. C., trans. *Lao Tzu: Tao Te Ching*. Harmondsworth, UK: Penguin, 1963.

Legge, James, trans. *The Lî Kî*. 2 vols. In *The Sacred Books of China: The Texts of Confucianism*. Delhi: Motilal Banarsidass, 1976.

———. *The Chinese Classics*. 5 vols. Hong Kong: Hong Kong University Press, 1960.

———. *The I Ching*. New York: Dover, 1963.

Maeda Tsutomu. *Heigaku to Shushigaku, Rangaku, Kokugaku*. Tokyo: Heibonsha, 2006.

Masai Yasuo. *Edo Tōkyō daichizu: Chizu de miru Edo Tōkyō no konjaku*. Tokyo: Heibonsha, 1993.

Masuda Toshimi. "Yoshino Michi no shōgai: Sono tegami o tōshite." In *Edo jidai no joseitachi*, edited by Kinsei Joseishi Kenkyūkai, pp. 115–44. Tokyo: Yoshikawa Kōbunkan, 1990.
McClain, James L. "Space, Power, Wealth, and Status in Seventeenth-Century Osaka." In *Osaka: The Merchants' Capital of Early Modern Japan*, edited by James L. McClain and Wakita Osamu, pp. 44–79. Ithaca, NY: Cornell University Press, 1999.
McMullen, I. J. "Non-Agnatic Adoption: A Confucian Controversy in Seventeenth- and Eighteenth-Century Japan." *Harvard Journal of Asiatic Studies* 35 (1975): 133–89.
Nenzi, Laura. "To Ise at All Costs: Religious and Economic Implications of Early Modern *Nukemairi*." *Japanese Journal of Religious Studies* 33, no. 1 (2006): 75–114.
Nishiyama Matsunosuke, ed. *Edo chōnin no kenkyū*, vol. 1. Tokyo: Yoshikawa Kōbunkan, 1972.
Ōedo happyaku yachō. Edited by Edo-Tōkyō Hakubutsukan. Tokyo: Edo-Tōkyō Hakubutsukan, 2003.
Ōguchi Yūjirō. *Josei no iru kinsei*. Tokyo: Keisei Shobō, 1995.
——. "The Reality Behind *Musui Dokugen*: The World of the *Hatamoto* and *Gokenin*." *Journal of Japanese Studies* 16, no. 2 (1990): 289–308.
Ōishi Kyūkei. *Jikata hanreiroku*. Edited by Ōishi Shinzaburō. 2 vols. Tokyo: Kondō Shuppansha, 1969.
Seigle, Cecilia S. *Yoshiwara: The Glittering World of the Japanese Courtesan*. Honolulu: University of Hawai'i Press, 1993.
Shively, Donald H. "Bakufu Versus Kabuki." *Harvard Journal of Asiatic Studies* 18, no. 3/4 (December 1955): 326–56.
Skene Smith, Neil, ed. "Materials on Japanese Social and Economic History: Tokugawa Japan (1)." *Transactions of the Asiatic Society of Japan*, 2nd ser., 14 (1937).
Smith, Thomas C. *The Agrarian Origins of Modern Japan*. Stanford, CA: Stanford University Press, 1959.
Stanley, Amy. *Selling Women: Prostitution, Markets, and Morality in Early Modern Japan*. Berkeley: University of California Press, 2012.
Sugano Noriko. *Edo jidai no kōkōmono: Kōgiroku no sekai*. Tokyo: Yoshikawa Kōbunkan, 1999.
——. *Kankoku kōgiroku*. Tokyo: Tōkyōdō Shuppan, 1999.
Takeda Izumo, Miyoshi Shōraku, and Namiki Senryū. *Chūshingura: The Treasure of Loyal Retainers*. Translated by Donald Keene. New York: Columbia University Press, 1971.
Takeuchi Makoto. "Festivals and Fights: The Law and the People of Edo." In *Edo and Paris: Urban Life and the State in the Early Modern Era*, edited by James L. McClain et al., pp. 384–406. Ithaca, NY: Cornell University Press, 1994.
Takigawa Masajirō. "Kaisetsu." In *Seji kenbunroku*, edited by Honjō Eijirō, pp. 8–56. Tokyo: Seiabō 1966.

Tamamuro Fumio. *Edo jidai no Sōtōshū no tenkai*. Tokyo: Sōtōshū Shūmuchō, 1999.

Teeuwen, Mark. "Early Modern Secularism? Views on Religion in *Seji Kenbunroku* (1816)." *Japan Review* 25 (2013): 3–19.

———. "The Way of Heaven in 1816: Ideology or Rhetoric?" In *Uncharted Waters: Intellectual Life in the Edo Period*, edited by Anna Beerens and Mark Teeuwen, pp. 109–28. Leiden: Brill, 2012.

Totman, Conrad. *Early Modern Japan*. Berkeley: University of California Press, 1993.

Tyler, Royall. *Pining Wind: A Cycle of Nō Plays*. Ithaca, NY: China-Japan Program, Cornell University, 1978.

Vaporis, Constantine N. *Tour of Duty: Samurai, Military Service in Edo, and the Culture of Early Modern Japan*. Honolulu: University of Hawai'i Press, 2008.

Walthall, Anne. "Fille de paysan, épouse de samouraï: Les lettres de Yoshimo Michi." *Annales. Histoire, Sciences sociales* 54, no. 1 (1999): 55–86.

———. *Social Protest and Popular Culture in Eighteenth Century Japan*. Tucson: University of Arizona Press, 1986.

Watson, Burton, trans. *Records of the Historian: Chapters from the Shih chi of Ssu-ma Ch'ien*. New York: Columbia University Press, 1969.

West, Mark D. "Private Ordering at the World's First Futures Exchange." *Michigan Law Review* 98, no. 8 (2000): 2574–615.

Wigmore, John Henry, ed. *Law and Justice in Tokugawa Japan*. 9 parts [19 vols.]. Tokyo: University of Tokyo Press, 1969–1986.

Williams, Duncan. "The Purple Robe Incident and the Formation of the Early Modern Sōtō Zen Institution." *Japanese Journal of Religious Studies* 36, no. 1 (2009): 27–43.

CONTRIBUTORS

JOHN BREEN is a professor at the International Research Center for Japanese Studies, Kyoto, where he edits the journal *Japan Review*. His research focuses on issues of state and religion in Japan.

FUMIKO MIYAZAKI is a professor emerita at Keisen University, Tokyo. Her research focuses on Tokugawa religion and society.

KATE WILDMAN NAKAI is a professor emerita at Sophia University, Tokyo. Her research focuses on Tokugawa and modern history, with an emphasis on intellectual developments.

MARK TEEUWEN is a professor in Japanese studies at the University of Oslo. He is a historian of Japanese religion, with a special focus on the history of Shinto.

ANNE WALTHALL is a professor emerita at the University of California, Irvine. Her research focuses on society and gender during the Tokugawa period.

INDEX

absconding, 17, 109, 134, 145n19, 146, 200
actors, 19, 26, 62, 183n30, 213–22
acupuncture, 130, 130n5, 132
adoption: and farmers, 78; and merchants, 135, 152, 166–67; and temple registers, 115, 116n18; and warriors, 7, 57–59, 68; and women, 226, 227
adultery, 83, 138, 179, 233
agriculture, 9, 23, 24, 27, 85, 94, 96, 101. *See also* farmers (*domin; hyakushō; kokumin*)
Amaterasu, 32
Amida Buddha, 119, 119n22, 120, 212n13, 217
Analects, 248
arson, arsonists, 83, 145, 147, 185, 186, 200, 236; and prostitution, 201, 210
artisans, 5–6, 83, 100, 148, 244; and farmers, 84–86, 100; and land, 173; and warriors, 68

bannermen (*hatamoto*), 6–7, 8n11, 10, 12, 16, 18, 25, 27, 46–49, 53–55, 152n3, 231n23, 245; and adoption of heirs, 58, 73; and the blind, 130, 135; debts of, 49, 53, 91; and farmers, 55; and lawsuits, 63; and rice agents, 158–62. *See also* fief holders (*jitō*)
beggars, 188, 189, 237; and outcasts, 18, 20, 189, 204, 238
blind, the, 19–20, 56, 59, 71, 128–35, 168, 187, 211, 237n5
bribery: and farmers, 78, 87; and lawsuits, 144, 145; and priests, 10, 105, 116, 125; and outcasts, 18; and prostitution, 210; and townspeople, 68, 142; and warriors, 51, 67–68, 89–90, 143, 155
Buddha (Śākyamuni), 118, 119, 123, 124, 218, 240
Buddhism, 11, 118, 124, 212, 218, 239–41, 247. *See also* Honganji sect

Buddhism (continued)
(True Pure Land; Jōdo Shinshū; Ikkō); priests and monks; temples
Bunsei reforms (1827), 27

capital (*motode, motodekin*): and the blind, 132; and farmers, 13, 96; and priests, 109, 120; and townspeople, 142, 177, 178; and warriors, 134, 141, 160n6
census registers (*ninbetsuchō*), 6, 10, 17, 87, 110, 211. See also unregistered persons (*mushuku*)
Christianity, 10
cities, 8, 9, 13–15, 17, 192, 243, 250; administration of, 15; vs. countryside, 78, 83, 94, 97, 98–102, 174–77, 189, 206; crime in, 182–85; Kabuki in, 217, 220; prostitution in, 211–12, 221
class structure, 5–22
clothing: and the blind, 132; of concubines, 72, 228–31, 234; extravagance in, 62, 71; of farmers, 14, 78, 88; of Kabuki actors, 26, 213, 214, 217; laws on, 245; of merchants, 151, 154, 162, 166; of outcasts, 238, 243; of priests, 103, 105, 109; of prostitutes, 194, 199, 208; of townspeople, 186, 222, 224; of warriors, 53, 56, 66
concubines, 228, 229, 233; and farmers, 79, 102; and Kabuki actors, 214–19, 221–22; and priests, 107; and townspeople, 26, 135, 151, 154, 164, 196–200, 235; and warriors, 42, 70, 72–74
Confucianism, 4, 26, 184, 224, 239–40, 247, 251; vs. military Way, 29, 65, 249. See also *Analects*; *Great Learning* (*Daxue*)
corveé labor, 13, 14; and farmers, 76, 87n5, 91, 95, 97, 148, 206–7; and townspeople, 174, 223

court nobility, 6, 9–10, 11, 12, 19, 61, 92n9; and money lending, 116, 178; and temples, 10, 116, 125n29
court rank, 9, 78; and the blind, 129n2, 130; of priests, 112, 116, 117, 119, 124, 126
credit associations, 106, 118
crime, 14, 17, 146, 246, 249; and farmers, 115, 176; of illicit sex, 233–34; in Kabuki, 217; and priests, 108, 119; and prostitution, 81, 200, 201; and townspeople, 182–87. See also lawsuits; punishment; troublemakers (*akutō*)

Daigaku wakumon (*Questions and Answers Regarding the Great Learning*; Kumazawa Banzan), 28
daimyo, 7–8, 12, 42–45, 54, 74, 214–15, 222–23; and the blind, 129, 130; and concubines, 73, 228–29; in Edo, 8, 15, 149, 173; and farmers, 95, 98, 101, 121; financial affairs of, 8, 16–17, 20, 52, 69, 76, 91, 129, 172, 244; and lawsuits, 146; and merchants, 150, 152–56, 160, 164–69; and priests, 115, 123; wives of, 238
daimyo compounds (*yashiki*), 8, 15, 17, 153n4, 173, 231n23
Danzaemon, 18, 19, 235
Debt. See loans
derelicts (*haijin*), 35, 35n2, 51, 147, 187–90, 204, 206, 241
Discourse on Government. See *Seidan* (*Discourse on Government*; Ogyū Sorai)
Divine Land, Japan as a, 32, 123, 239
Divine Lord (Shinkun, Tokugawa Ieyasu), 5, 22, 30–40, 75, 90, 101, 124, 148, 189, 252. See also Tokugawa Ieyasu
Dōjima (Osaka), 170, 171
drunkenness, 118, 198
Dutch imports, 167, 168, 196

Edo Town Office (Machi Kaisho), 189, 190n34
Eiheiji, 124n28, 126
emperor, 9, 31, 110n8, 125n29, 129, 213. *See also* court nobility
entertainers (*yūgeisha*), 5, 62, 251; female, 73, 183, 211, 214, 216, 221, 228, 229; in restaurants, 226–27. *See also* geisha; jesters (*taikomochi*)
entertainment, 22, 31, 212–13; and farmers, 79, 80, 85; and merchants, 153, 169; and prostitution, 221–26; and temples, 106n2, 114n15; and warriors, 44, 61, 70, 75. *See also* Kabuki theater; music; poetry
etiquette: of high and low, 160, 161; of marriage, 232; of warriors, 61, 66, 141

famine, 25, 172, 182, 224, 250; and riots, 190, 191
farmers (*domin; hyakushō; kokumin*), 5, 6, 12–14, 23, 27, 29, 35, 76–102, 130, 140, 163, 207; classes of, 12–13; and laws, 84, 245; and lawsuits, 92–94; poverty of, 22, 86, 175, 191, 238, 243–44; and prostitution, 206; small-scale, 85, 89, 90, 95–97; and temples, 10, 109, 113, 115, 127; tenant, 95, 97, 98; and townspeople, 140, 149, 150, 158, 159, 163, 164, 170, 194; uprisings, 95–96, 205; and urbanization, 25, 98–102, 174; and warriors, 48–50, 54–55, 64, 66, 154; water-drinking, 79; wealthy, 78–80, 95, 251
festivals, 80, 106n3, 166, 168, 169, 212n13, 220
fiction (*gesaku*), 22, 25, 224, 224n21
fief holders (*jitō*), 6, 13, 14, 46–50, 55, 78, 79, 91, 98, 146, 148, 165, 244. *See also* bannermen (*hatamoto*)
fiefs: and farmers, 91, 120, 122; of nobility, 10; of temples, 11, 12, 126;

of warriors, 6, 7, 27, 42, 46, 48–55, 62, 75, 167, 174, 245
filial piety: *vs.* Buddhism, 241; and concubines, 222; and fiction (*gesaku*), 224; and Ieyasu, 39; and Kabuki, 217, 223; and prostitution, 21, 196, 204, 206; and townspeople, 168, 183; of warriors, 41
financiers, 16, 25, 126
floods, 148, 170, 190, 250
food: extravagance in, 70, 151, 160, 196, 208, 214, 219, 222, 229; of farmers, 76, 86; of outcasts, 236, 237; of priests, 103, 105, 107, 109, 178; at restaurants, 139, 226; supply, 85, 96, 98, 100, 102, 243, 251
funerals, 11, 46, 67, 106, 111, 116, 130, 135, 169, 186, 207, 237

gambling: of brothel keepers, 196; and merchants, 160; and outcasts, 236; on the price of rice, 170; and priests, 107, 114; and prostitution, 234; and troublemakers, 19, 80–84, 146, 183, 244
geisha, 153, 168, 210, 211, 219
Genroku-Kyōhō periods, 22, 24, 36, 136, 137, 214, 242
gods, 32, 44, 87, 98, 113–18, 127, 178–80, 184, 207, 220, 239–42, 246–49. *See also* Buddhism; Shinto; spirits (*kishin*) of mountains and rivers
Gozasso (*Wuzazu*), 196, 197n2
granaries, 25, 189, 190
Great Learning (*Daxue*), 23n23, 28
guilds (*nakama, kumiai*), 16; of the blind, 19–20, 128n1, 130–34; of merchants, 24, 25, 27, 31, 68, 152, 176, 180, 244; of rice agents, 159. *See also* Tōdōza (guild of the blind)

hairstyles: of concubines, 72, 229–32; extravagance in, 80, 168, 234;

hairstyles: of concubines (*continued*) Kabuki actors, 217; of outcasts, 238; of prostitutes, 194, 199, 203, 208
Heike monogatari (*Tale of the Heike*), 19
Hiei, Mount, 114, 114n17
Hihon tamakushige (*Jeweled Comb-Box: A Private Memorial*; Motoori Norinaga), 28
Honda Masanobu, 29
Honda Toshiaki, 4
Hōnen, 119, 119nn21–22, 123
Honganji sect (True Pure Land; Jōdo Shinshū; Ikkō), 119–24; and Mikawa uprising, 90n6, 122; and outcasts, 235, 236; and prostitution, 123, 124, 212
Honsaroku (*The Records of Lord Honda*; Honda Masanobu), 29, 31
housemen (*kenin*), and daimyo, 42–43. *See also* retainers
housemen, shogunal (*gokenin*), 7, 52–53, 59–60, 63; buying of positions, 59, 135; and rice agents, 16, 25, 49, 158–62
house owners (townspeople), 16, 134n13, 164, 174n23, 190n34
hungry spirits, 106, 113, 113n14

idlers (*yūmin*), 5, 6, 17, 19, 20, 22, 23, 29, 31, 35, 73, 76, 206–7; concubines of, 227; and entertainment, 216, 223; extravagance of, 226; and farmers, 101, 102; freedom of, 191; increase in numbers of, 66, 77, 85, 99, 173, 243, 246; and lawsuits, 93; nobility as, 10; priests as, 12; reduction in numbers of, 245, 250; and warriors, 64; as worms, 192, 249
Ikkō Buddhism. *See* Honganji sect (True Pure Land; Jōdo Shinshū; Ikkō)
Imagawa Ujizane, 222–23
infanticide, 123n27. *See also* thinning (*mabiki*)

intendants (*daikan*), 59, 59n17
interest: high, 59, 178–81; and the blind, 56, 131; and court nobility, 10, 178; and daimyo, 244; and farmers, 80, 85, 101, 205; and pawnbrokers, 57; in prostitution, 209; rates of, 56n13, 131n8, 180; and rice agents, 17, 25, 49, 158, 160n6; and the shogunate, 27, 48, 48n5, 49, 190n34; and temples, 108, 113, 117, 178–79; and townspeople, 77, 180; and warriors, 17, 48, 52, 56, 57, 71, 153, 156
Ise Shrines, 164
Itakura Katsushige (Shirōzaemon), 30

Japanese spirit (*yamato-damashii*), 248
jesters (*taikomochi*), 227
Jikata ochiboshū (Buyō Inshi), 2n1
Jōdo. *See* Pure Land (Jōdo) Buddhism
Jōdo Shinshū. *See* Honganji sect (True Pure Land; Jōdo Shinshū; Ikkō)
jōruri story chants, 74, 212

Kabuki theater, 19, 22, 183n30, 212–21; restrictions on, 213; and warriors, 62; and women, 216, 217, 219, 221, 222, 228
kagura dances, 220
Kaiho Seiryō, 4
Kajūji house, 10, 125
Kansei reforms (1787–1793), 24–26, 159, 160n6, 189, 206n9, 214
Kantō region, 14, 27, 91, 93, 115, 207
kept women (*kakoimono*), 22, 73, 108, 114, 183, 221, 227–32, 234
kirisute (right to kill commoners), 9
Kojiki, 192n36
Kōkaku, Emperor, 9
Kokugaku (nativist) thought, 4, 32, 253n12
Korea, 187
Kōya, Mount, 114

Kumazawa Banzan, 28
Kuramae rice agents, 158–62
Kuruma Zenshichi, 18, 235
Kyōhō period. *See* Genroku-Kyōhō periods
Kyōhō reforms, 24
Kyoto, 14, 75, 87, 93, 148, 164, 165, 171, 244; concubines in, 232; court nobility in, 6, 19, 125; crime in, 207; governor, 30; merchants in, 150, 156, 163; outcasts in, 235–36; priests in, 121; prostitution in, 209; townspeople in, 173, 243

land: in Edo, 173–74, 180, 209, 210; and farmers, 12, 13, 44, 66, 80, 85, 95, 96, 100, 169; and outcasts, 18; shogunal, 6, 54, 59n17, 150; surveys of, taxes on, 55, 79, 87–88, 91, 95, 97, 101, 121, 159, 168, 206, 244; and temples or shrines, 11, 15, 108, 112n11, 113, 114, 117, 126, 245; and warriors, 7, 48–49, 54
Laozi, 146n20
laws, 49, 53; and Buddhism, 123n26; decline of, 124, 146–47, 220, 249; domainal, 7; and illicit sex, 233; ineffectiveness of, 245; and merchants, 176–77; and priests, 107, 112, 126, 127; and prostitution, 196, 199, 199n4, 204; shogunal, 162, 177, 245, 248, 250, 252; sumptuary, 24, 25, 84; and townspeople, 157, 162, 192; on trade, 198; and unnatural deaths, 201; and warriors, 159
lawsuits, 136–47; bribery in, 144, 145; and Buyō, 3; costs of, 91; and farmers, 79, 91, 92–94; and magistrates, 15, 136; and priests, 114, 115; private settlements in, 20, 91, 94, 138–40; for profit, 138, 177, 181; and townspeople, 63; and warriors, 9, 140, 142

loans, 179; from the blind, 20, 48, 56, 71, 131–34; and Buyō, 3; and court nobility, 10; and daimyo, 8, 49, 70, 78, 156–57, 244; and farmers, 80, 96, 97; and lawsuits, 138, 181; and merchants, 17, 150, 154; and pawnbrokers, 57, 57n14; and priests, 108, 113, 117, 118; and rice agents, 16, 25, 158, 161; and shogunate, 24, 48n5, 52, 179; and temples, 11, 48n6, 178, 179; and townspeople, 173; and troublemakers, 81; types of, 180, 180n27; and warriors, 8, 48, 55, 56, 60, 71
lotteries, 11, 84, 104, 106, 118, 146
Lotus Sutra, 119

mabiki. *See* thinning (*mabiki*)
magistrates, 10, 55, 88, 93, 139, 147, 217, 245; finance, 59n17, 93n10; and lawsuits, 181; town, 15, 71, 93n10, 136, 161, 177, 183n31, 213, 213n15
marriage, 232, 238; and the blind, 129; of farmers, 78; of warriors, 62, 68, 73
Matsudaira Sadanobu, 24–25
Matsuemon, 18, 235
Mencius, 23
merchants, 5, 16–17, 40, 148–49; cities, 16–17; clerks of, 164; and daimyo, 8, 68; extravagance of, 164, 175, 227; and farmers, 85, 86, 87, 89, 96, 100; guilds, 20, 24, 27, 31, 176, 244; and loans, 20; and prices, 169–72; *vs.* priests, 109; and profit, 84, 162; riots targeting, 191; as shogunal purveyors, 150–53; and shogunate, 25, 243; and troublemakers, 83
Mikawa uprising, 90, 90n6, 122, 241
military Way (*budō*), 5; and benevolent government, 30; *vs.* Confucianism, 65, 249; decline of, 65, 75, 192, 223, 246; *vs.* frivolous entertainment, 223; restoration of, 29, 75, 251;

military Way (continued)
  Tokugawa Ieyasu, 5, 11, 31, 75; vs. townspeople and idlers, 31, 192, 246; and warriors, 61, 73; and the way of Heaven, 31–32, 39, 248
Minamoto no Yoritomo, 11
money lending. See loans
monks. See priests and monks
Motoori Norinaga, 28
moxa, moxibustion, 208, 246
music, 19, 22, 74, 79, 130, 153, 168, 210n12, 212, 216, 223, 237
Musui's Story (Katsu Kokichi), 3, 52n11

nenbutsu dance, 212
Nichiren, 119, 123n26, 127n31
Nihon shoki, 192n36
Nikkō highway, 91, 92n8
Noh, 60, 253n11; vs. Kabuki, 212

Oda Nobunaga, 223n20
officials, 10, 59, 90, 100–101, 177, 245, 250, 252; agents of, 184; and bribery, 67–69, 87, 210; and Kabuki actors, 26, 214, 215; and lawsuits, 63, 93, 94, 137–47; and merchants, 153, 156; shogunal, 15, 92n9, 217, 236; and transport system, 112n12; village, 12–13, 78–82, 89, 97, 113, 116n18. See also magistrates; shogunate
Ogyū Sorai, 28, 29
Ōoka seidan (*Tales of Ōoka's Decisions*), 136n16
Ōoka Tadasuke, 136–37
Osaka, 6, 14, 15, 148, 165; commercialization in, 87, 243; and Edo, 27, 244; and lawsuits, 93; merchants in, 154, 156, 163, 173; outcasts in, 235, 236; prostitution in, 209, 232; rice market in, 8, 16, 170–72
outcasts (*eta*; *hinin*), 6, 17–19, 235–39, 244; and beggars, 189; bosses or chiefs, 18, 235; and concubines, 228; vs. farmers, 101, 243; and Kabuki, 212; and prostitution, 195, 204; and warriors, 60

palanquins: and the blind, 135; and brothel keepers, 196; guilds, 244; and merchants, 150, 153; and priests, 111, 112; and townspeople, 227, 231; and warriors, 54, 69
pawnbrokers, 25, 53, 83, 153, 162, 180
pawning: of leased goods, 180; by priests, 107; by warriors, 53, 57, 71
physicians, 6, 59, 173
pilgrimages, 32n31, 234; and kidnappings, 207; of merchants, 196; and women, 229
poetry, 10, 75, 78–79, 212, 223n20; *haikai*, 60, 79
Policy for Great Peace. See *Taiheisaku* (*Policy for Great Peace*; Ogyū Sorai)
post stations, 14, 83, 87, 92, 92n9, 99, 112, 150, 165, 166n10; and prostitution, 212
poverty: and benevolent government, 116; in cities, 175; and crime, 44; of farmers, 85, 86, 94, 95, 101, 207, 243; inequality of poverty and wealth, 5, 22, 40, 94–97, 174, 206, 230, 239, 250; and lawsuits, 144; and merchants, 170, 171; of outcasts, 18; and prices, 169; and priests, 119, 123; and prostitution, 204; and urbanization, 100, 191; of warriors, 48, 53, 166, 192, 243
prices, 26, 35, 169–72; bidding, 68; control of, 25, 172n17; in Edo, 173, 176, 194, 225; and farmers, 86, 95, 96, 100, 244; and guilds, 152, 176; of rice, 8, 17, 25, 109; rising, 27, 219, 243; of temples, 105, 126
priests and monks, 6, 10–12, 103–27, 185, 228, 246, 251; chief, 105, 108, 112, 126; and court nobility, 10, 116, 125–26; donations to, 107, 111, 122; as

idlers, 19, 76, 227; and money lending, 113, 179; and prostitution, 114, 195; and shogunate, 29, 31, 173n22
prints, erotic (*shunga*), 22, 224
prostitution, 19, 20–21, 123–24, 193–212; and arson, 220; brothel keepers in, 195–97, 208; causes of, 204–7; and chastity, 203; and concubines, 233; costs of, 194, 232; and farmers, 79, 83–84, 99; and filial piety, 83, 205–6, 230; increase of, 209–12, 224, 232, 234; and Kabuki, 221, 231; and kidnapping, 207–8; life in, 198–202; at post stations, 83; and temples, 114; and townspeople, 217, 227; and troublemakers, 81; unlicensed, 21, 83–84; and warriors, 62, 72–74, 228
protests. *See* uprisings
punishment: of criminals, 83n4, 182; of farmers, 54, 55, 115; from Heaven, or the buddhas and the gods, 20, 32, 128, 129, 182, 247; of priests, 109, 118; of prostitutes, 198, 200, 201, 208; of servants, 66; and sexuality, 65, 233–34; and shogunate, 39, 44, 147, 151, 176, 248; of townspeople, 151, 176, 181; of troublemakers, 81; of warriors, 44, 55, 151
puppet theater, 22, 223
Pure Land (Jōdo) Buddhism, 119n21, 120

qi (*ki*; psychophysical energy), 35n1

rations (*fuchi*), 49, 50, 68, 70
rear vassals (*baishin*), 8n11, 63, 63n20, 67, 111, 134, 157
Records of Lord Honda. *See Honsaroku* (*The Records of Lord Honda*; Honda Masanobu)

Records of the Grand Historian (Sima Qian), 203n7
restaurants, 21, 68, 139, 218, 225–27, 234; and prostitution, 210, 226–27, 231
retainers: of blind, 135; honorary status as, 78; nonhereditary, 135n15, 183n30; personal, 59, 142; relations with lord, 42, 45, 50–51, 54, 66; as retinue, 41, 53, 60; stipends of, 8, 49, 54, 70, 154; of townspeople, 164. *See also* rear vassals (*baishin*); vassals; warriors (*buke, bushi, samurai, shi*)
retirement allowance, 58, 152
rice agents (*fudasashi, kurayado*), 16, 24, 25, 49, 50n9, 56; of Kuramae, 158–62
riots. *See* uprisings
rōnin (masterless warriors), 8, 52, 59, 78, 161n8

Segawa Kikunojō Rokō (Segawa Kikunojō III), 215–16
Seidan (*Discourse on Government*; Ogyū Sorai), 28
servants, maidservants, 14, 19; castle (*obōzu*), 173, 173n22; of farmers, 78, 207; farmers as, 14, 81, 98, 99; of Kabuki actors, 214; of kept women, 229; of merchants, 151, 168; prostitutes as, 200; wages of, 230–31; of warriors, 43, 44, 47, 49, 53, 54, 64, 65–67, 68, 227; warriors as, 59
Shin kokinshū, 192n36
Shinran, 119, 123
Shinto, 123, 124, 247. *See also* gods
Shirakawa house, 10
shogunal purveyors (*kanjōsho goyōtashi*), 150–53, 173, 190n34
shogunate, 30, 36, 171, 245; administrative posts in, 7, 60; and the blind, 19–20, 130n15; Buyō on, 3; and court

shogunate (continued)
  nobility, 9–10, 112n12, 126; and crime, 186–87, 244–45; and the domains of daimyo, 8, 69, 153, 155, 157, 165; and farmers, 78, 91; and filial piety, 206; and guilds, 152; and Kabuki, 213n14; land, 2, 6, 54, 59n17, 150, 173n20, 174; and lawsuits, 92, 93n11; and loans, 24, 27, 48, 48n5, 49, 70, 131n8, 131n9, 138n17, 179, 180; and merchants, 25, 149, 150–52, 160–62; and military Way, 29, 65; and outcasts, 18; and prices, 172n17; reforms by, 26–27, 31; and taxes, 13, 207; and temples, 11, 110n7, 112n12, 120n23; and townspeople, 190; and warriors, 58, 64
Sima Qian, 203n7
Skene Smith, Neil, 4n7
Smith, Thomas C., 4n7
Sōjiji, 124n28
Sōtō Buddhism, 124–26
spirits (kishin) of mountains and rivers, 250
steeplejacks (tobi no mono), 73, 185–86
stipends: of Danzaemon, 18; of domainal purveyors, 153; reductions of, 8, 26, 154; and rice agents, 16–17, 158–62; supplementary (tashidaka), 46, 46n4, 47; of temples and priests, 109, 112, 237; of warriors, 6–8, 46–50, 54, 57, 58, 60, 70, 70n23, 165, 169, 213n15, 252
storehouse agents, 17, 153–56
subsidies assistant (shiokuri yōnin), 50
Suganuma Sadamitsu, 90
Sugiyama Wa'ichi, 130, 130n5
suicide: double, 202; and prostitution, 200, 202; seppuku, 157
sumo wrestling, 22, 196, 219–20
sumptuary laws and regulations, 24, 25, 27, 69, 84
Supreme Judicial Council (Hyōjōsho), 15

swords: and brothel keepers, 196; and outcasts, 236; right to use family names and carry swords, 50, 78, 150, 153; and riots, 192; and townspeople, 168; and warriors, 56, 61, 64, 69, 161, 223

Taiheisaku (Policy for Great Peace; Ogyū Sorai), 28
Taikoya Matabei, 235
Tale of the Heike. See Heike monogatari (Tale of the Heike)
Tales of Ōoka's Decisions. See Ōoka seidan (Tales of Ōoka's Decisions)
taxes: annual land tax, 54, 79, 85, 87, 88, 91, 95, 97, 101, 121, 148, 159, 174, 244; in daimyo's domains, 7, 8, 121, 244; and farmers, 12, 13, 27, 55, 76, 92n9, 207; and idlers, 223; imposed by fief holders, 46, 48, 121; and prostitution, 205, 206; rice paid in taxes, 154, 172n18; and temple lands, 112n11; and townspeople, 16, 168, 206; and warriors, 62
tea ceremony, 19, 60, 75, 79, 106, 113, 212, 225
tea shops or stands, 21, 107, 114, 159, 183, 210, 218, 220, 227, 231, 234
temples, 10–11, 12, 15, 32n31, 44, 104–26, 169; and imperial court, 110–14, 116, 125, 178; income of, 109–10; and loan funds, 48n6, 106n4, 112–13, 179–80; and lotteries, 11, 104, 106, 118; and post-stations, 92, 112; and prostitution, 114; and registry system, 10–11, 115–16
Tenmei famine, 24, 190, 191
Tenpō reforms (1841–1843), 31
thinning (mabiki), 97, 123
Tōdōza (guild of the blind), 19–20, 128n1, 130n4
Tōkaidō highway, 83
Tokugawa Iemitsu, 130, 130n5
Tokugawa Ienari, 6

Tokugawa Ieyasu, 5, 12, 26, 29–30, 223n20; benevolent government of, 30, 39, 101, 189, 252; as Divine Lord (Shinkun), 39n1; founds Edo, 148; and Mikawa uprising, 90, 122, 123n26; and military Way, 5, 30, 32, 75; peace established by, 12, 31; and Sōtō Zen, 124. *See also* Divine Lord (Shinkun, Tokugawa Ieyasu)

Tokugawa Tsunayoshi, 24, 130n5

Tokugawa Yoshimune, 24, 46n4, 136n16

townspeople (*chōnin*), 5, 6, 14–17, 148–92; and benevolent government, 30; and the blind, 130; and bribery, 68, 142; clothing of, 84, 245; consumption by, 31, 166–69; and crime, 182–85, 186; dependence of warriors on, 149, 154, 158, 161, 162, 165–66; and farmers, 101, 102; and festivals, 168; and fires, 185–86; freedom of, 64, 140, 141, 151, 152, 172; increase in numbers of, 99, 173, 243, 246; and Kabuki, 213, 216, 222, 223; and land, 174; and lawsuits, 63, 71, 93, 143; and loans, 48n6, 134, 150, 180; lower, 17, 175–92; machinations of, 29; need to reduce numbers of, 5, 77, 243, 245, 250–51; and noble arts, 10; and poverty, 135, 175, 177; and priests, 76, 109, 113; and profits, 163, 170; and prostitution, 228; and riots, 191; and taxes, 16, 206, 207; and warriors, 49, 59, 68, 71, 73, 74, 149–50, 159, 161; wealth of, 24, 28; as worms, 192, 249. *See also* house owners (townspeople); idlers (*yūmin*); merchants

Toyotomi Hideyoshi, 209

troublemakers (*akutō*), 19, 27, 80–84, 161n8, 244; and farmers, 80–84, 99, 243; and gambling, 146, 183; and lawsuits, 145–47; and outcasts, 236; priests as, 114, 115; and prostitution, 204; reduction in numbers of, 246, 251; and townspeople, 186, 187; as undercover agents, 184

True Pure Land Buddhism. *See* Honganji sect (True Pure Land; Jōdo Shinshū; Ikkō)

Tsuchimikado house, 10

unregistered persons (*mushuku*), 6, 17–18, 27, 81–84, 99, 101, 146, 243, 251. *See also* outcasts (*eta; hinin*); troublemakers (*akutō*)

uprisings: in Edo, 25, 26; by farmers, 95–96, 205; Mikawa, 90, 90n6, 122, 241

vassals: hereditary vs. nonhereditary, 135n15; relation between lord and vassal, 39, 43–45, 49, 51, 52, 54, 59, 66, 249, 252; of Tokugawa, 7, 8, 90n6, 123. *See also* rear vassals (*baishin*), retainers

vermilion-seal grants, 11, 112–14, 117, 126

village officials (*mura yakunin*). *See* officials

villas (*bessō*), 153, 164, 173

warriors (*buke, bushi, samurai, shi*), 5, 6–9, 41–75, 250; and adoption of heirs, 57–60; and benevolent government, 12, 23, 24; and the blind, 20, 56, 130; and bribery, 67–70; and Buddhism, 122–23, 127, 241; and Buyō, 3; in cities, 14, 15; clothing of, 62, 66; and concubines, 72–75, 228; and court nobility, 9, 10, 61, 75; and decline of, 22, 26, 27, 29, 40, 83, 239, 249; and farmers, 13, 50, 55, 78, 89, 101; "fixers," 3, 50–52; footmen (*wakatō*) and foot soldiers (*ashigaru*), 53, 66, 68, 112, 135, 149; high-ranking,

warriors (*continued*)
42–45; and illicit affairs, 63, 66, 222; impoverishment of, 48–50, 52–57, 135, 192, 238, 243, 244; and Kabuki, 216, 219, 223; and kept women, 227; and lawsuits, 9, 63, 140–43, 186; and loans, 8, 56, 71, 113, 133, 134, 156–57, 161, 179; men-at-arms (*kachi*), 112, 135, 149; mounted rank (*ikki*), 60, 60n18; and outcasts, 19; and prostitution, 200; and rice agents, 17, 158–62; and right to use force, 9, 55, 63, 64–66; small-scale (*shōshin*), 47; and taxes, 76; and temples, 44, 109, 111–13; and townspeople, 16, 63, 65, 71, 141–43, 148–50, 152, 154, 163, 165–68, 169–70, 174, 179, 191. *See also* bannermen (*hatamoto*); daimyo; fief holders (*jitō*); housemen, shogunal (*gokenin*); retainers; *rōnin* (masterless warriors)
watchmen (*banta*), 18, 111, 235. *See also* outcasts (*eta; hinin*)
Way of Heaven (*tendō, tentō*), 23, 31, 32, 39, 87, 127, 237, 238, 242, 246–50; and prostitution, 195, 203, 204, 212

women, 22, 62, 83, 184; as brothel keepers and handlers, 197, 198; and Buddhism, 105, 114, 122, 218; chastity of, 21, 195, 203, 234; extravagance of, 162, 166, 238; and fiction, 224; and illicit affairs, 64, 66; and Kabuki, 212, 213, 216–20, 221–23; kept, 22, 73, 108, 114, 183, 221, 227–32, 234; and priests, 114, 117; warriors behaving like, 42, 61; Way of men and women, husband and wife, 232–34. *See also* concubines; geisha; marriage; prostitution
wool, as luxury item, 167, 168, 168n13, 196, 231

Yamakawa Jōkan, 130n5
yin-yang divination (*onmyōdō*; Way of yin and yang), 10
Yoshida house, 10
Yoshiwara (Edo brothel district), 20, 21, 114n15, 193, 194, 200, 208, 210

Zen (Sōtō), 124–27
Zenshichi. *See* Kuruma Zenshichi

TRANSLATIONS FROM THE ASIAN CLASSICS

Major Plays of Chikamatsu, tr. Donald Keene 1961
Four Major Plays of Chikamatsu, tr. Donald Keene. Paperback ed. only. 1961; rev. ed. 1997
Records of the Grand Historian of China, translated from the Shih chi of Ssu-ma Ch'ien, tr. Burton Watson, 2 vols. 1961
Instructions for Practical Living and Other Neo-Confucian Writings by Wang Yang-ming, tr. Wing-tsit Chan 1963
Hsün Tzu: Basic Writings, tr. Burton Watson, paperback ed. only. 1963; rev. ed. 1996
Chuang Tzu: Basic Writings, tr. Burton Watson, paperback ed. only. 1964; rev. ed. 1996
The Mahābhārata, tr. Chakravarthi V. Narasimhan. Also in paperback ed. 1965; rev. ed. 1997
The Manyōshū, Nippon Gakujutsu Shinkōkai ed. 1965
Su Tung-p'o: Selections from a Sung Dynasty Poet, tr. Burton Watson. Also in paperback ed. 1965
Bhartrihari: Poems, tr. Barbara Stoler Miller. Also in paperback ed. 1967
Basic Writings of Mo Tzu, Hsün Tzu, and Han Fei Tzu, tr. Burton Watson. Also in separate paperback eds. 1967
The Awakening of Faith, Attributed to Aśvaghosha, tr. Yoshito S. Hakeda. Also in paperback ed. 1967
Reflections on Things at Hand: The Neo-Confucian Anthology, comp. Chu Hsi and Lü Tsu-ch'ien, tr. Wing-tsit Chan 1967
The Platform Sutra of the Sixth Patriarch, tr. Philip B. Yampolsky. Also in paperback ed. 1967
Essays in Idleness: The Tsurezuregusa of Kenkō, tr. Donald Keene. Also in paperback ed. 1967
The Pillow Book of Sei Shōnagon, tr. Ivan Morris, 2 vols. 1967
Two Plays of Ancient India: The Little Clay Cart and the Minister's Seal, tr. J. A. B. van Buitenen 1968
The Complete Works of Chuang Tzu, tr. Burton Watson 1968
The Romance of the Western Chamber (Hsi Hsiang chi), tr. S. I. Hsiung. Also in paperback ed. 1968
The Manyōshū, Nippon Gakujutsu Shinkōkai edition. Paperback ed. only. 1969
Records of the Historian: Chapters from the Shih chi of Ssu-ma Ch'ien, tr. Burton Watson. Paperback ed. only. 1969
Cold Mountain: 100 Poems by the T'ang Poet Han-shan, tr. Burton Watson. Also in paperback ed. 1970
Twenty Plays of the Nō Theatre, ed. Donald Keene. Also in paperback ed. 1970
Chūshingura: The Treasury of Loyal Retainers, tr. Donald Keene. Also in paperback ed. 1971; rev. ed. 1997
The Zen Master Hakuin: Selected Writings, tr. Philip B. Yampolsky 1971

Chinese Rhyme-Prose: Poems in the Fu Form from the Han and Six Dynasties Periods, tr. Burton Watson. Also in paperback ed. 1971

Kūkai: Major Works, tr. Yoshito S. Hakeda. Also in paperback ed. 1972

The Old Man Who Does as He Pleases: Selections from the Poetry and Prose of Lu Yu, tr. Burton Watson 1973

The Lion's Roar of Queen Śrīmālā, tr. Alex and Hideko Wayman 1974

Courtier and Commoner in Ancient China: Selections from the History of the Former Han by Pan Ku, tr. Burton Watson. Also in paperback ed. 1974

Japanese Literature in Chinese, vol. 1: Poetry and Prose in Chinese by Japanese Writers of the Early Period, tr. Burton Watson 1975

Japanese Literature in Chinese, vol. 2: Poetry and Prose in Chinese by Japanese Writers of the Later Period, tr. Burton Watson 1976

Love Song of the Dark Lord: Jayadeva's Gītagovinda, tr. Barbara Stoler Miller. Also in paperback ed. Cloth ed. includes critical text of the Sanskrit. 1977; rev. ed. 1997

Ryōkan: Zen Monk-Poet of Japan, tr. Burton Watson 1977

Calming the Mind and Discerning the Real: From the Lam rim chen mo of Tsoṇ-kha-pa, tr. Alex Wayman 1978

The Hermit and the Love-Thief: Sanskrit Poems of Bhartrihari and Bilhaṇa, tr. Barbara Stoler Miller 1978

The Lute: Kao Ming's P'i-p'a chi, tr. Jean Mulligan. Also in paperback ed. 1980

A Chronicle of Gods and Sovereigns: Jinnō Shōtōki of Kitabatake Chikafusa, tr. H. Paul Varley 1980

Among the Flowers: The Hua-chien chi, tr. Lois Fusek 1982

Grass Hill: Poems and Prose by the Japanese Monk Gensei, tr. Burton Watson 1983

Doctors, Diviners, and Magicians of Ancient China: Biographies of Fang-shih, tr. Kenneth J. DeWoskin. Also in paperback ed. 1983

Theater of Memory: The Plays of Kālidāsa, ed. Barbara Stoler Miller. Also in paperback ed. 1984

The Columbia Book of Chinese Poetry: From Early Times to the Thirteenth Century, ed. and tr. Burton Watson. Also in paperback ed. 1984

Poems of Love and War: From the Eight Anthologies and the Ten Long Poems of Classical Tamil, tr. A. K. Ramanujan. Also in paperback ed. 1985

The Bhagavad Gita: Krishna's Counsel in Time of War, tr. Barbara Stoler Miller 1986

The Columbia Book of Later Chinese Poetry, ed. and tr. Jonathan Chaves. Also in paperback ed. 1986

The Tso Chuan: Selections from China's Oldest Narrative History, tr. Burton Watson 1989

Waiting for the Wind: Thirty-six Poets of Japan's Late Medieval Age, tr. Steven Carter 1989

Selected Writings of Nichiren, ed. Philip B. Yampolsky 1990

Saigyō, Poems of a Mountain Home, tr. Burton Watson 1990

The Book of Lieh Tzu: A Classic of the Tao, tr. A. C. Graham. Morningside ed. 1990

The Tale of an Anklet: An Epic of South India—The Cilappatikāram of Iḷaṅkō Aṭikaḷ, tr. R. Parthasarathy 1993
Waiting for the Dawn: A Plan for the Prince, tr. with introduction by Wm. Theodore de Bary 1993
Yoshitsune and the Thousand Cherry Trees: A Masterpiece of the Eighteenth-Century Japanese Puppet Theater, tr., annotated, and with introduction by Stanleigh H. Jones Jr. 1993
The Lotus Sutra, tr. Burton Watson. Also in paperback ed. 1993
The Classic of Changes: A New Translation of the I Ching as Interpreted by Wang Bi, tr. Richard John Lynn 1994
Beyond Spring: Tz'u Poems of the Sung Dynasty, tr. Julie Landau 1994
The Columbia Anthology of Traditional Chinese Literature, ed. Victor H. Mair 1994
Scenes for Mandarins: The Elite Theater of the Ming, tr. Cyril Birch 1995
Letters of Nichiren, ed. Philip B. Yampolsky; tr. Burton Watson et al. 1996
Unforgotten Dreams: Poems by the Zen Monk Shōtetsu, tr. Steven D. Carter 1997
The Vimalakirti Sutra, tr. Burton Watson 1997
Japanese and Chinese Poems to Sing: The Wakan rōei shū, tr. J. Thomas Rimer and Jonathan Chaves 1997
Breeze Through Bamboo: Kanshi of Ema Saikō, tr. Hiroaki Sato 1998
A Tower for the Summer Heat, by Li Yu, tr. Patrick Hanan 1998
Traditional Japanese Theater: An Anthology of Plays, by Karen Brazell 1998
The Original Analects: Sayings of Confucius and His Successors (0479–0249), by E. Bruce Brooks and A. Taeko Brooks 1998
The Classic of the Way and Virtue: A New Translation of the Tao-te ching of Laozi as Interpreted by Wang Bi, tr. Richard John Lynn 1999
The Four Hundred Songs of War and Wisdom: An Anthology of Poems from Classical Tamil, The Puṟanāṉūṟu, ed. and tr. George L. Hart and Hank Heifetz 1999
Original Tao: Inward Training (Nei-yeh) *and the Foundations of Taoist Mysticism,* by Harold D. Roth 1999
Po Chü-i: Selected Poems, tr. Burton Watson 2000
Lao Tzu's Tao Te Ching: *A Translation of the Startling New Documents Found at Guodian,* by Robert G. Henricks 2000
The Shorter Columbia Anthology of Traditional Chinese Literature, ed. Victor H. Mair 2000
Mistress and Maid (Jiaohongji), by Meng Chengshun, tr. Cyril Birch 2001
Chikamatsu: Five Late Plays, tr. and ed. C. Andrew Gerstle 2001
The Essential Lotus: Selections from the Lotus Sutra, tr. Burton Watson 2002
Early Modern Japanese Literature: An Anthology, 1600–1900, ed. Haruo Shirane 2002; abridged 2008
The Columbia Anthology of Traditional Korean Poetry, ed. Peter H. Lee 2002
The Sound of the Kiss, or The Story That Must Never Be Told: Pingali Suranna's Kalapurnodayamu, tr. Vecheru Narayana Rao and David Shulman 2003
The Selected Poems of Du Fu, tr. Burton Watson 2003
Far Beyond the Field: Haiku by Japanese Women, tr. Makoto Ueda 2003

Just Living: Poems and Prose by the Japanese Monk Tonna, ed. and tr. Steven D. Carter 2003
Han Feizi: Basic Writings, tr. Burton Watson 2003
Mozi: Basic Writings, tr. Burton Watson 2003
Xunzi: Basic Writings, tr. Burton Watson 2003
Zhuangzi: Basic Writings, tr. Burton Watson 2003
The Awakening of Faith, Attributed to Aśvaghosha, tr. Yoshito S. Hakeda, introduction by Ryuichi Abe 2005
The Tales of the Heike, tr. Burton Watson, ed. Haruo Shirane 2006
Tales of Moonlight and Rain, by Ueda Akinari, tr. with introduction by Anthony H. Chambers 2007
Traditional Japanese Literature: An Anthology, Beginnings to 1600, ed. Haruo Shirane 2007
The Philosophy of Qi, by Kaibara Ekken, tr. Mary Evelyn Tucker 2007
The Analects of Confucius, tr. Burton Watson 2007
The Art of War: Sun Zi's Military Methods, tr. Victor Mair 2007
One Hundred Poets, One Poem Each: A Translation of the Ogura Hyakunin Isshu, tr. Peter McMillan 2008
Zeami: Performance Notes, tr. Tom Hare 2008
Zongmi on Chan, tr. Jeffrey Lyle Broughton 2009
Scripture of the Lotus Blossom of the Fine Dharma, rev. ed., tr. Leon Hurvitz, preface and introduction by Stephen R. Teiser 2009
Mencius, tr. Irene Bloom, ed. with an introduction by Philip J. Ivanhoe 2009
Clouds Thick, Whereabouts Unknown: Poems by Zen Monks of China, tr. Charles Egan 2010
The Mozi: A Complete Translation, tr. Ian Johnston 2010
The Huainanzi: A Guide to the Theory and Practice of Government in Early Han China, by Liu An, tr. and ed. John S. Major, Sarah A. Queen, Andrew Seth Meyer, and Harold D. Roth, with Michael Puett and Judson Murray 2010
The Demon at Agi Bridge and Other Japanese Tales, tr. Burton Watson, ed. with introduction by Haruo Shirane 2011
Haiku Before Haiku: From the Renga Masters to Bashō, tr. with introduction by Steven D. Carter 2011
The Columbia Anthology of Chinese Folk and Popular Literature, ed. Victor H. Mair and Mark Bender 2011
Tamil Love Poetry: The Five Hundred Short Poems of the Aiṅkuṟunūṟu, tr. and ed. Martha Ann Selby 2011
The Teachings of Master Wuzhu: Zen and Religion of No-Religion, by Wendi L. Adamek 2011
The Essential Huainanzi, by Liu An, tr. and ed. John S. Major, Sarah A. Queen, Andrew Seth Meyer, and Harold D. Roth 2012
The Dao of the Military: Liu An's Art of War, tr. Andrew Seth Meyer 2012
Unearthing the Changes: Recently Discovered Manuscripts of the Yi Jing (I Ching) and Related Texts, Edward L. Shaughnessy 2013

Record of Miraculous Events in Japan: The Nihon ryōiki, tr. Burton Watson 2013

The Complete Works of Zhuangzi, tr. Burton Watson 2013

Lust, Commerce, and Corruption: An Account of What I Have Seen and Heard, *by an Edo Samurai,* tr. and ed. Mark Teeuwen and Kate Wildman Nakai with Miyazaki Fumiko, Anne Walthall, and John Breen 2014

Exemplary Women of Early China: The Lienü zhuan *of Liu Xiang,* tr. Anne Behnke Kinney 2014

The Columbia Anthology of Yuan Drama, ed. C. T. Hsia, Wai-yee Li, and George Kao 2014

The Resurrected Skeleton: From Zhuangzi to Lu Xun, by Wilt L. Idema 2014

The Sarashina Diary: A Woman's Life in Eleventh-Century Japan, by Sugawara no Takasue no Musume, tr. with introduction by Sonja Arntzen and Itō Moriyuki 2014

The Kojiki: An Account of Ancient Matters, by Ō no Yasumaro, tr. Gustav Heldt 2014

The Orphan of Zhao *and Other Yuan Plays: The Earliest Known Versions,* tr. and introduced by Stephen H. West and Wilt L. Idema 2014

Luxuriant Gems of the Spring and Autumn, attributed to Dong Zhongshu, ed. and tr. Sarah A. Queen and John S. Major 2016

A Book to Burn and a Book to Keep (Hidden): Selected Writings, by Li Zhi, ed. and tr. Rivi Handler-Spitz, Pauline Lee, and Haun Saussy 2016

The Shenzi Fragments: *A Philosophical Analysis and Translation,* Eirik Lang Harris 2016

A Record of Daily Knowledge and *Poems and Essays*: Selections, by Gu Yanwu, tr. and ed. Ian Johnston 2017

The Book of Lord Shang: Apologetics of State Power in Early China, by Shang Yang, ed. and tr. Yuri Pines